MADI RAE CRONIN

JOSHUA WHEELER

ACID WEST

Joshua Wheeler is from Alamogordo, New Mexico. He teaches creative writing at Louisiana State University.

ACID WEST

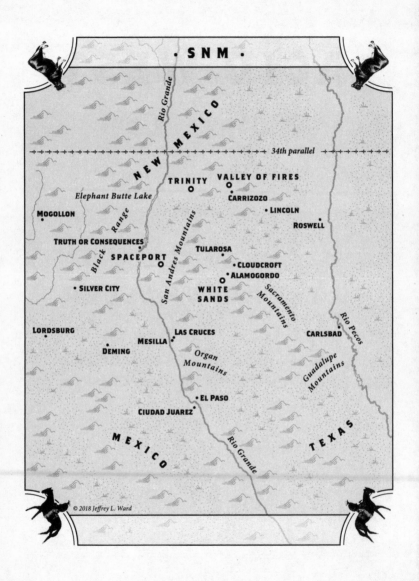

· S N M ·

NEW MEXICO

Rio Grande

34th parallel

TRINITY

VALLEY OF FIRES

Elephant Butte Lake

CARRIZOZO

• LINCOLN

MOGOLLON

ROSWELL

Range

Black

TRUTH OR CONSEQUENCES

San Andres Mountains

SPACEPORT

TULAROSA

• CLOUDCROFT

ALAMOGORDO

WHITE SANDS

Sacramento Mountains

• SILVER CITY

LORDSBURG

LAS CRUCES

CARLSBAD

Rio Pecos

MESILLA

DEMING

Organ Mountains

Guadalupe Mountains

• EL PASO

CIUDAD JUAREZ

MEXICO

Rio Grande

TEXAS

© 2018 Jeffrey L. Ward

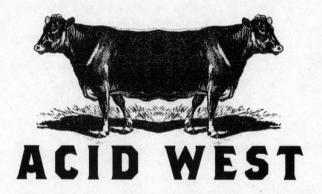

ACID WEST

· ESSAYS ·

JOSHUA WHEELER

MCD X FSG ORIGINALS · FARRAR, STRAUS AND GIROUX

NEW YORK

MCD × FSG Originals
Farrar, Straus and Giroux
175 Varick Street, New York 10014

Map and title page illustrations from iStock.
Illustration on page 395 copyright © 2018 by Na Kim.

Library of Congress Cataloging-in-Publication Data
Names: Wheeler, Joshua, 1984– author.
Title: Acid West : essays / Joshua Wheeler.
Description: First edition. | New York : MCD x FSG Originals, 2018. |
    Includes bibliographical references.
Identifiers: LCCN 2017047910 | ISBN 9780374535803 (pbk.)
Subjects: LCSH: Home—New Mexico. | New Mexico—Social
    conditions. | Technological innovations—United States—Social
    aspects. | Popular culture—Effect of technological innovations on—
    United States. | National characteristics, American. | United States—
    Social conditions—21st century.
Classification: LCC PS3624.H44 A6 2018 | DDC 814/.6—dc23
LC record available at https://lccn.loc.gov/2017047910

Designed by Abby Kagan

Our books may be purchased in bulk for promotional, educational, or
business use. Please contact your local bookseller or the Macmillan
Corporate and Premium Sales Department at 1-800-221-7945, extension
5442, or by e-mail at MacmillanSpecialMarkets@macmillan.com.

www.fsgoriginals.com • www.fsgbooks.com
Follow us on Twitter, Facebook, and Instagram at @fsgoriginals

1   3   5   7   9   10   8   6   4   2

For Magic Momma and Pops
and all my blood,
backward and forward

Write the things which thou hast seen,
and the things which are,
and the things which shall be
hereafter

—THE APOCALYPSE 1:19

Well, alright.

—JOHN WAYNE

Acid Western \'æsɪd 'we-stərn\ *n.*
(subgenre, cinema, c. 1970)

. . . the color looks cheap and bright, unreal in
that gaudy way . . . cacophonous music alter-
nating with camp music, screeching bird
sounds . . . a version of the classic Western
reconfigured as some sort of nightmare . . . a
death romp . . . in skulls on drugs . . . an inability to distinguish inner consciousness from
external reality . . . desert . . . piled high with
deformity . . . prophecies, transformations,
miracles, and a sacrificial, somewhat paranoid
vision . . . a drug-like handling of time . . .
associating our westward journey with death
rather than rebirth . . . a cartoon catalogue of
evils . . . more and more desert . . . savage frontier poetry to justify a hallucinated agenda, a
laconic magical realism . . . a horror circus . . .
conjuring a crazed version of America at its
most solipsistic, hankering after its own lost
origins . . . over the sandy plains . . . an empty
stage . . . a bad trip . . .

CONTENTS

ACID WEST

SNM

Beyond Deadman Canyon but just this side of Purgatory Canyon lies the Sleeping Lady. I watch her from the yard of the haunted house where I've been staying since coming home again like I can't quit doing because I can't quit leaving. The Sleeping Lady is a formation of peaks and mesas and ridges in the Sacramento Mountains that spoon this house. She is made of our mountains, her rocky breasts presiding over town, over the whole of our desert basin, the peaks of her chin and nose in the clouds, striations of limestone and sandstone in a cliff of tremendous hair flowing behind her. During the days, I lie in the yard, burning out the ghosts, taking summer heat to the core as a reminder that whatever the intensity of whatever series of thoughts I've worried down to a single shooting pain in my brain or chest or ass, it is not real. After an hour, when the sweat has stopped, the mirage literally rises from my skin. If there is a god of infinite love and scorn, it is the New Mexico sun, and so I lay myself bare before her, getting it all off my chest, letting it all hang out, a lazy naked prayer, but there are few neighbors this close to the mountains. There is only the Sleeping Lady. The mirage rises from her too. Together we bathe in the rays of our Lord like a couple of rattlesnakes cooking the night's cold hex from our veins.

This house is haunted because Granddaddy died here, because Grandmommy went blind here and lost her mind here, enough to finally get wrenched from the only place she could still navigate by memory, haunted because seven generations of my blood have run through this desert basin at the feet of the Sleeping Lady but now this house is empty except for me and I hear a strange sound that crescendos when the sun goes down. This house is haunted because it is home, because I am home but am leaving again soon and that makes it feel haunted too, haunted by me. I grew up in this house as much as my own, which is just down the street, where Grandmommy now lives out her last days with my parents, confused about my relation to her. It is strange to have swapped like this, to see her in my old bedroom, to be surrounded by her whole life in boxes waiting to be dumped or sold or donated, to spend nights on the floor of her old bedroom, tossing and turning because there is a sound that won't quit, a hum or a drone, getting up at all hours to unplug all possible culprits, navigating around the boxes of Bibles and needlepoints and sheet music and so many framed photos of Ronald Reagan, trying to get at lamps and fans and the refrigerator, cutting their power, circling even outside the house with an ear to the ground, hopping around from all the cockleburs impaling my feet as I fail to discover the sound's origin and finally collapse again inside, eyes bugging and spine like a tuning fork resonating with the ungodly frequency, making my blood run with it, the sound I increasingly suspect is the stirring of the Sleeping Lady.

I began lying with her when I was young, when she was all majesty and no stir. From the couch in the living room and from the top of the playground slide at Heights Elementary and from the roof where I sat with Granddaddy counting stars or shooting fireworks or watching the horizon turn to haze and static when a windstorm filled the air with sand from the white dunes west of town. From these vantage points I could lie on my side and close one eye and stretch my arm out and it'd look like I was holding her, resting next to her and keeping her close, not desperately but just sort of lounging, draping one limb nonchalantly over my big mountain lady.

They did not always call her a lady. At first she was only Steamboat Ridge. The desert made my ancestors thirsty for anything nautical. Or they were prudes who didn't hanker to live in the shadow of breasts. But haven't we always feminized the land, out of hope it is fertile? Please perpetuate and sustain us, Mother Earth. It is hard to suckle at the teat of a steamboat. We long to be coddled, but also seeing ourselves in the land is a defiant declaration of victory. Which of us won in that ancient battle against nature? You, mountain, are in our image. See our conquering queen rest. Still, from some angles around town, the Sleeping Lady disappears, leaving only the outline of a steamboat's smokestacks looming over our home. And anyway, these days, rising out of the Sleeping Lady's forehead: a cluster of steel cell towers and broadcast antennas.

When I say *home*, I mean this town, but also I mean all of Southern New Mexico, the cities and villages down here spread out but stuffed into the same feverdream. When you hear I'm from New Mexico, you may have visions of saguaro, towering green beacons of lawless freedom, but there are no saguaros here. You will only ever see a saguaro in New

Mexico when you are high on drugs. They do not grow here, but no one believes us. They are your icon of the West. For us they are signposts of a myth we didn't make, tentacles of the hallucination. When you hear I'm from New Mexico, you may have stories of Albuquerque and Santa Fe and Taos, the famous towns up north. There is no easy way to explain that here in the underbelly, south of the 34th parallel, which cuts the state in half, things are different. We use the abbreviation SNM for our home, and maybe that is a good explanation, how there is something awkward but accurate in the way it comes off the tongue like S&M. Most of us SNM-ans feel some pride or gratification in the way our half of the state is robbed or abused or forgotten entirely—like it makes us the better half because we endure the most fiscal pain or Border Patrol harassment or tourism-department shafting or general ignorance about our existence. We are just the bottom. And we like it. But I guess this feeling of pleasure about the pain inflicted by one's place of origin is not unique to SNM and most folks likely feel a bit sadomasochistic about their home region. We are just lucky enough to get that feeling caught up on the tongue whenever our name is shorthanded by mouth. Grins and sideways glances abound anytime some-one mentions SNM Power Company or the Ballard-esque SNM Speedway or the probably more accurate than we real-ize SNM Surgical Associates or, my favorite, SNM Human Development, which is a rehab where you go to get set straight for doing too much of the bad things that make you feel good. You have always been a very bad boy if you are at SNM Human Development.

Or maybe I should tell you the motto of our desert is Land of Mañana, which we mean to signify that we are laid-back, that everything will happen in good time, that there is

no rush, we will get around to it tomorrow. Today is for siestas. But Land of Mañana is also the sense that time here is
folded over on itself. Today we are the land of tomorrow. As
soon as you cross below the 34th parallel, you feel yourself
projected in this way, made polyphonic in time, experiencing at once all the epoch-making wonders born of the underbelly: the Apache and conquistador and cowboy, rocketry
and atom bombs and ETs, Firebees and Hellfires and spaceships. Our lady of the mountain has slept through it all. But
now she stirs.

If I tell you I hear the noise of this land, you will think
about the twang of country guitar or the horns of mariachi
or the pulsing falsetto of peyote song or just the evening
screech of coyotes. The howl of a wolf. The scratch of sandy
wind through ocotillo. And surely all that still echoes, but
these nights there's something new, a noise of vacillation,
resonating on the brink of chaos, a wavering: a wobble, deep
and electronic. Down here where so much of our land is
grayed out on maps because our military installations require secrecy or because we are in an unmappable warp or
wrinkle or glitch—here be desert dragons: the Sleeping
Lady wobbles.

I mean wobble as a metaphor for that feeling of polyphonic projection but also as the literal sound, like the sudden walls of synthetic bass ubiquitous in dance music these
days. The drop, they call it. A digital wobble that comes from
a failure to emulate the sound of an electric bass guitar,
which itself failed to emulate the sound of an acoustic bass
guitar, which itself failed to emulate the sound of an upright
bass, which itself failed to emulate the deep sounds of our
ancient instruments that harnessed wind, the sound of the
wind itself whenever the earth stirred or shook or broke and

made us cry out for a god. A failed emulation of a failed emulation of a failed emulation of a sense of existential lone-liness. She wobbles with echoes of that ancient blast catching new wind, the sound of us shocking it back to life again and again with our newfangled paddles and knobs and buttons and screens—gadgets—keeping it booming, beating, just barely breathing, radiating out from deep inside the Sleeping Lady. The Apaches, who have wandered her mountains longer than any of us, use just one word for what our language breaks into separate notions. *Ni'* means land. *Ni'* means the mind. *Ni'* means earth and consciousness. *Ni'* is the revelation that mem-ory and joy and sorrow and prophecy do not exist without geography, are nothing but geography. Did you know "revela-tion" is what our word *apocalypse* used to mean? The Sleeping Lady knows something. She wobbles with apocalypse.

She was struck by lightning a few years back. Seventy-five acres of her chest caught fire. The sheriff got swamped with calls. *There's a giant woman on fire! The Sleeping Lady is smoking trees! Those tits are looking mighty hot today!* The Smokey Bear Hotshots came with Pulaskis and chain saws, dug line around her shoulders and dripped flame from their buckets and burned her more to save her from being en-gulfed entirely. I search for her scars as we bathe in the rays of our Lord, but they are gone.

If ever snow comes our way, it sticks only to her. Then we say she has slipped into a wedding gown, we confuse her with the Lady of the Sands, an apparition that appears on the other side of town when the wind kicks the gypsum dunes of our White Sands into the ghost of a wandering woman, widowed on her wedding day, searching for her murdered groom or the conquistadors who gutted him. In the snow, our grieving sand bride transforms into a mountain, to rest. The white gown is lovely, but we know from our myths it means only that she is hungry for revenge. There are no ghosts, only unfinished stories. There are no horrors other than the familiar ones, made unbearable by our hunch they have no end.

The Pueblo, who have wandered this desert longer than any of us, have in their Tewa language a name for the force of existence, the genesis energy coursing through everything in this desert: *po-wa-ha*, flowing through animate and inanimate alike. "Water-wind-breath" if you want to be literal about the translation. Don't be. No words mean what they should.

One day I'll meet a boy named Yogi in an asylum in Juárez. He'll touch things, pet them really, all objects and plants and people, touching almost like a DJ scratching and twisting and fading everything around him up and down, in and out. He traces *po-wa-ha*, and some days I'll convince myself he commands it. I close one eye and stretch my hand out in front of me and run my fingers through the Sleeping Lady's cliff of hair and down to her noble thighs. I try to twist the mournful synth into a shriek. I try to mute it, try to change it in any way at all. I fail. *Po-wa-ha* is in the desert and the mountains, the cottonwoods and ocotillo, the people and rocks and sand and snot and bison and then also in the conquerors and their horses and cows and guns and snot and their guns' cracks and bangs and smoke and then also in more conquerors and horses and guns and also their bombs and missiles and drones and the cracks and bangs and smoke of all that too. *Po-wa-ha* is deep like bass because it is our rhythmic foundation, but now it wobbles, the harsh pulse of the Sleeping Lady skipping beats, the throb of her entrance music, bass so strong you can see its waves coming like the aftershock of a bomb. Did you know our brains evolved to hear all notes in relation to the lowest pitch? And here it is: the underbelly of the West, our manifest hallucination, the lowest pitch of the American myth, the sound of the unfinished story that keeps me up at night, that gets me naked in the yard with the mirage rising up out of my skin, waiting for a time the Sleeping Lady wakes for good, all the loose ends of SNM ghosts coalescing, the rattlesnakes and coyotes and the last of the endangered jackrabbits tumbling down her torso, the yuccas flung from her arms like a million tiny daggers, her standing and shaking out a cliff of hair, looking rough from being ripped asunder outside time, slouching through the basin as she slops war paint over her barbwire stitches, pulls a space helmet down over her alien eyes and settles a cowboy hat on top of everything, kicks up mushroom clouds of white sand with every step as she walks through the underbelly headed not into the sunset, but for it—looking to pick a fight with the god of infinite love and scorn that let us do all of this.

THE LIGHT OF GOD

AMERICA'S PASTIME IN THE AGE OF DRONE WARFARE

•

In the Year of Our Lord 2012

At the elbow of Highway 54, where the road bends back toward Jornada del Muerto, there we are, just before it veers north and climbs from the Tularosa Basin, just before the straight shot of asphalt between the dark green stretch of Lincoln National Forest and the big pure splotch of White Sands, just before it rips straight to the Valley of Fires, the hardened guts of the earth coughed up all molten five thousand years ago, cooled to black and stuck midflow like the shadow of a mighty bird hovering, covering the sun, a dark scar across SNM, a mean streak grinning toward Trinity where they discovered destroying whole worlds by cracking atoms, radiated sand still glowing green just north of where we are, me and Pops eating hot dogs, holding our hearts, and standing atop flimsy aluminum bleachers for "The Star-Spangled Banner" blaring from a stereo in the press box, which is a closet above the garage where they sell beer at the ballpark in Alamogordo— my home, sweet home. Can't you see that American flag, popping in the wind? My god, look at that sunset. Take 54 south and there's a porn shop and the very tip of the spout of Texas and then there's Juárez, where 11,202 people have been murdered in six years.

Maybe seventy fans are here at the height of summer in 2012, all milling around, not exactly excited because of the heat and because this is only the Pecos League of Professional Baseball Clubs. But there is minor league anticipation; this is a rivalry game—White Sands Pupfish vs. Roswell Invaders. Tickets were six bucks. The players get two hundred a month if they get paid at all. The beer is three bucks, except when the cleanup batter strikes out; then it's two for the rest of the inning.

Pops is keen to retire after thirty years as a public school administrator, tired of dealing with guns like never before, tired of education reduced to standardized tests, tired of his cartoon ties and the click of his cowboy boots on the asbestos tile up and down the halls of Heights Elementary—Where Everyone Is a Winner—just tired. I worry he will drown in his La-Z-Boy, so we start here with plans to go north and see all the baseball we can, trying to remember why we care to be alive and American.

The Sacramento Mountains rise over nine thousand feet just beyond the outfield fence of chain link covered in tattered banners for Margo's Mexican Food. The white lines to first and third run ninety feet to their bases and, by regulation, at least 325 to the outfield fence, but the rules say nothing of a maximum. "These perpendicular lines theoretically extend to infinity."* Follow the right-field line straight into

* A. Bartlett Giamatti, the seventh commissioner of Major League Baseball, writes this about foul lines in his essay "Baseball as Narrative," where he also writes, "To know baseball is to continue to aspire

the rolling Sacramentos and there is the New Mexico Museum of Space History, tucked in with the boulders and yuccas, the glossiest building in town, all glass and shimmery and surrounded by a bunch of dead rockets aimed at the sky, a dead ape named Ham buried at the door: Ham the Astrochimp who rode the *Mercury-Redstone* 2 to outer space and floated around, yanking at different levers. From his grave, the astrochimp stares into the mountains at our Sleeping Lady. If the left-field line chalked on for five miles, it would cut in half Our Lady of the Light Catholic Church, making her insides both fair and foul. Home plate is the point of the diamond that points directly at Holloman Air Force Base, where Ham the Astrochimp was trained, where the F-117A Nighthawk flew and the F-22 Raptor flies and booms and cracks the ceiling in our kitchen, crumbles adobe all over town with blast waves from outracing sound, scratches up the sky with vapor trails like zippers unzipped in the firmament everywhere around the nowhere desert base where they now train young airmen of the 29th Attack Squadron for just a few months and then set them operational as remote pilots of MQ-9 Reaper drones. Some of the Pecos League guys have been playing semipro ball for five years and may play for ten years more and never get anywhere close to Major League Baseball's minor leagues.

Pops and I throw Cracker Jacks at a guy in a pupfish outfit, our mascot: Gordo. Everybody teases Gordo. One kind of pupfish lives on the brink of extinction in our White

---

to the condition of freedom, individually and as a people, for baseball is grounded in America in a way unique to our games." Another of his baseball essays begins, "It breaks your heart. It is designed to break your heart."

Sands, bubbling up in springs that trickle through the hardened gypsum, tiny guys that glow iridescent when they mate, blue or purple, gleaming translucent the way any of us might if we found ourselves in the miracle of one puddle in a white-hot desert with a boner and another fish. No one understands why Pupfish is the name of our baseball club—of all the Old West culture, cowboys and outlaws, of all the Native American lore, of all the war machines and aerospace technology, we ride a scrawny, glowing fish to America's most storied field of play. Last year the Pupfish were banned from Applebee's for ripping apart the dining room while trading blows with a bunch of airmen who got to giggling about the team's name. Gordo's mascot getup is the epitome of semipro: the fins only come to his elbows, so his bare arms and hands and fingers are on display, and his bowed legs are sticking out of the yellow foam fillets from the thigh down and his manface looms in the dark of his gaping fishmouth. Too much of the human visible. The way we dream up a transformation and give it a half-assed go and get ourselves stuck looking silly. A swing and a miss and the beer's a buck cheaper.

Wedged in the fence behind home plate is a camcorder and its ponytailed operator, who mostly just stands around puffing cigarettes, but sometimes he flips open the side viewer and ducks down and jabs his smoking fingers at the buttons and smooths his ponytail and studies the video. Redneck nearly instant replay. Five miles west, as the Reaper flies, two airmen sit in recliners in a steel cargo container, far from war but dressed for it with flight suits and headsets, one manning a control stick and a couple of pedals, the other on a scroll ball, both airmen staring at six screens each, GPS and sensor video feed and data and data and data. The ponytail ashes and grins and slaps his screen closed when he knows a call was either right or wrong, but he's just some guy so it doesn't matter much. In the major leagues of our national pastime the powers that be are all tore up about the role of replay, about the extent to which they're charged with making sure every call is right, tore up about bringing already-common video technology to the old sport and whether that will skew its soul. Pops says, *Keep the tradition of using your eyeballs.* All the talk is of eyeballs. Last week the Boston Red Sox skipper went on a rant about science proving the human eye misses out on the final five feet of a pitch, how hurlers are now so good their pitches cut and split and move all over in that last five feet, how we need cutting-edge technology to get it right. *Your lens doesn't snap that photograph,* the skipper says. *So if you can't see it, why are we asking umpires to call it? They can't see it. They're humans. We're asking humans to do a feat a human can't do.** Our eyeball wasn't built to track something so imminent—we were meant to flee or fight back, anything but hold still in judgment.

Tonight the umpire behind home plate is a kid, younger looking than most of the players, mostly swallowed up under his chest pillow, a little lanky like he would have been great on the mound, but he's signed up for a job of jeers and he doesn't care. He sings strikes like opera. He flails his fist way out from his body and hollers each one sustained and soprano

---

* As early as 1954, *Sports Illustrated* was publishing scientific research that showed a batter never saw his bat hit the ball, lost sight of the ball eight to fifteen feet from the plate. Seeing the ball pass through the strike zone has never been integral for successful batting. And even the best batters fail most of the time, hitting maybe three times out of ten. This high rate of failure is accepted as part of the game for the players; the umpires, however, are expected to be perfect.

just in case the foul lines do extend to infinity and somebody deep along the way gives a damn. He's not worried about second-guessing. He's confident about his eyeballs, how they rolled from the goop of his brain early in development but never let go, stayed tethered by the optic nerve, started the lifelong turn of light into neural twitches into thought into decisions about holding still and calling strikes—how the complexity of the human eye is the hardest thing for evolution to explain. The fans are tired of trusting it. Most are leaning toward an everything-but-the-strike-zone policy for instant replay in the big leagues. This season they can review home runs, and next season they may add the review of line drives that are hell for an eyeball to judge because they come off the bat like a bullet, like a missile, absolutely no sense of the arc, no chance to predict a path, where it will land or on which side of the line. And then tags and then trapped balls in the outfield and then everything but the strike zone will be decided by rewinding the world a few seconds, by taking another look at the same tiny moment, rewound and replayed again and again, just that one instant until somebody staring at a couple of screens is confident we've got all the information to understand it exactly right, that tiny moment, then on to the next.

The Invaders' third-base coach sends signals to his batter, a handswipe across the chest and a touch to the bill of his cap and a wipe down the length of each arm followed by banging his fists and doing some wacky twisting of his wrists. A primitive form of communication. The Invader at the plate gets the gist and turns to the batter's box but pauses before digging in, grabs his crotch, tugs at his belt, taps at his cleats with the bat, bends left, spits, bends right, spits, tugs his helmet down and chokes up and spits again and tugs at the left shoulder of his jersey and grabs his crotch and does the whole thing again just exactly the same before every pitch. A primitive form of religion. The Pupfish catcher gets in his squat and reaches with his ungloved hand under his right thigh and rubs back to his ass, holding still like that for a moment before bringing his hand up under his mask, to blow on his fingers, or lick them. From where I sit he appears to be eating his own shit, a pantomime not exactly gross but provocative—like this might have been a more effective design for us, scrolling the same chunk of fuel through our bodies for an entire lifetime. Why were we designed just so, to such arbitrary specifications, with eyeballs like ours and desire for more than our own shit? And then the crack of the bat. An Invader gets to first on a fielder's choice. Pops sends me for another round of dogs and beer. I walk in stride with an Invader who has left the field of play, headed to check a phone he's plugged into the generator behind the food cart.

The awful great thing about baseball is that it's boring as hell to watch. I can get lost in pondering all of existence, but I've got the crack of the bat to snap me back into the story, ground me in the game, in life for just a moment before I drift again into a lazy anxiety about the universe. Even the players spend most of their time spitting. Pops keeps his dip in his lip as he watches the game. I've never seen him spit the stuff out. His gut is a steel vat bubbling with wintergreen Skoal, but he looks calm always and keeps pretty quiet. I say, *I'm bored*, not because I am bored but because baseball fosters a feeling of boredom so the crack of the bat, when it happens, stings and echoes like an epiphany. You just gotta wait for it. Wait for it. Pops looks at me and says nothing because it is only the bottom of the fourth and the Pupfish are already trying to rally from five runs down.

Thirty years ago the thirty-third inning of the longest game in baseball history was played two months after the game first began. Those minor leaguers only really played about nine hours over two days, but damn—a baseball game can last nine hours and sometimes it seems even longer. The sport embodies timelessness: no game clock, all the action moving counterclockwise around the diamond, all the cyclical rhythms of its agrarian origins spilling out in the rebirth of spring training and the freeze of the Fall Classic and the hacking away and the whackers and the apple-knockers and the rhubarb and brushback and bush league and rain check and snake jazz, which is the curveball that first got us knocking at apples in the garden, obsessed with knowledge and the idea that we might get things wrong. The game could go on forever and that's the rub with replay, that it will slow the game down even more, that we will go on forever indulging our information lust, trying to get every call right and never making it to the end unless we bore ourselves to death.

Crack.

A Pupfish homers. A Pupfish doubles. A Pupfish gets caught stealing third to end the inning.

The sun is pretty well set now. Two fans pull out their cowbells. A group of teens down the third-base line have hurried through a bunch of beer and started up the taunts. One girl yells at the Invaders, *My balls are bigger than yours!* Her taunt does not get lost in a crowd of taunts or drowned out by a crowd of cheers or chatter, but because almost no one is here, her taunt lingers in the air over what is clearly an only slightly modified Little League baseball field, and her taunt sours in the quiet and stretches over the grass, with the shadow of the meager press box crawling across the infield toward the Sacramento Mountains until the park lights sizzle to life and all darkness is pushed back just enough for the game to keep on boring us until it incites us. Five miles west, as the Reaper flies, the remote pilot and sensor operator are in the steel cargo container dealing with the same problem of doldrums as they fly what military brass call "the unblinking eye." One of them says, *Highly skilled, highly trained people can only eat so many peanut M&M's or Doritos or whatnot.* The other one says, *For most missions nothing happens. Your plane orbits in the sky, you watch and you wait . . . It's very boring.*

The 29th Attack Squadron is in Alamogordo training so they can avoid what the Air Force calls the two biggest causes of civilian casualties from drone strikes: lack of positive identification and lack of tactical patience. Out in the White Sands just on the edge of town, you can visit the sites where they filmed *Jarhead* and *Transformers* and *Transformers: Revenge of the Fallen* and *The Men Who Stare at Goats* because this place, they say, is so much like that place: the Middle East. The studio execs grin and call our land NewMexistan. If you look, they say, at each desert just so, through a camera, on a screen: they're practically the same.*

I lean back on the bleachers and sigh to the heavens, but

---

* Maybe the Hollywood fakery is more accurate than we know. In September 2011, our drones assassinated an American citizen for the first time and without any kind of U.S. trial. He was killed in the Middle East deserts of Yemen but was born just down the road from here, in Las Cruces, New Mexico. He was born while his father was in Las Cruces on a Fulbright fellowship, studying how people of the Yemeni desert could learn from New Mexican agricultural practices because the desert of SNM is so much like the desert of Yemen. So little water. So much sand. All life in these areas is miraculous. The assassinated— New Mexico–born—American citizen was the radical imam and al-Qaeda recruiter Anwar al-Awlaki.

I don't see much between me and the stars, though I know a handful of Reapers hover above us, their remote pilots getting a feel for their screens and how a desert looks on them and getting a feel for the feel of being bored until they get the itch to strike. Or until a Reaper hits the ground. Reapers crash at twice the rate of manned aircraft. If a Reaper crashlanded on the diamond right now, in the bottom of the sixth, skidding from one foul territory to the other, and stopped on the infield grass between the mound and home plate, the wings would span the distance from the laces of the ball leaving the hand of the Pupfish pitcher at the top of his hurl, over the dirt of his mound and over the perfectly manicured grass to the dirt around home, over the Invader's choked hands and the barrel of his bat exploding toward the crescendo of his swing—a whiff—and the tip of the Reaper's wing would extend just over the thud in the catcher's mitt to stop exactly at the hand of the umpire as he unballs his fist and stands up straight after calling the strike, sustained and soprano just in case the foul lines chalk on to infinity and somebody deep along the way gives a damn. But Reapers don't need to land so often. They were built to stay aloft all day and night or maybe just fourteen hours if they're heavy with a payload of Hellfire missiles. They're small for a plane and they fly high and are relatively quiet, but oddly, they are conspicuous in the skies over Waziristan, like we want everyone on the ground to know we are there, like Reapers evolved for surveillance and then for killing but also there's the advantageous mutation of terror. Villagers all over North and South Waziristan tell stories of the maddening sound: *I can't sleep at night because when the drones are there . . . I hear them making that sound, that noise. The drones are all over my brain, I can't sleep. When I hear the drones making*

*that drone sound, I just turn on the light and sit there looking
at the light.*

Not two months after the destruction of the World Trade
Center an F-117A Nighthawk, the pinnacle of our stealth-
aircraft engineering, flew over Bank One Ballpark in Phoe-
nix to launch Game 7 of the 2001 World Series between
the New York Yankees and the Arizona Diamondbacks. The
plane flew low and loud just as Jesse McGuire trilled out the
last notes of "The Star-Spangled Banner" on his trumpet.
The crowd went wild, and Jesse blew out the very bottom of
his lungs and got to fist pumping and jumping and pumping
his trumpet at the sky while the whole stadium shook from
the boom of the flyover and the boom of fifty thousand fans
giving up the last of their lungs too, even before the first
pitch, because no matter who won the game, it was great to
be alive and American. The Nighthawk was the plane I grew
up with, black and sharp with so many slick facets, like an
Apache arrowhead commandeered by Darth Vader. We
used to get our school pictures taken standing in front of the
thing. The pilots were heroes around town. Now the Night-
hawks are all retired to graveyards and the U.S. arsenal swells
to nearly seven hundred Predators and Reapers, but I don't
guess we will ever get a triumphant drone flyover to com-
mence a ball game, the small plane hovering slowly, just
barely visible above the stadium, all the fans holding their
breath to hear the slight, steady buzz of the propeller, like the
motor of a distant neighbor's lawn mower as he rides over
the same patch of grass all of Saturday afternoon, just to get
out and see what's going on. But I know right now at this ball
game, Reapers do hover over us—there is no better place to
train for boredom, to overcome lack of tactical patience.

The Elysian Fields of Hoboken, New Jersey, was the first

place the game of baseball ever bored anyone, in this month of June, 166 years ago.* In Greek mythology the Elysian fields are a paradise where gods send heroes of war after making them immortal. No one will ever die piloting a Reaper. I wonder if eternal paradise is something we can manifest and if it will ever bore us. "The lack of tactical patience is not a problem that can be solved technologically," says an official Air Force report on diminishing civilian casualties from drone strikes. "That is a matter of training American soldiers to live in a surreal moral universe."†

Crack.

A Pupfish fights off the inside heat and then takes a ball and stumbles back to avoid losing his head when the pitcher hurls some chin music. The aggression begins when the Invader pitcher launches a fastball toward the lone Pupfish at bat, or the aggression begins before that when the Pupfish steps to the plate and waves a stick, or the aggression is sparked by the catcher crouching behind the batter, adopting his perspective, sending covert signals to his pitcher asking

---

* This is the first known game of organized baseball, in 1846. Some of the first baseball ever played in New Mexico was played in the south of the territory by soldiers at Fort Cummings and Fort Bayard in the 1870s. They were taking a break from killing Apaches, a group of people America declared war on because they were in our way, and it was easy to portray them as savage desert terrorists.

† The USAF report focuses on how to diminish civilian casualties resulting from drone strikes. The report found that the design of chairs in ground-control stations leave drone operators ergonomically prone to boredom and therefore deadly mistakes. The implication: Less comfortable seating may make our drone pilots more morally acute. I'm thinking, of course, of stadium seating, which never lets one's ass get lax. Imagine all future wars fought from bleachers.

for a strike or some dangerous chin music. "Is it so clear who is the defense, who is the offense?"* Obama has a "kill list" and a stack of "terrorist suspects' biographies on what one official calls . . . macabre 'baseball cards.'" But most Hellfire missiles get loosed in Pakistan not because we know a guy's biography or even his name, but because we've observed his "pattern of life" in the desert of Waziristan, extrapolated the imminence of his threat to us by putting the eye of a Reaper on him from five thousand or twenty thousand or sixty thousand feet above, watching like a kid learning mad science, holding a magnifying glass between the sun and an ant. Signature strikes, they're called, and only the powers that be know what that signature is, what confluence of data streaming into our screens from our drones halfway around the world adds up to a "positive identification" of a "pattern of life" that deserves to be snuffed out.† "Among the elements that could combine for a lethal signature," writes Andrew Cockburn, "was a man's mode of urinating. Someone informed the targeters that while Pashtun men urinate standing up, Arab

---

* Giamatti again, this time in his essay "Baseball and the American Character." His question eventually leads him to conclude, "In baseball and daily life, Americans do not take sides so much as they change sides in ways checked and balanced. Finally, in baseball and daily life, regardless of which side you are on and where you stand, shared principles are supposed to govern."

† A Reaper's video stream does not actually beam halfway around the world. From Pakistan it first hits a satellite in space, and from there it hits a relay satellite on the ground in Europe, and then it travels by cable under the Atlantic Ocean to America. The relay satellites are on the ground in Germany, at Ramstein Air Base, in a clearing just beyond the fences of Ramstein American High School's baseball field.

men squat." This was "duly incorporated in the targeting al-
gorithms." And all those Invaders gathering at the mound, the
infielders and the catcher and the skipper out there to check
on his pitcher, huddling up in the dirt and jawing for a bit—a
Reaper on high is bound to notice such an assembly, and the
remote operators staring at their screens, running low on
Doritos after twelve hours in a steel cargo container, are
bound to find a pattern in it. The Invaders pitcher gives up
the cowhide and heads for the dugout, done for the night.
The rest of them linger around as the reliever arrives. The
catcher returns to his squat. I can almost see it as ruins—the
baseball there, unstitched and steaming. The mound is a crater. Flesh sizzles on the rim.

Nobody can say for sure how many civilian casualties
have resulted from American drone strikes in Pakistan, and
that is maybe because the drones move on, the stream of
data moves on to suck at another target, drones in the air
twenty-four hours a day gathering data and data and data,
enough data to make the exact right decision about whose
life has the scariest pattern when watched from twenty thousand feet, but then the gathering of data about that target
stops because the target is totally "dismembered, mutilated,
and burned beyond recognition" by Hellfire missiles. We
cannot prove the innocence of someone we never bothered
to identify and cannot now recognize.

The Invaders strike out the side in the bottom of the
sixth and now the seventh-inning stretch is in full swing.
Some lady hollers a drunken rendition of "Take Me Out to
the Ball Game." There are prizes. The announcer throws
one T-shirt from the press box but the fans want more, so he
grabs a half-gone box of Daylight Donuts and hurls them
down one at a time. Folks on the bleachers get ferocious

about the donuts even though they are stale. Everyone in town knows Daylight Donuts closes at noon. One lady climbs to the top bleacher, snags an airborne donut with each hand, then returns to her seat and munches. She's German, at the game with her kid and probably in town with the German Air Force, which also trains at Holloman. She feels better now, with the donuts, and even though the game is nearly over, she turns to me and asks what all the numbers on the scoreboard mean. I say, *Runs, hits, and errors*. She says, *Errors?* I say, *Yeah, when somebody makes a mistake, an error*. Tonight there are only two errors, both committed by the Invaders. She says, *Why would they put "errors" on the scoreboard?*—but says it mostly to herself and gets lost again in the donuts.

Pops says, *I guess with replay we'd miss the fights*. He means the institutionalized spectacles of rage, when a skipper charges from the dugout and puts his red face up to the stone face of an umpire, hat thrown to the ground, dirt kicked on pants, spit flying in faces, gum even, ripping the bases from the earth and tossing them into the nowhere of center field as protest against a call he knows will never be changed. I guess the soul of baseball is somewhere in those rages. There'd be no reason to rage with replay. If the call is always absolutely right, then you could only ever weep with regret. The Reaper's wings are prone to get icy when it flies high or at night and so the edges are made to bleed ethylene glycol from areas covered in things called microscopic weeping holes. Pops says, *Keep the tradition of using your eyeballs*. Crack. An Invader hits a sacrifice fly to center field, bringing his teammate home from third. This is what makes our pastime indelibly human: the possibility of sacrifice. First they were called drones and then they were unmanned aerial vehicles and now they are remotely piloted aircraft because we are increasingly anxious to clarify our relationship to our technology—we are there and not there at all. With Reapers, it's whether our moral barometer for taking lives slips or loosens wildly or totally implodes; and with replay, it's whether we cling to our infallibility. These problems have drastically different stakes but are blurred by the same struggle to keep a hold on how we define ourselves as Americans.

By this time next year many Reapers will be fitted with the Gorgon Stare sensor package, which will add up to sixty-five full-motion video feeds to the bird's eye, creating "data at rates of 10 to over 1,000 times projected communications data transmission capacities, and will far exceed human analytic capability." To keep this glut of data from being wasted, to make it useful in "pattern of life" recognition, the USAF Scientific Advisory Board recommends "automated processing." By this time next year the Institute of Electrical and Electronics Engineers will announce they're designing baseball equipment—bats, balls, and gloves—that can be networked with sensors and transmitters installed around the stadium to provide verdicts for every call in the game. "The new technology should be accurate to an extent that human observers simply cannot match, even with tools such as automatic replay."

Pop says, *We're all human.* I'm not sure what he means.

When a reporter gets into the Reaper Ground Control Station at Holloman Air Force Base, he sees the video feed and asks, *Is that a civilian car on the road?* Major Trey says, *It is a civilian car, here in New Mexico . . . simply to train drone pilots to be able to follow a moving target . . . the cars do not know we are following them.* The targeting system on the screen moves along Highway 54, the road Pops and I will take north in a few hours, along the bend back toward the Jornada del Muerto into La Luz desert, the climb from the Tularosa Basin, the straight shot of asphalt between the green stretch of Lincoln Forest and the big pure splotch of White Sands, me and Pops at the start of a road trip to see as much baseball as we can, trying to remember why we care to be alive and American. Major Trey says, *We do not simulate or actually engage those vehicles.*

Tomorrow morning, after a stop in Roswell at the Super Meat Mart to buy hot beef jerky, Pops will get chili flakes in his eyes as he gnaws and they will swell and tear, and I'll wake in the passenger seat as he steers the truck with his knee, one hand prying open a fiery eye and one hand dumping a bottle of water into that fiery eye while the truck's cruise control hurtles us at seventy-five and all four wheels veer onto the shoulder. Tomorrow morning, when we don't die but his eyes are swollen shut, Pops justifies his decision to keep speeding even though his eyes were melting out of his face by saying, *I didn't want to stop getting to where we were going.*

Crack.

A Pupfish homers in the bottom of the ninth, a long bomb to right field, but it means little. The final score is 10–4. The Pupfish fall to the Invaders. Our pupfish are endangered because they survive in only two sad excuses for springs, Salt Creek on the White Sands Missile Range and Lost River on Holloman Air Force Base, both areas off-limits to the public. The military promises to keep an eye on the population count and let us know when they are gone for good. So now you know our ball team's name is an elegy. We were born to lose.

The ballplayers pack up, and some kids run onto the field. They jump around the mound as a lady snaps a photo of them on her phone and hollers for them to stay out of the dirt. Few photos of victims of drone strikes in Waziristan have been published because the area is dangerous for reporters, because the Hellfire missile destroys everything, because of a "double-tap" tactic that keeps the drones hovering just long enough to launch additional Hellfires at any first responders. One of the few photos I've seen is of three children whose parents are dead, have not yet been dead one day or one night. The children's little hands clutch the rubble, hold the rubble out for the camera, chunks of Dande Darpa Khel, where they will never live again, where their parents have died, have not yet been dead one day or night, staring, her into the eye of the camera and him at the rubble like treasure in his hands, and the small one in the middle looks to her right, in profile, her eyeballs invisible, their lips all dipping at the corners, but these are not frowns—I can trace the sink of a frown but see smiles on their faces, have in my belly, despite the flames behind them, despite the rubble, despite the sinking, a sensation of smiles, a discrepancy called shock and awe that will not last into the night. The government reported no civilian casualties for this strike. Two Hellfire missiles hit exactly what they targeted, just as they always do, because our Reaper uses what marines call the Light of God, a laser fired from a Multi-Spectral Targeting System on the nose of the drone, fired really from a steel cargo container in an American desert or an office in Langley, but beaming down on Dande Darpa Khel in the desert of North Waziristan, a beam that, seen from the ground, might extend up to infinity, *light that looks like it's coming from heaven*, says one drone pilot. *Right on the spot. Coming out of nowhere from the sky. It's quite beautiful.* But, of course, it is green like an alien thing, and you will only ever see it with the right goggles. Even then it comes only in pulses. You see, for a moment, the pitcher's mound lit up, and for a briefer moment, you don't. Then you see the target lit up again with the pulsing green Light of God. Then comes the explosion when you can't see anything at all but light.

CHILDREN OF THE GADGET

In the Year of Our Lord 2015

July 18, 2015

Hundreds of twinkling lights, five hundred brown paper sacks with candles in them, luminarias around the mound and spilling out into the base paths and a family of three with singing bowls on the infield grass, the biggest singing bowls I've ever seen, like singing buckets between their legs and them dragging mallets along the glass rims to make the air drone, for hours the air drones as one by one the luminarias are extinguished by roving figures in the dark, and when another wisp of smoke from a smothered wick dissipates, then we are done remembering, for this year, one more victim of the Gadget, the Manhattan Project's crowning achievement at Trinity, the world's first atomic blast, seventy years ago, right here in Southern New Mexico. The guy sitting in front of me on the bleachers has a John Wayne koozie around his drink. He sips and sips from John Wayne. Up in the press box a trio of announcers takes turns reading pages of names of all the people in the Tularosa Basin who have died of cancer caused, they say, by radioactive fallout from the first breath of the atomic age. For hours, name after name like the slow grind of a macabre graduation ceremony. So then this is how the twenty kilotons of the Gadget's blast fades, not up into the mushroom cloud and gone in under a minute, but filtered through seventy years and still a few more names, and still a few more flames to be extinguished.

Out beyond center field is a rusty merry-go-round, the kid-powered playground kind with the kids running in circles to get it spinning at unsafe speeds and jumping on and getting immediately flung off, and all through the reading of names and extinguishing of luminarias, that merry-go-round never stops creaking and spinning, the children of Tularosa never stop running and hollering and getting flung into the night. It's almost like they don't even know they're the children of the bomb. Or, the Gadget. Children of the Gadget. Out of New Mexico came two different versions of the bomb and then there was a superbomb and eventually many tens of thousands of each including warheads on missiles and torpe-does, but they were all born of the same moment of warfare singularity when mass destruction became less of a campaign and more of a decision. The Trinity Site: just forty-five miles northwest of those children discovering the nauseous joy of physics on the merry-go-round. Every bomb is the Bomb. But that first one at Trinity was called the Gadget—a code name for secrecy's sake, a name diluted by the technicality that it was only a test device, a name meant to hide the significance of what we were about to do. Just a gizmo or a widget. A little doohickey. Nothing but a goddamn gadget. Just toying with the nauseous joy of physics.

Henry Herrera sits up in his lawn chair next to the

bleachers and says, *The thing went off and the fire went up and the cloud rose and the bottom half went up that way.* He gestures over my head toward first base. *But then the top part, the mushroom top started coming back this way and fell all over everything.* He waves both his arms back toward us and all around us, big swoops of old, thin, and crooked arms over his head like he might be able to accurately pantomime an atomic blast or like he's invoking its spirit or just inviting the fireball to rain down again so the rest of us can really understand.

Henry's sort of a celebrity in this crowd, one of the only remaining residents of Tularosa who actually witnessed the Gadget's blast, a guy who's beat cancer three times already and says he'll lick it again if he gets the chance. I've heard him repeat the story, word for word, to anyone who will listen, for years now. He sits next to me, fiddling with the pearl snaps on his Western shirt, petting his white hair down in back behind his big ears, telling the tale in spurts, little stanzas between long gaps of pondering, those rests of silent reflection that never stop growing as we age, like ears, like I guess all our really old storytellers have big ears and the will to ride a lull for as long as it takes until an aphorism or anecdote has marinated on the tongue and is ready to serve. He serves one up: *I'll bet ten dollars to a donut your momma never blamed you for the atomic bomb.* True enough. And the rest of his story sidles out as the luminarias burn.

Henry was eleven and up early, just before dawn, to fill the radiator in his daddy's Ford, always his first morning chore. The radiator on an old Model A had to be drained every night and filled every morning if you couldn't afford fancy additives like water lube or that newfangled antifreeze.

And the Herreras couldn't afford anything fancy. This was 1945 and they were just like all their neighbors in Tularosa, most everyone Hispanic and working ranches, growing and raising as much of their own food as they could and collecting most of their summer drinking water from the monsoon rains. So there's little Henry with his skinny arms holding a bucket over the fill hole in the grille of the Ford, and what he remembers most is that his momma had laundry hanging on the line to dry. He remembers the laundry blowing in the wind. *Kinda strange to have wind like that right before dawn. All her white stuff,* he says. *Linens and shirts and underwear flapping around.* And then the flash: on the polished steel of the Ford's grille and the dull steel of the bucket and the flapping white linens and the retinas of little Henry's eyes. *Light. Night turned to day,* he says. *Like heaven came down.** And then the blast and the shaking and then dark again. Silence. Nobody ever thought much of a bomb going off because bombs were always going off over at the Alamogordo Bombing and Gunnery Range since our Second World War began, but this explosion was different. *It was huge and after*

---

* There's a hymn I sang often in my youth, from a pew in a warehouse chapel over on Cuba Avenue: "Heaven Came Down." I'm certain that in his description of the Gadget, Henry is referencing, however subliminally, this very hymn. I sang it so many times, those lyrics that make simultaneous the historic event of the crucifixion and the divine experience of the singer receiving grace thousands of years later, as if every time you repent, Jesus is crucified again, just for you. Those lyrics that meant one thing about joy until Henry says them about the Gadget: *My sins were washed away and my night was turned to day / Heaven came down and glory filled my soul!* Now *heaven came down* will become a refrain in this essay about the Gadget and mean the opposite of joy, which is sorrow, and also, I think, nervousness.

a few minutes comes this little filmy dust, Henry says. *Fine dark ash just came down and landed all over everything. Momma's clothes hanging out there turned nearly black, so she had to wash them over again. You talk about a mad Mexican.* He laughs at the thought of his momma's face, seeing all her whites turned to grays, screaming, *What the hell did you explode out here, Henry?*

So that's the story of how Henry's momma tried to blame him for the atomic bomb. *It's funny until you know we was drinking it and eating and everything else. But we didn't know that for years. Not really until we started dying.*

For so long the story of the Gadget's explosion at Trinity has included some version of this: history made in an uninhabited stretch of the high lonesome desert in New Mexico. A 2015 PBS documentary about Trinity begins, "Here, miles and miles from anywhere . . ." Even the most acclaimed history, *The Making of the Atomic Bomb*, by Richard Rhodes, an otherwise stellar eight-hundred-page tome that covers everything from the most minute details of late-nineteenth-century theoretical physics to the rate of venereal disease at the Trinity outpost (proudly the lowest in the nation), glosses over that many thousands of New Mexicans lived within fifty miles of the blast. "A bomb exploded in a desert damages not much besides sand and cactus and the purity of the air," writes Rhodes. More recent articles about Trinity occasionally use the phrase "sparsely populated region." And it is true that a few thousand mostly Hispanic or Native ranchers and villagers living within fifty miles of the Gadget pale in comparison to the nearly half million Japanese who felt the Bomb in Hiroshima and Nagasaki in 1945. But that kind of math is little solace for folks such as Henry who feel they've been poisoned in the shadows, forgotten or swept under the rug by their own victorious nation.

Henry intertwines his tale of the Gadget with one about being in the military ten years later, touring Hiroshima and Nagasaki after the war because he'd become obsessed with what he'd seen as a kid—*night turned to day, like heaven came down*—and he needed to see also what the Bomb had done to our enemies, and he surely saw it all: the complete devastation, the rubble and ash and shadows stuck to walls and *just imagine all those families*, he says. His eyes get watery, crying the way all these old tough guys from the desert do, a quivering lip and the eyes barely dripping but gritting his teeth to offset it all, gritting so hard it appears he's trying to stop not just his own tears but trying to will away all the sorrow in the world all by himself, the presence of any tears really secondary to the wrought of his face in relating not just sadness about Japanese civilians killed in the bombings or sadness about American civilians killed by the test but also rage about the inevitability of it all. *We did it*, he says. *We Americans did that. We had to, I know. But nobody remembers we did it here first.*

So here they are having a vigil, three generations of families from the Tularosa Basin, a stretch of desert southeast of Trinity, between the San Andres Mountains and the Sacramento Mountains, from Carrizozo down past Alamogordo with the village of Tularosa smack-dab in the middle. And the luminarias on the village ballpark are their way of saying after all this time, *We were there. The desert you blew up was not so lonesome. We are here still but we are dying. If you cannot save us, then let us tell our story.*

July 18, 1945
(Two Days After the Gadget's Blast)

There's the head of a jackrabbit, blown from its body. Little chunks of them are everywhere, and maybe this one's body is in pieces nearby or maybe it evaporated. There are so many heads and legs and piles of charred guts or just shadows on the sand, burns where all the sand is scorched except where a jackrabbit stood, perked up at the sight of a warning rocket, then blocked the heat of the big blast for a shake until it was blown away, leaving only the specter of its long, jagged ears on the sand. The official report will use the word *eviscerated.* How else to explain a whole spattering of lucky feet not far from the crater where just the other day sand was melted to green glass by heat ten thousand times hotter than the surface of the sun. So it was jackrabbits. And snakes and cicadas and maybe a coyote or two. First blood of the Gadget. Someone reports a stench in the air from eviscerated animals, but that is the only time any death will ever be officially linked to the first breath of the atomic age.

The Gadget's explosion was only announced retroactively after its cousin Little Boy wiped out Hiroshima. The *Alamogordo Daily News*, the paper of record for the Tularosa Basin, wrote it up like this on August 9, 1945, printed this as the Gadget's twin, Fat Man, was falling toward Nagasaki:

> Some of the biggest news ever to break on man's understanding has exploded this week—a terrifying type of bomb, the Russian declaration of war upon Japan, etc., etc. Since our readers get the details in the dailies and magazines and by radio, we will not attempt to even review it. In fact

we are forced to leave out much news of local import for lack of space.

    And in the BIG NEWS: Alamogordo probably is now a heard-of place to people all over the world, as the site of the final atomic-bomb test.

This is the entirety of the announcement of the Gadget's birth in our hometown newspaper. Because the Trinity test happened on the Alamogordo Bombing and Gunnery Range (now White Sands Missile Range), Alamogordo is often credited as the site of the bomb's birth. But the village of Tularosa is closer to Trinity—forty-five miles southeast. Carrizozo is closer still—thirty-five miles east. Alamogordo is sixty-two miles south of Trinity and I guess that's about as close as the government wanted the press to suggest any Americans lived. The announcement in the *Daily News* is small, and half of it is an apology for lack of space. There are two *et ceteras* (abbreviated, of course, for space). Maybe this was the beginning of us not telling the full extent of the story. But Alamogordo was only three thousand folks large and the paper was only a weekly, so maybe it can be excused for extreme brevity regarding "the biggest news ever to break on man's understanding," if not for what comes directly below the small announcement of the Bomb, just an eighth of an inch away, separated only by a slight line with a small circle in the middle, a second announcement that dwarfs the first, dominates the page:

Early on the morning of Friday, August 17th, with the rumbling of heavy trucks, the neighing of horses and ponies, the screeching of monkeys, the trumpeting of Susie Q, the elephant, everyone will know that BUD E ANDERSON'S ALL AMERICAN CIRCUS has arrived at the Tularosa circus lot.

It has always been spectacular to watch the arrival of a circus and how with precision, truck after truck of material and animals are run on the lot, unloaded, and in just a few hours the big top, with its pennants floating in the air, the side show with its colorful banners, all have been erected in the twinkling of an eye, forming a complete little city of its own, ready for the sound of the calliope, the blare of the brass band which announces that all is in readiness for another day of good wholesome family fun and entertainment.

The circus coverage barrels on for another three grafs, down to the bottom of the page, just as flowery as it began, mentioning the "monkies" a few more times and adding the "Great Wilkins Family of aerial artists" along with "Buckley's Troop of trained dogs" and "Rodeo Ranger with his well known educated white Stallion Tonto" and finally bringing things to a close with the promise every reader eagerly awaits: "clowns, clowns, clowns."

Just below the circus ad is an invitation to the Church of Christ in Alamogordo—the warehouse chapel my family has attended for much of the seven generations we've been here. They invite you in August 1945 to attend a study of chapter 10 of the Book of Revelation, aka Revelation, aka the Apocalypse. The name of the sermon this week is "A Mere Form, or a Mighty Force; Pretence or Power," preached by Minister Tice Elkins. His congregation had been working their way through the Apocalypse for months, one chapter at a time, meaning they started way back in May, long before they had any notion of the Bomb. When the Gadget exploded in secret early on the morning of Monday, July 16, the church had just finished, the evening before, reading aloud from chapter 8, which ends with the writer proclaiming, "And I beheld, and heard an angel flying through the midst of heaven, saying with a loud voice, Woe! Woe! Woe to the inhabiters of the earth!" The angel says woe because the angel holds a key to some awful force and has every intention of using that key, which the angel does straightaway: "And there arose a smoke out of the pit, as the smoke of a great furnace; and the sun and the air were darkened by reason of the smoke of the pit."

As we sit at the ballpark, listening to names of the dead, luminarias flickering and merry-go-round spinning, Henry Herrera and I try to talk about something other than the Bomb. We talk about how he plays guitar every Sunday at mass, about how his favorite thing in the sky these days is hot-air balloons, about how he knew my granddaddy and uncles from work out at the missile range in the seventies, after the Department of Defense had gobbled up so much of the land in SNM and was offering the only decent-paying jobs around. But I can't shake the clowns and so I put it to Henry: *Did you go to the circus a few weeks after the Gadget's blast?* He doesn't remember. He can't say for sure. *But, yes, every now and again, there'd be a circus right here.* Then he waves his arms again just like he did when he was showing how the fallout came down, saying from where we sit along the third-base line over to Highway 54 running north to Carrizozo, right in that thousand or so feet of sand and mesquite is where Bud E. Anderson's All American Circus raised their big top seventy years back. We're more or less sitting on top of the old Tularosa circus lot. And so the neighing of horses and ponies, the screeching of monkeys, the trumpeting of Susie Q, all that happened right here but back then and in the wake of the Gadget. Susie Q stomping her giant feet in the radioactive ash. The Great Wilkins Family of aerial artists swinging on their trapeze high above all the settled ash. Trained dogs and Rodeo Ranger and clowns, clowns, clowns, traipsing around in it. And maybe Henry but definitely plenty of the other residents of Tularosa who were children then, many of those whose names are no doubt being read in the endless list over the PA, all of those first children of the Gadget running around excitedly and hollering and the screams of the kids on the merry-go-round out past center field are the screams of all these luminarias rolled back in time and reformed into the light inside the children they once were, running around with their peanuts and big eyes and experiencing magic for the first time right here at the circus in the world's first radio-active fallout.

July 17, 1945
(One Day After the Blast)

Twenty miles northeast of Trinity, M. C. Ratliff and his wife and their grandson and dogs and livestock have been wondering why their house and fences and land are covered in gray snow in the middle of summer. The Army sends out two doctors to investigate a canyon they've just named Hot because it keeps sending the needles on their Geiger counters into a tizzy. The doctors wander onto the ranch in Hot Canyon and are surprised to see the family going about their chores, gathering food and shoeing horses. All the official Army reports claim nobody lives in this area. The doctors do not identify their reason for visiting the Ratliff ranch and do not explain the snow of ash, which will continue to appear at dawn and dusk for many days, blanketing the roof and garden and livestock, sinking into the soil. The Ratliffs appear alive enough and are left to go about their business, dusting the soot from their animals and vegetables, collecting ashy rainwater from their roof for drinking and washing after a long day of chores.

The luminarias are extinguished and Henry heads onto the baseball field with nearly everyone else in the stands, people currently suffering from cancer and people who have loved ones who are suffering from cancer and people who have survived by the skin of their teeth, all to get blessed by the village priest, who lays his hands on their heads one by one as a medicine man, an Apache from the Mescalero reservation in the nearby mountains, dances and drums and sings and kneels down in the dirt around home plate and rubs his hands in the dirt and tosses the dirt up into the air like he's trying to show all things it has contained over time. Dust to dust, ashes to ashes: the simplest story ever told because the whole human part is erased.

When I arrived at this ballpark vigil for the Tularosa Basin Downwinders Consortium, there was a fair amount of confusion at a table where people were gathering and compiling the names of the dead. Some folks wanted to add a name to the list but didn't know if they could because the person didn't die from cancer. And the list makers said, *Well, this is just for those that are dead.* And the family with the name said, *Oh, yes, our father is dead.* And the list makers said, *Oh, well, this is for those that had the cancer.* And the family said, *Oh, yes, he had the cancer but that's not what killed him.* After a long back-and-forth regarding the exact factors that went into the father's death and all the illnesses he suffered and all his addresses of residence, his name was added to the list, a luminaria lit in remembrance of him.

It is so hard to know, seventy years on, exactly whom the Gadget hurt. The explosion killed no one yet the fallout fell all over this desert. In a world where the causes of cancer seem to seesaw between everything and most things and absolute randomness, the issue has become what you might call muddled. The National Cancer Institute is in the midst of a years-long study in Tularosa, but there's not a whole lot of hope that it's a real priority because they only interviewed a half dozen residents of the village and, according to Henry, their questions were dumb. The state's own Tumor Registry claims cancer rates for Anglos, Hispanics, and Native Americans in the Tularosa Basin are similar to those throughout New Mexico, that there is nothing anomalous. So I hold a three-page homemade health survey in my hands, a thorough inquiry of family background and medical history and a page listing over thirty types of cancer, each with a box next to it for writing your year of diagnosis or your family member's year of diagnosis. The village wants to finally collect their own proof that they were downwind of something terrible that now creeps through every new generation too.

The notion of downwinders, American citizens exposed to fallout from nuclear tests, wasn't part of the national consciousness until the 1970s, even though aboveground nuclear weapons testing stopped because of environmental and safety concerns in 1963. The horrors of death by radioactive fallout were well-known, despite government obfuscation, as early as 1946 with John Hersey's publication of *Hiroshima*. But somehow we convinced ourselves that nuclear weapons detonated in the name of science rather than war (if such a distinction can exist) caused little or no harm, despite all evidence to the contrary. In 1954, U.S. tests of a hydrogen bomb at Bikini

Atoll made the Marshall Islands the most contaminated place in the world. That fallout eventually killed a Japanese fisherman on the boat *Lucky Dragon 5* along with eighteen Marshallese children who played in the downfall of what they called snow. Their deaths would lead to compensation payments just two years later for all Marshall Islanders, the first-ever restitution to people affected by nuclear weapons testing, and the last of that kind for nearly four decades. The year 1954 included live television broadcasts of the Bikini test, and a flood of press about the dead fisherman and Marshallese children, and an aftermath of men in full hazmat suits closing down fish markets on California's coast, and a blockbuster film, *Them!*, about giant killer ants, mutants born out of the Gadget's blast at Trinity—all of that and still there was little political pressure to do much of anything about the plight of American downwinders. Not until 1979, and about 750 more nuclear tests on our soil, did Ted Kennedy first try (but fail) to pass a radiation-exposure compensation act for American citizens.

Then John Wayne died.

In November 1980, seventeen months after Wayne lost his long battle with lung, throat, and liver cancer, *People* magazine ran his photo on their cover with the question "Did atom bomb tests give him and other stars cancer?" Their story raised the possibility that, while filming *The Conqueror* in Utah in 1954, John Wayne, Susan Hayward, and many others in the cast and crew were exposed to radiation from a test site at Yucca Flat, Nevada, about one hundred miles from their shooting location. The year before production began, there had been eleven nuclear explosions at the Nevada site, including the infamous atmospheric test of Dirty Harry, which resulted in the highest downwind contamination ever measured in the United States. Ninety-one of *The Conqueror's* 220 cast and crew were diagnosed with cancer by 1980, with forty-six of them already dead, including Wayne. No definitive link between these nuclear tests and the cancers of those from *The Conqueror* production has ever been established. Wayne's penchant for six packs of Camel smokes a day didn't help to resolve anything. But the possible nuking of an American icon finally helped imprint the plight of downwinders on the national conscience. Apparently the only thing more horrifically un-American than the filming of *The Conqueror*, a historic flop in which John Wayne plays the monstrous Mongol emperor Genghis Khan, is the thought that while John Wayne played Genghis Khan, we murdered him with our Bomb.*

---

* *Please, God, don't let us have killed John Wayne*, a nuclear defense scientist told *People* magazine. This prayer contains the obvious and pragmatic desire to avoid extremely bad press, but it's also, when you ponder it deeply, a desperate plea about the whole narrative of our nation, a plea that's caught up not just in our Bomb's possibly having killed one of our most defining (for better or worse) icons, but that the possible poisoning happened as a result of the singularly mind-boggling film *The Conqueror*.

And maybe nobody understood this prayer better than the film's financier and producer, the man who wanted *The Conqueror* to be the great epic of his film career, Mr. Howard Hughes. When *The Conqueror* was panned by critics as one of the worst films of all time, Hughes reportedly spent millions buying up every print in existence. Different sources record his obsession over eliminating the film from public view as either a matter of shame over its awfulness or devotion to its greatness or some of the obsessive-compulsive disorder that dominated his later years. But most agree that he spent a four-month period in 1957 locked in a screening room in Hollywood watching films by

Joseph Masco's got this idea in his book *The Nuclear Borderlands* that he calls the nuclear uncanny: "Fear of radioactive contamination has . . . colonized psychic spaces and profoundly shaped individual perceptions of the everyday from the start of the nuclear age, leaving people to wonder if invisible, life-threatening forces intrude upon daily life, bringing cancer, mutation, or death." Masco writes mostly about Northern New Mexico, the strange collision of Pueblo culture and weapons scientists around the nuclear laboratories at Los Alamos where the Gadget was built, where most all iterations of the Bomb were designed after the Manhattan Project, where all contemporary nuclear weapons science is increasingly happening in immersive computer simulations, where the horrors of the Bomb have become, quite literally, only virtual. You've likely never heard of Masco's

---

himself, naked and eating chicken, watching a few films over and over, and one of the lucky few films for this audience of one was *The Conqueror.* Hughes watched it over and over by himself, even blindfolding the projectionist to maintain the total solitude of the screening. He continued the ritual even after that four-month psychotic break, watching *The Conqueror* over and over when nobody else would or could, through the sale of his airline, which made him the richest man in America, through his gobbling up and development of the largest single stake on the Las Vegas Strip, through his exile in the Bahamas with the Mormon mafia, always watching *The Conqueror* and probably always still with that poor blindfolded projectionist.

Or maybe the blindfolding of the projectionist was not a crass act to maintain the solitude of the screening but an act of grace to save the poor projectionist's life, because maybe in the story of *The Conqueror* is some powerful truth, some wicked axiom about the existence of America, some unutterable prophecy about humankind, the witnessing of which will drive you insane just like Hughes went insane and watched *The Conqueror* over and over and died with six hypodermic

book because we don't read about the Bomb much anymore, we don't talk about it much except as a plot device in our blockbusters or a chess piece in foreign policy charades. The Bomb is shorthand for all sorts of fear and unimaginable devastation that we'd rather not ponder too deeply, and so we keep it at arm's length, a symbol encompassing so much that it might as well be empty. We are becoming numb to the Bomb despite it pervading nearly every aspect of our lives, which is exactly Masco's thesis and why you'll likely never read his book: the Bomb has become a bore, an un-imaginative plot point to inflate the stakes of any film or book or political discussion. But Masco argues that we still feel daily the worry and fear of the nuclear uncanny even as we have made the thing that causes that fear a cliché so in-nocuous by our pop-cultural representations of it that we

---

needles broken off in his skin, needles for injecting codeine right into his muscles, steel needles to maybe dull the pain of knowing the unut-terable prophecy of *The Conqueror*. Or maybe Hughes is a necessary part of the story, of the unutterable prophecy that comes out of the experience of the whole backstory of *The Conqueror*, and the only one with any real understanding of the unutterable prophecy in its full context is the only one who was in the room with Hughes as he watched the film: the blindfolded projectionist.

So here we are: a blindfolded projectionist with the blindfold just barely cinched up on our face through some vigorous smiling motions or cheek stretches and projecting *The Conqueror* for the zillionth time for Mr. Howard Hughes. If we tilt our head back, we can see a sliver of the world beneath our blindfold, and in that sliver is the light of the projector, all the dust particles reflecting the light, the beam expanding as it shoots past the back of Hughes's head, a head that these days just sticks up out of a naked and emaciated body like the top of a raggedy mop, his playboy looks wasted away and his white hair in scraggles and its thinness really clear—transparent—in the light of the projector,

can no longer remember why we feel so fearful all the time. And that makes the fear worse, and useless.

The guy in front of me on the bleachers at the downwinders vigil with the John Wayne koozie is George. I met George a few weeks ago at a downwinders meeting in the village town hall, where he also brandished his Duke koozie.

"The dislocation and anxiety produced by these moments of tense recognition," writes Masco, is "the *nuclear uncanny* . . ."

George hasn't seen *The Conqueror* and didn't know about Wayne's possible downwinder status but waves his koozie at me, showing me he's still got it.

". . . The nuclear uncanny exists in the material effects, psychic tension, and sensory confusion produced by nuclear weapons and radioactive materials . . ."

———————

The Conqueror beamed through the billionaire's scraggles: John Wayne in the Western Costume Co.'s absurd interpretation of a thirteenth-century Mongol tunic, John Wayne in yellow face complete with rubber bands to slant his eyes, John Wayne as Genghis Khan, warring and marauding with his hundreds of warriors, extras cast from reservations of Paiute and Navajo in the southwest of Utah where the film was shot— Snow Canyon, Utah, where the sand was full of fallout from hundreds of nuclear weapons tests just across the border at Yucca Flat, Nevada.

And we can almost see through the billionaire's thin skin too, see with the light of the projector through his thin skin and watch *The Conqueror* play on his blood, on the 150 milligrams of Valium circulating through his system every day. And on the 45 grains of codeine circulating too, in the reflection of the needles broken off in his skin as he stares at the screen, watching John Wayne, whose own blood circulates with 150 milligrams of Dexedrine, speed to shape him up, to help him pass as the sleek but powerful Genghis Khan. What makes America so red-blooded, full-blooded, poison-blooded? And Hughes stares even deeper, beyond the Dexedrine in Wayne, looking for the radiation,

George sat through a whole rant of mine about Wayne and *The Conqueror* and the existence of the nuclear uncanny and how I found his use of that particular koozie, that seemingly innocuous object, at a downwinders meeting to be a kind of anxiety-inducing deal.

". . . It is a perceptual space caught between apocalyptic expectation and sensory fulfillment . . ."

George doesn't have enough fingers to count up the number of people in his life with cancer. This became evident as he was counting them on his fingers for me and, when he ran out of fingers, just pointed to people in the room, telling me how he knew them and which cancer they had or, if it was someone who had already passed, shaking his head and shrugging because he had nowhere to point.

". . . a psychic effect produced, on the one hand, by liv-

---

the tumors that will develop in Wayne's gut and the woman whom Wayne-as-Khan keeps raping, played by Susan Hayward, the smoky-voiced Hollywood vixen who always called Hughes *Mr. Magic* when she fucked him, who bragged openly that she would marry Hughes until suddenly he was married to some other vixen and so Susan Hayward moved on from Hughes until twenty tumors in her brain kept her from moving at all, little clouds so slowly mushrooming in her brain. Did he do that to her? Did his film put the cancer in her like it put the cancer in Wayne? Is Hughes the signal of a paradigm shift from Wayne as the symbol of the American spirit, frontiersman to capitalist, or is Hughes just the logical evolution of the same terrible myth of the conqueror that has slouched through history since Khan and before?

I stole you. I will keep you. Before the sun sets, you will come willingly to my arms, says Wayne-as-Khan to his bride.

Khan's empire came at the cost of around 40 million lives. The American spirit (and policy) of Manifest Destiny that John Wayne embodied cost anywhere from thirty thousand to seventy thousand Native lives during the Indian Wars, not to mention millions of others lost to

ing within the temporal ellipsis separating a nuclear attack and the actual end of the world, and on the other, by inhabiting an environmental space threatened by military-industrial radiation."

George finished his pointing and shrugging and said, *There's nobody but us to remember how these people died. There's no monument. No recognition and no compensation and no monument to anyone. The only monument we got is for the Bomb.*

George talks about compensation because that's exactly what many downwinders have already received. In 1990, thirty-six years after the first payments for nuclear-weapons-test fallout were given to Marshall Islanders, the U.S. government passed RECA—the Radiation Exposure Compensation Act—which provides up to $50,000 of compensation for

---

smallpox and famine since the coming of Europeans and then also all the Native lives lost to all manner of subsequent American fuckery. The two atom bombs dropped in our Second World War killed around 225,000 in Japan. And what has the capitalist spirit of Hughes wrought?

We can hear them now, can literally feel the atomic bombs.

We, the blindfolded projectionist, are at the Desert Inn in Las Vegas where Hughes spends some of his last years pouring money into developing our national City of Entertainment—our Sin City—at the Desert Inn just seventy-five miles from the very same Nevada test site that irradiated Snow Canyon, Utah, where *The Conqueror* was filmed. Hughes watches *The Conqueror* yet again as nuclear blasts shake the walls of his penthouse every three days and shake the projection of the film off the screen. Hughes yells, *Straighten the picture* and *God damn the Bomb.* And it is our job—we, the blindfolded projectionist—to anticipate the shock waves of the Bomb and stabilize the projection despite our blindfold. But we know the trick of seeing a sliver of the world out the bottom of our blindfold and have been peeking like this for years and we could easily straighten the picture but we must not let on

downwinders and up to $100,000 for uranium miners, mill workers, transporters, and any other workers exposed to radiation at nuclear test sites. RECA covers exposures of private citizens in Nevada, Utah, and Arizona but fails to acknowledge that anyone may have been hurt by the Gadget in Southern New Mexico.

I don't have the expertise to convince anyone that the Gadget is responsible for all or any of the cancer in the Tularosa Basin. But I can tell you Henry's story. And I can quote the government's own 2009 report: "Exposure rates in public areas from the world's first nuclear explosion were measured at levels 10,000-times higher than currently allowed." And I can give you Masco's summation of the character of our species' nuclear weapons testing:

> The international nuclear complex is estimated to have already produced over four hundred thousand cancer deaths worldwide simply from the dispersion of radioactive materials into the environment. It also has consistently targeted minority communities for the most dangerous nuclear projects, creating a new form of global environmental discrimination some have called radioactive colonialism. Put differently, even as the sole remaining superpower, the

---

that we are peeking or we will raise the ire of the billionaire so we let the blasts in the distance shake the film from the screen, we let it play like that, Wayne-as-Kahn cockeyed across the wall of the casino penthouse, warring with his thousands of Navajos-as-Mongols, the whole scene wobbling in the shock waves and we just pull the blindfold down and pray the lunatic dies before too long and aren't we always the blindfolded projectionist just letting the uncanny unfold like that, like we couldn't ever change things anyway, didn't have our fingers on the power switch the whole goddamn time.

United States is also the most nuclear-bombed country in
the world, having detonated nearly one thousand nuclear
devices within its own territorial borders.

So then this is really why we're at the ballpark, why the
downwinders of Tularosa have organized into a consortium,
why there are letters of support from U.S. senators and representatives being read from the press box—the victims of the
very first atomic blast want an apology and a chance at compensation. The standard RECA settlement, $50,000, might
help pay for a few months of chemotherapy but wouldn't
even begin to settle the full bill for someone such as Henry,
who's battled the sickness multiple times. Really the folks of
Tularosa want recognition, acknowledgment that the first of
nearly one thousand nukes exploded on American soil had
some consequences for the citizens nearest Trinity. *We were
lab rats*, says Henry. *That ought to make us hero patriots or
something. Which we are. But nobody gives a damn.*

Henry's eighty-one now and his story of the Gadget likely
has all the refinements any of our stories might after seventy
years of retelling. In some ways it's just another anecdote
mapping the birth of a new age our scientists now call the
Anthropocene Era, an epoch in which the earth is affected
by human technology more than all natural forces com-
bined, an epoch whose beginning we often pinpoint at exactly forty-six seconds past 0529 hours on July 16, 1945: the
moment of the explosion at Trinity. A miner felt the blast
forty miles east in White Oaks. Windows broke 180 miles
southwest at a bar in Silver City. A whole passenger train
gawked at the flash 235 miles to the north. On a highway
between Socorro and Albuquerque a blind woman, Miss
Georgia Green, exclaimed, *What's that?!* In Tularosa, little

Henry's eyes lit up and his bones shook and his momma blamed him. But the part of Henry's story that runs against the grain of the official narratives is that most vivid part: the white linens and underwear flapping in the wind on the clothesline and then all of it going gray in the snow of fallout. The government has always claimed that the wind on the morning of July 16, 1945, blew the radioactive plume of the Gadget's fiery mushroom cloud northeast toward the plains in that corner of the state that truly was sparsely populated, that the cloud of fallout simply missed the towns of Carrizozo and Tularosa and Alamogordo in the basin to the south. The whole issue of whether anyone in the Tularosa Basin will ever get any recognition or apology about the Bomb in their backyard relies entirely on weather conditions over about twelve hours on a morning seventy years ago. The answer, my friends, is blowing in the bygone winds.

1620 Hours—July 16, 1945
(Ten Hours Fifty Minutes After the Gadget's Blast)

The beta-gamma meter in Carrizozo goes off scale. So much radiation is in the north part of the Tularosa Basin that scientists openly debate evacuation. Monitors continue to chase the Gadget's fallout cloud beyond Carrizozo but lose radio contact with base camp at Trinity. They are not equipped with long-distance radios. They never expected to chase the fallout so far.

The Army has drawn up plans for evacuating everyone within a forty-mile radius of the blast, if necessary. The evacuation would include Carrizozo but not Tularosa. But their evacuation plans contain little more than maps of villages and ranches in the area—a sham plan to pacify concerned scientists. The Army would never risk exposing their big secret. Tomorrow they'll discover ranches covered in fallout that they had no clue existed because even their maps were a sham. But for now the radios are silent, the fallout monitors out of contact. And no evacuation is ordered. The official reasoning: *There is no immediate threat.* But if some evacuations are ordered now, perhaps fewer people will collect fallout-tainted rainwater from their roofs, fewer people will slaughter irradiated cows or swallow those cows' fresh milk. They will think twice about harvesting their vegetables growing along arroyos flowing with ash. But no evacuation is ordered. Four decades from now one of the doctors who discovered the M. C. Ratliff ranch caked in fallout will pen a memoir that says, "A few people were probably overexposed, but they couldn't prove it and we couldn't prove it. So we just assumed we got away with it."

July 14, 2015

Four days before the downwinders' vigil, two days before the seventieth anniversary of the Gadget's blast, and I'm at the New Mexico Museum of Space History in Alamogordo because the *New Horizons* spacecraft has made a 3-billion-mile journey to Pluto and the man who discovered that lonely rock, Clyde W. Tombaugh, lived in these parts and his ashes are on that spacecraft and this is a ceremony to proclaim today Pluto Day forever after in the Tularosa Basin. In the gift shop of the museum they sell T-shirts sporting a fiery mushroom cloud and the slogan HAVE A BLAST AT TRINITY, NM. This is perhaps an object of the nuclear uncanny like

George's koozie of John Wayne, but it is also just a dumb-ass cash grab and bad humor to boot and the kind of thing whose real value is only in helping us identify with some certainty the morons in our lives because they are the ones proudly wearing the shirt that reduces the whole complex human triumph/tragedy of the Gadget to a corny and insensitive pun. I buy the shirt anyway (size medium, $25.99), but only because I know that at times it is comforting (and empowering and necessary for getting out of a supreme depression) to reduce immense tragedy to a corny pun. But even as you read this, I will not yet have worn the shirt because it will only work once, will only help defuse one imponderable paradigm shift toward greater savagery before it becomes inert like the ugly Christmas sweater at the back of the closet that will never bring you joy again. Sometimes, when so many wars and murders and rapes are on the news, the Trinity T-shirt will call out to me from the drawer, but I will never convince myself that this is as bad as it's gonna get and so I leave it for another day. Mostly I forget it exists.

The museum has only a few exhibits on the Gadget, saving most of their space for space. But recently I found an AP story from November 12, 1945, that reminds me how our explorations of space are totally intertwined with the Bomb: "Hap Predicts Space Ships Dropping Atom Bombs": "General Hap Arnold advises that atomic bomb warfare waged from interstellar space ships is 'within the foreseeable future' . . . Said he: 'War may descend upon us by thousands of robots passing unannounced across our shorelines—unless we act to prevent them.'" We haven't yet waged war on invading robots with spaceships, but we've got plenty of spaceships and they're going far, fueled by the same stuff that made the Gadget blast.

New Horizons uses a radioisotope thermoelectric generator (RTG) to power its over-3-billion-mile journey. The RTG
runs on about twenty-four pounds of plutonium. Though it
is not quite the same weapons grade as the fifteen pounds of
plutonium that made the Gadget blast, it's a nuclear power
whose origins can be traced to the science of the Manhattan
Project and Trinity. And the whole Manhattan Project was
a model for Kennedy's moon shot in the sixties, was the
only real predecessor of NASA, was proof of how the highly
regulated concentration of scientific minds under the pressure of military conflict could change the trajectory of human
existence.

Also, there's the rather obvious Pluto connection: the planet
is named for the Greek god of the underworld, and the element plutonium is named for the planet. Apparently the
naming of the elements neptunium and uranium had
started a pattern that could not be broken, a pattern of naming the little things we were discovering after the biggest
things we had already discovered. But plutonium's once-
removed connection to the god of the underworld manages
to fit too. The underworld of Pluto was often described by
the Greeks as being in perpetual darkness, and the planet
is far enough from the sun to be in perpetual darkness, and
the element in the form of the Bomb has the ability to one
day cast us all into, you guessed it, perpetual darkness. But the
ancient god of the underworld was not an entirely bad guy,
and though he controlled your fate after death, it was not
necessarily a depressing afterlife—there were plenty of fields
in which those who had won the god's favor could frolic.
Pluto could offer rebirth and was often considered the god
of wealth because he was in the ground from which agriculture and minerals arose. So too is plutonium by turns

terrifying and generous. I sit in the theater at the space museum watching video from *New Horizons*' trip to the edge of our solar system and know that the Gadget's legacy, the legacy of the primordial element at its core, includes both the means for escaping our home and the means for destroying it.

In the theater, gobs of schoolchildren hold up little models of *New Horizons* and signs that say WE LOVE PLUTO and PLUTO IS OUR PLANET!!! Technically, scientists have demoted Pluto to a dwarf planet, but in SNM we are stubborn, and proud because Pluto was discovered by one of us—we cling to its glory days as if it were a far-flung chunk of our own desert home. The mayor reads a proclamation declaring this day Pluto Day at the exact moment the video feed from NASA declares the spacecraft is passing by the outer planet, snapping souvenir pics.

In two days, NASA will release the first close-up images of Pluto taken by *New Horizons*, and the world will adore its newfound intimacy with this distant, oft-spurned peewee orb pockmarked by nitrogen glaciers. It will be on the front page of *The New York Times* and you will not be able to scroll through any Net feed without seeing its gnarly surface in amazing detail. On July 16, 2015, we will be in love with the face of Pluto, and almost no one will mention that on this exact same day, seventy years ago, the Bomb took its first breath at Trinity.

July 16 is one of those uncanny days. In it you can already see forming the history of our species' running from its biggest mistake, its own destruction. When the lucky few of us look back at the history of Earth, we'll be like, *Damn. July sixteenth was an uncanny day.* Our president of Mars will gather us in our habitat bubble and give a speech like this:

On this day in 1945 at 0530 hours the first atomic explosion occurred, solidifying our fate. On this day in 1965 we obtained the first close-up photos of Mars, where we now live. On this day in 1969 Apollo 11 launched toward the moon, really beginning our history of travel to other celestial bodies. On this day in 1979 at 0530 hours, ninety-four million gallons of radioactive waste spilled into the Puerco River from a uranium mine in Church Rock, New Mexico, the largest single spill of liquid radioactive waste in U.S. history. We have been morons, my fellow Martians. On this day in 1980 Ronald Reagan was nominated by his party as a candidate for president and would eventually preside over a massive nuclear arms buildup even as he signed nuclear disarmament treaties that would, on this day in 2014, be declared defunct. We have been morons. On this day in 2015 the first close-up photos of Pluto are transmitted to Earth, on the seventieth anniversary of the first atomic blast, showing a planet all cratered and brown, finally solidifying our suspicion that all worlds were just as cold and desolate as our own.

Along with the ashes of Tombaugh, *New Horizons* has another memorial of sorts, the Venetia Burney Student Dust Counter. This instrument is named after the British schoolgirl who, in 1930, suggested Tombaugh use the name Pluto for his newly discovered planet. She liked that the new planet, like the god of the underworld, seemed to disappear even though we can always sense its pull. Because she named the planet, Venetia is also indirectly responsible for the name of the element that fuels the spaceship carrying the dust counter named after her, responsible for the name of the plutonium at the core of the Gadget that made it go boom. What a thing to pin on a little girl! She was eleven when she thought of the name, the same age as Henry Herrera when his momma blamed the Bomb on him.

The purpose of the Venetia Burney Student Dust Counter is unclear. The instrument is meant to study—detect but not collect—how much dust is in the universe and the densities and fluxes of that dust's dispersion, but no one yet knows what might be learned from this data. For now, *New Horizons* sails through that distant perpetual darkness like an impotent vacuum, finding so much dust but not knowing what to do about it.

0900 Hours—July 16, 1945
(Three Hours Thirty Minutes After the Gadget's Blast)

One hundred and sixty enlisted men in vehicles spread out around Trinity, around Socorro and along highways to the north and west. Twenty-five members of the Army Counter Intelligence Corps are in towns within a hundred-mile radius, mostly to manage people if they get jumpy at the sight or sound of the blast. About this time, some enlisted men a few miles north of Trinity get a reading on their Geiger counter that makes them anxious. They immediately abandon the steaks they've grilled as part of an Atomic Age birthday celebration, going so far as to bury the meat underground for fear of radioactive contamination. A handful of enlisted men chasing the fallout south, toward Carrizozo and Tularosa, have been given respirators and they make use of them because the radioactive dust of the blast has begun to coat everything. At least one soldier forgets a respirator in his haste to chase the cloud, and as soon as the needle on his Geiger counter begins to twitch, he takes the officially sanctioned precaution of breathing through a slice of bread.

Some of these soldiers on fallout duty are equipped with gear for sampling the environment for later tests—mason jars for collecting soil samples and FilterQueen vacuum cleaners to suck fallout from the air or the sill of a restaurant window or the sleeve of a shirt. The FilterQueen 200 was introduced in 1939, the first vacuum to use centrifugal force to suck and trap dirt. An upgraded version can be used to filter or freshen air, spray paint, dry hair, sand wood, or polish floors, and, it seems, to collect nuclear fallout. The FilterQueen is a squat little beast of a machine with a hose attachment, the ads for which are everywhere in the 1940s and show housewives dancing with the machine or show the Filter Queen herself, a regal woman whose torso is the actual bulky canister of the vacuum, with the hose around her bare legs like a spiraling hoop dress. And so this is quite literally what transpires in a hundred-mile radius after the first-ever atomic blast: soldiers breathing through bread and carrying around FilterQueens, vacuuming up the fallout. Despite all that hard work, the dust collected by the FilterQueens will never be analyzed or tested. The jars will sit in storage until they are forgotten and lost.

July 10, 2015—Noon

I sit at the bar at Applebee's in Alamogordo next to Barb, a lifetimer in the Tularosa Basin, a white-haired lady who's a ton of fun on account of her sour disposition. She sits every day at the Applebee's bar beginning sometime before noon, sits here in her bathrobe, a shabby, molting vermilion situation. She's dolled up underneath the bathrobe, frilly shirt and a good bit of turquoise, but the frumpy bathrobe is how she chooses to finish off the outfit because nobody in SNM owns a real coat and she is *freezing my ass off here every day*, she yells at no one in particular, *since they started blasting the goddamn AC*. She points up at the air vent in the ceiling and shakes her finger at it and says, *A demon lives there and every day I am battling that demon*. She takes a sip of beer. I only just met Barb, but I agree our Applebee's is a little bit haunted.

On the wall behind Barb, Applebee's has installed a mural of the Trinity Site, not a picture of the Gadget's blast but just a picture of the monument to the test, a lava obelisk that now sits out in the desert of the missile range. Also in the mural is a road sign that is in reality nowhere near the obelisk. The sign, as signs do, explains things: "The world's first atomic explosion occurred on July 16, 1945, at the Trinity Site near the north end of the historic Jornada del Muerto. It marked the beginning of the nuclear age, and the culmination of the Manhattan Project. The site, now part of the White Sands Missile Range, is closed to the public."

Surely you know all about Applebee's quest to be your neighborhood bar and grill since 1986. This quest involved widespread deployment of a highly nostalgic décor, little red wagons and old baseball mitts and rusty rifles and lots of tin signs for gas stations, all manner of stuff that suggests the general feeling of the old white owner's ideal of an American neighborhood. Sometime around the year of our Lord 2010, Applebee's launched a revitalization campaign intended to make their nostalgia blitz more specific to each of the over two thousand neighborhoods in which their restaurants operated. I do not know the intricacies of the process they must have used in those two thousand neighborhoods to ensure that each of their chain restaurants incorporated exactly the right amount of location-specific nostalgia to make all the rest of the crap on the walls seem unique too. But I don't imagine there was much careful consideration of the political or moral contexts surrounding those decisions because most of the revitalization choices are pretty banal. For instance, my experience at a wide range of Applebee's throughout the Southern, Southwestern, Midwestern, and Western regions of America suggests that most of the Applebee's revitalizations consisted of hanging recent team photos from the local high school's sports programs on the wall. But here in Alamogordo we have a mural, a whole wall complete with overhead spotlights, dedicated to the stretch of desert where the Bomb took its first breath, memorializing not even the Bomb or its mushroom breath or its creators but just memorializing the memorial itself, the obelisk made of lava rock that stands in the place of the Gadget's test. And memorializing also, for some reason, a road sign about the memorial. The choice of the obelisk and sign suggests they (whoever is at the top of the Applebee's pecking order for this particular restaurant or region) had an actual conversation about the possible implications of memorializing the invention of the world's deadliest weapon on the walls of their family-friendly, community-centered, happiness- and nostalgia-obsessed eatery, a place that has, for over two decades, had the primary goal of offering so many generic food, drink, and décor options that it quite literally became so bland that it no longer seemed to

belong anywhere and required location-specific revitalization. These Applebee's regional middle managers said to
themselves, *Oh, let's not show the destructive power. Oh, that
might be in poor taste. Oh, let's not even reconsider, though,
the idea to memorialize the thing that will likely bring the
world as we know it to an end, but let's have the mural show
only the memorial to the Bomb, just that innocuous obelisk;
oh, and also throw in a fucking road sign, so that our mural
of the Bomb is so far removed from the idea of the Bomb and
its destructive power that almost all of the people who walk
into our family-friendly, community-centered, happiness- and
nostalgia-obsessed eatery will not have any idea that they are
enjoying their Quesadilla Burgers or Grilled Chicken Wonton
Tacos while looming over them is a memorial to the thing that
will likely bring the world as we know it to an end.*

It doesn't bother me none, says Barb. *I never even really
noticed it.*

Barb talks about how back in the day her husband and
two sons collected a million arrowheads and how she would
still to this day have them all except that her son married a
woman who loved arrowheads too, but then it turned out she
didn't love him and loved money most of all. And so the million arrowheads have all been sold. Or most of them, anyway. She still has a box or two of the good ones in some old
shed alongside her massive collection of movies on VHS.
Barb tightens her bathrobe and switches from beer to a glass
of wine that she implores be filled right to the brim. Her collection of VHS tapes is so massive, she used a computer to
make a file that indexes all the movies she's recorded from
TV onto the VHS tapes over the years. She has the computer file printed out somewhere. She says there's something
like three thousand movies on the list but then remembers

she could generally fit three movies on one VHS, so really it's maybe only about a thousand videotapes. That still sounds to me like an impressive collection until she switches back over to the arrowhead story and says, *Yeah, my husband and boy collected those arrowheads all over the Southwest. They got all kind of rocks too. You know, you'll love this . . . they got some of that green stuff from the Bomb.*

Trinitite, also called Alamogordo glass, is the name of the stuff created when the Gadget's blast melted the desert sand. Everybody around here has some. My family has plenty and the bartender chimes in that she's got some in her nightstand and Barb says her husband and her boy probably got one whole box full of it. I ask if her greedy ex-daughter-in-law absconded with the trinitite and she says no, she's sure that's still in the old shed. I tell her I hope she wasn't too fond of her VHS collection. Even though trinitite is more or less safe to handle, a whole box of it probably has more than enough radiation to, over many decades in a storage shed, erase the VHS tapes sitting next to it. I've seen it erase X-ray film stored beneath it on a closet shelf. In 1945, radiation from the Gadget made it all the way to Indiana, where it ruined whole production runs of film at Kodak's manufacturing plant. Likely all Barb's recordings of *The Conqueror* have been erased by trinitite. She stops talking to me after this revelation. I keep picking at my Wonton Tacos.

Masco writes this about the 1955 Apple-2 atomic bomb test in Nevada, when the military conducted "a civil defense exercise designed to measure how a 'typical' American community would look after a nuclear attack . . .

An elaborately rendered town was built on the test site, consisting of a fire station, a school, a radio station, a library, and a dozen homes in the current building styles. These buildings were carefully constructed, furnished with the latest consumer items (appliances, furniture, televisions, carpets, and linens), and stocked with food that had been specially flown in from Chicago and San Francisco. Residences were populated with mannequins dressed in brand-new clothing and posed with domestic theatricality— at the dinner table, cowering in the basement, or watching television.

You've no doubt seen video of this. The footage of Apple-2 exploding life-size dollhouses known as Survival Town was widely circulated in civilian preparedness videos throughout the Cold War but has, these days, become a kind of cliché, a joke. The archival footage of JCPenney's mannequins exploded by an atomic blast has been used so often, as B-roll in so many shows and films, that we laugh when we see it. *What were we thinking?! Ha-ha. So naïve we were!* But even as we recognize our past ignorance, we internalize the image of those smithereened mannequins as the worst thing the Bomb ever did to America. The Campbell's soups lined up perfectly in the pantry. The midcentury furnishings. The pencil skirts and the Studebakers. A whole lot of staging of now-vintage décor. The ideal of a contemporary American neighborhood that was nuked back in 1955 looks a lot like the inside of a nostalgia-obsessed Applebee's in 2015. I concoct a plan to replace the Applebee's mural of the lava obelisk at Trinity with a looping projection of Apple-2's destruction of the ideal American community to see how that affects people's appetites. Then Barb and I head out for a smoke.

Another thing that happened during Apple-2: weapons scientists employed a system of parabolic mirrors to channel the flash (and heat) of the twenty-nine-kiloton blast into a thin beam they then used to light their cigarettes. "The massive destructive power of the atomic age," writes Masco, "is marshaled to accomplish that most mundane—and purely sensual act—of smoking."

I use only a Bic. Barb persists in not talking to me though, so we just stand there, gandering at our smoke in the wind.

0545 Hours—July 16, 1945
(Fifteen Minutes After the Blast)

The energy developed by the test is several times greater than expected. The cloud column mass now reaches a phenomenal height: fifty thousand to seventy thousand feet. The mass will hover over the northeast corner of the Trinity Site for several hours. This will be sufficient time for the majority of the largest particles to fall out. But now various levels move in different directions. In general, the lower one-third drifts eastward, the middle portion to the west and northwest, while the upper third moves northeast. Many small sheets of dust move independently at all levels, and large sheets remained practically in situ . . . The distribution over the countryside is spotty and subject to local winds and contours. Basically the fallout is going everywhere and could go anywhere and, they say officially, it's hard to say.

July 1, 2015—Breakfast

Tina says many times, *We're the ultimate patriots,* a line that has become the rallying cry for Tularosa Basin Downwinders

Consortium. She's battled thyroid cancer just like half the people she knows. Her father died from jaw cancer. Both of her grandfathers died of stomach cancer within a decade of the Gadget's blast.

Tina Cordova is a cofounder of the consortium, the person responsible for the meetings and the protests and the luminaria vigil that will happen later this month. She is tireless in her organization of people and politicians in an effort to get the children of the Gadget recognized and compensated as the world's first downwinders. We're at IHOP debriefing because she's recently hosted U.S. senator Tom Udall in Tularosa, had him sit through a few hours of stories of sickness and death from Henry Herrera and Margie Trujillo and Edna Hinkle and Louisa Lopez and dozens of other downwinders. They preached at him and sobbed at him and begged for him to take their sorrow back to Washington and lay it at the feet of lawmakers with power to amend the RECA legislation. Udall will go back to Washington and say, *These downwinders are the ultimate patriots.*

Ultimate patriots—that means we've died for our country, Tina says when I keep asking about that phrase, which sounds mismatched to the subject, like a group of comic-book superheroes rather than cancer-stricken villagers. Many downwinders have endured lifetimes of discrimination because of their Mexican heritage. All are at an economic disadvantage in this poor state. Some, such as Edna Hinkle, have had their ranchland taken by the government for use in the missile range. The abuses compound and still they love their country. I get the sense there is no other choice. A patriot makes a conscious sacrifice. A victim, on the other hand, is powerless. It is a remarkable contortion to call your involuntary exposure to an atomic blast a sacrifice, but when your whole life has been a struggle against powerlessness, you bend to keep from breaking.

Tina wears a black bandanna in her hair and a small crucifix around her neck. The area beneath her eyes is always damp from heat, from the sweat of running around. She touches her forehead with her fingertips as she talks, both hands and the fingers just sort of lightly on her temples, as if she's got a lifelong headache she still believes can be willed away. She presses harder when she talks about her father, who was just three years old at the time of the blast. Milk was his beverage of choice, and before all this mess, everyone used to marvel and tease about how much milk that kid drank. But now they realize the error of their joking—those irradiated cows.

It was probably also a mistake to do so much picnicking out at the Trinity Site, Tina says. For up to five years after the blast, locals would drive out to the site for lunch, spend the afternoon eating from baskets and filling those baskets with souvenirs of trinitite.

We eat as she relates how first they removed the right side of her father's tongue and jaw on account of the cancer. A few years later when he was diagnosed with prostate cancer, it was no big deal after all the jaw surgeries. Then they found cancer in the left side of his face, a totally separate cancer from that first one on the right side. The doctors kept telling him how incredibly rare this was, to have two different cancers on one face. She mentions again how much milk he drank as a young boy. All around IHOP are glasses of milk and little pots of milk to pour into coffee, skillets of ground beef and burritos of ground beef and big slabs of breakfast steak.

The first of the creatures mutated by the Bomb were promptly eaten. These were the cows. Other animals died, of course. The government records only the eviscerated jackrabbits, but on September 12, 1945, the AP reports, "Snakes were killed. Ground squirrels and other small animals died. A bat was found miles away, hanging apparently unharmed, but so shocked that it did not attempt to get away from men.* There was the stench of death for about three weeks, all from small animals." This report doesn't mention the cows, but by September, ranchers all around Trinity noticed their livestock had changed, were a different color on the sides that had faced the blast. By October the

* This invincible bat hanging in the wake of the first atomic blast was undoubtedly a Mexican free-tailed bat, a species that almost kept us from creating the Bomb at all. These bats fly out of Carlsbad Caverns in SNM by the millions during the summer, an emergence that darkens the evening redness 150 miles southeast of Trinity. Early in 1942, reeling from the surprise attack of Pearl Harbor, a Harvard researcher visited the caverns and snagged about three hundred emerging bats. He wanted to know if their bony wings had the power to carry time-delayed explosives—seventeen grams of napalm. The superweapon on his mind was a fleet of American bombers retrofitted to carry tens of thousands of bats, bats that could be released over Japan, bats that would roost in the wooden houses of the Japanese, bats that would explode after a day or two and ignite the houses and create firestorms that would level cities. President Franklin Roosevelt had approved the project, writing, "This man is not a nut. It sounds like a perfectly wild idea but is worth looking into." The Army and the Navy pursued bat bombs, achieving suitably destructive results, including the accidental incineration of an airfield in Carlsbad, New Mexico. But the army of bats was abandoned when the project developed too slowly and the directive came down to allocate all available military resources to the Manhattan Project. Go watch the bats emerge at dusk in Carlsbad. Millions in a wondrous roar from the underbelly. Every bat a civilian family burned to death. And still we could imagine something more monstrous.

first of these irradiated cows were sold to slaughter. The November 1945 issue of *New Mexico Stockman* magazine ran the headline "Red Hair of Hereford Cattle in Region Surrounding Site of Atomic Bomb Test in New Mexico Turns White." But this link to the Bomb didn't matter much when it came time to sell to slaughter. Or, it only affected the price. "The cattle all appeared healthy, but because of the strange color markings, the purity of the pedigree was questioned, and the ranchers had to take a cut in their price." Bad pedigree was an explanation that all could wrap their brains around, especially when the country was in the midst of that strange dance with the Bomb, in awe of its power, in a daze from the end of our Second World War, but also with our government swearing up and down that the Bomb was nothing too crazy.

The first public tour of the Trinity Site was organized in September of 1945 "to show first hand," the AP reported, "that the facts do not bear out Japanese propaganda that apparently tried to lay the foundation for claims that Americans won the war by unfair means." This was an Army-led media tour with writers and photographers donning "white canvas foot-bags" to protect against radioactive sand and with warnings that "spending a day and night right in the crater [was] a possibly risky business," but with assertions that "no horrors other than the familiar ones" were inflicted on the enemy. Even as the writers and the scientists tiptoed around "the great jade saucer" and left the "complete annihilation center" after just an hour when their Geiger counters got to jumping too high, the Army maintained that, for the enemy, in the destroyed cities, just eleven days after the Bomb, "it was safe to move permanently into the center of the blast area and live there all his life."

"No horrors other than the familiar ones," they said.

The mutated cows that weren't quickly sold to slaughter to keep from incurring too much of a price cut ended up as celebrities. By November of 1945 many more cattle with "discoloration" or "burns" were rounded up and displayed at the Alamogordo zoo. Kids came on field trips and sewing circles spent their afternoons in the zoo park gazing over their needlework and drunks stumbled over from the Plaza Pub across the street to do their cross-eyed gawking. The newspaper called them "Atomic Cows" and they traveled like a sideshow from Alamogordo to El Paso and back again. In December, Paramount Pictures came to town and "secured some good pictures of the cattle and also of two cats which have changed coloring." This stretch of fame did not last long. The military took note and started rounding up the mutated cattle that hadn't already been slaughtered, about three hundred head, and sent some as far away as Oak Ridge, Tennessee, where they were poked and prodded and bred until they were raw. Only twice in the 1950s would the atomic cows at Oak Ridge hit the headlines, both times to say they were fine or dying of natural causes or didn't seem to be passing on any mutations to their offspring.

The effects of internal radiation from inhalation and the consumption of contaminated food are hotly debated, even in the wake of more recent nuclear fallout situations such as the reactor meltdown at Chernobyl in 1986, where estimates of sickness from this kind of exposure range from a few hundred people to millions. *More studies are needed* is the refrain Tina Cordova keeps hearing. But she has little hope for the ongoing cancer studies in Tularosa. Like Henry Herrera, she thinks the people conducting the studies have so little understanding of the villagers' way of life that they will never reach the appropriate conclusions. She can't, for instance, ever remember them asking about the cows. Tina shifts gears, talks about her fifteen-year-old niece, who has expressed concern about whether she should have children because they might be born deformed. Tina talks about her own anxiety, worry over when her cancer will come back or when the next member of her family will be diagnosed. She knows of two young men from the community who committed suicide after they were diagnosed. *Having seen their neighbors' faces and breasts and guts removed,* she says, *they just didn't want anything to do with it.*

This kind of fear is a big part of the nuclear uncanny, and some studies suggest the emotional toll is ultimately costlier than the measurable physical effects of fallout. A 2011 study of the aftermath in Chernobyl:

> The information policy of the Soviet government which deliberately concealed the scale and the danger of the accident in 1986 and thereby gave room to rumours about disastrous health consequences, the unresolved scientific debate on expected long-term health consequences as well as the inability to assess one's own type of affectedness have provoked deep rooted fears and uncertainty in the population. As a consequence, even physically healthy individuals might be afraid of falling ill. This worry and anxiety might manifest itself in lower subjective well-being, psychological distress or mental disease . . . Significantly higher suicide rates among the Chernobyl affected population indicate the high mental toll associated to the catastrophe.

The study also suggests children exposed to fallout have lower educational outcomes, which in turn makes it more likely their children will have lower educational outcomes, which has a ripple effect throughout the generations. But the same can happen to people who believe they've been exposed to fallout even if no objective evidence supports that belief. Compensating for this anxiety, depression, fatalism, and all of the educational and economic implications, the study concludes, would require 7 percent of the Ukrainian GDP in addition to the 5 to 7 percent already being spent on Chernobyl-related social programs. "The long-lasting toll of the Chernobyl catastrophe for the Ukrainian population," the report says, "works mainly through mental distress and subjective perceptions of poor health rather than through measurable somatic health effects." Another doctor investigating the Chernobyl disaster put it this way: "These people are sick. It's just not the type of illness they think. We have to realize that the psychological damage here runs very deep. And we need to treat that every bit as vigorously as we need to treat cancer."

Tina holds her forehead, rubs her temples.

There are no horrors other than the familiar ones.

0530 Hours—July 16, 1945
(Fourteen Seconds After the Gadget's Detonation)

It was a vision which was seen with more than the eye.

It just kept echoing back and forth in that Jornada del Muerto.

While this tremendous ball of flame was there before us,

and we watched it, and it rolled along, it became in time diffused with the clouds . . . Then it was washed out with the wind.

Words haven't been invented to describe it.

Now we are all sons of bitches.

April 4, 2015

Today is Holy Saturday. Tomorrow is Easter and I'll be down in the Valley of Juárez, where the drug cartels have shifted their war away from the city in search of other Mexicans to terrorize. But today I'm up early with Pops and we're headed to the northernmost part of Southern New Mexico, headed to the Trinity Site as part of the seventieth anniversary caravan of pilgrims. Hundreds of vehicles and a few chartered buses meet up at 7:00 a.m. in the parking lot of Tularosa High School. The caravan coalesces one thousand feet west of a baseball field that will be covered in luminarias in three months, coalesces directly across the road from the lot where Bud E. Anderson's circus raised its tents in August of 1945. As we snake out of the parking lot sometime after 8:00 a.m., we pass a group of people in folding chairs on the side of the road and people standing alongside the chairs, jumping and pumping signs and shouting. Some of their faces are painted like skulls in the manner common here around Día de los Muertos, but today is not Día de los Muertos. *Estos son los días de los muertos,* they say. Some of them have skull cutouts pasted to a stick. Many of them have signs that read TRINITY TEST FAILED US or YOUR RADIATION MADE US PATIENTS or SPEAKING UP FOR THOSE WHO HAVE BEEN SILENCED BY THE

BOMB. Some signs are just a picture of the international symbol for radiation, the trefoil, with a skull at its center. It is not immediately clear what these people are protesting, and many of the people in cars bearing license plates from out of state roll past them with scowls, upset anyone would try to sour their family vacation to such a historic landmark. The tourists must think these protesters are burnt-out hippies and their progeny, still tripping on ripples of the psychedelic era, still believing a world without nukes is possible or even desirable. But all these folks with signs and skulls are self-described *ultimate patriots*. They seem a sideshow until you spend hours listening to them read the names of their dead. They do not hate the Bomb or their country that made it. They just want their dues for being in the wake of the first breath. The caravan moves so slowly out of the parking lot that the protesters get a chance to make everyone feel uncomfortable, even if few understand why.

As we crawl along, it becomes evident that caravans packed this tight with minivans and SUVs are an extraordinarily inefficient way to travel. The kids of the families inside the minivans and SUVs keep having to stop along the side of the road to pee. On days when the Trinity Site is open, a solid stream of piss flows down the middle of White Sands Missile Range, down along the road to Tularosa. When we arrive, many hundreds of cars are already there, visitors having streamed in from the north gate, where participation in a caravan is not required for entrance. All those cars and trucks and RVs and buses in the middle of the open range certainly gives the sense something important is going on. And the media add to the frenzy, are already running around with cameras, working up their hot takes about the legacy of the first atomic bomb test in an "uninhabited region of the New Mexico desert."

Today thousands of us are milling around, pretty literally milling around because there is little to see or do. You can take a ten-minute bus ride to the McDonald Ranch House, where the Gadget was assembled. You can stand inside Jumbo, the steel blast barrier for the Gadget, which was never used. You can touch the black obelisk marking the exact site of detonation, maybe kick at the ground hoping to uncover a bit of trinitite. Everybody mills. Many chat. Some of it will end up in *The New York Times*:

> "This is kind of the mecca," said Cammy Montoya, a spokes-woman for the White Sands Missile Range. "This is the first. This is the marking point."
>
> "It's nice to sit back and let it sink in, and really get a sense of where you're at—you get to feel the wind, feel the sun and see the mountains," [a visitor] said. "It's so impor-tant for people to get here and touch and feel a place like this."

But most chatter will bounce off the obelisk and disappear:
I can't believe no one died.
No one died?
Well, I heard there was cows.
They were only irradiated.
Mutated? Like with superpowers? Superpower cows?
Cooked.
Atomic burgers. We ought to open a joint that sells 'em.
But a burger truck is already set up west of the obelisk.

The menu makes no mention of atomic cows, just as the official program for the Trinity Site open house makes no mention of downwinders.

By the time I was born, four decades after the Gadget's blast, nearly every rancher in the region had a story about how his cows or his daddy's cows had been hit by the Bomb, burned or bleached or grown a second head or mutated into elephantine beasts. The stories had become unbelievable. And this was true of our whole culture. By the time I came around the Bomb's power had long since been subsumed into myth, the origin story for countless superheroes and supervillains. Captain Atom and the Fantastic Four, Spider-Man and the Hulk, Firestorm and Starlight and Doctor Manhattan, all born of atomic power. Even if the Bomb was never again used, we were desperate to remember that it had inside it an otherworldly thing with the power to change us. All those superheroes were not just the hope that something good could come of the Bomb but that something could come at all, more than an infinite stalemate, that the Bomb and its power could change us from the bloodthirsty thing we've always been, force us into something infinitely better, or, with the supervillains, at least something infinitely worse so that we'd get on with going extinct. The atomic cows were the first walking sign of our foray into this age of desperation—that epoch the scientists now call Anthropocene, the first new geological era in 1.8 million years, predicated on humans as the primary destructive force on planet Earth—just a little *discoloration* here, a slight *burn* there, one flank fully bleached by fallout and the other still that old Hereford red. As a child when I heard about my great-granddaddy's cows bleached white on the side facing the Gadget's blast, I spun them around in my mind, seeing on one side the dusty color of the Old West and on the other side the glowing, irradiated world of Spider-Man and the Hulk and Doctor Manhattan. All of SNM sometimes feels like that now, after the Bomb, stuck with one foot in two epochs, the ancient and the futuristic ungracefully fused, a warning or a sideshow. All of us down here have been reared in that wobble. The Gadget was designed up north, on top of an extinct volcano at Los Alamos, but then, to blow it up, they just barely dragged it across the 34th parallel, which divides our state in half, that literally divided New Mexico territory in half during the Civil War. Union up north of the 34th. Confederacy down south of the 34th. Surely the whole state has suffered from the industrial nuclear complex, but up north they get it with a side of prestige in the form of two elite national laboratories.* Down here we get one black obelisk at 33°40′38″ N, just twenty-three miles south of the 34th parallel, twenty-three miles into the underbelly of the American West where atomic cows roamed. But now the cows are little more than a joke around the obelisk, which is itself

---

* I'm being too flippant here. The pretty clear cultural divide between Northern and Southern New Mexico is only partly about the Bomb, which has wrought its havoc throughout the state with devastating fairness. Masco writes plenty about the toll that the nuclear industry has taken on the people of Northern New Mexico. As does V. B. Price in *The Orphaned Land: New Mexico's Environment Since the Manhattan Project.* The gist: lots of exposed people, lots of sick Native American uranium miners, and lots of radioactive runoff into communities and rivers around the national labs near Los Alamos and Albuquerque. For instance, Acid Canyon, an area named as a result of large amounts of nuclear waste that flowed through it after being unceremoniously drained "down the mountain" from Los Alamos. Acid Canyon has been "cleaned up," they say, and now boasts a pretty sweet skate park for the

little more than a joke. There's a lot of space between debili-
tating fear and ignorant nonchalance, but why do we have
such a hard time walking that line? See the people with their
faces painted like skulls, holding skull cutouts pasted to a
stick, flashing the international symbol for radiation with a
skull buried at its heart. These are the children of the Gadget. There are no superheroes, no real Captain Atom or Fantastic Four, no Spider-Man or Firestorm, no Starlight. But
there are these downwinders, real people who are more than
myth. They have been sick and maybe they are sick still.
They have little power, super or otherwise. But they remind
us, at least, of what we are dangerously close to forgetting.
And that's exactly what any superhero story must do. If the
Bomb is the origin story for any superhumans, it must be
these ultimate patriots.

---

kids. And don't forget about the Church Rock uranium spill way up
north near Gallup, New Mexico, still the largest single incident of
radioactive contamination on American soil.

The Church Rock accident happened at 0530 hours on July 16,
1979, exactly thirty-four years, to the minute, after the Trinity test. The
uranium mine's disposal pond burst and poured into the Puerco River.
The exact consequences of this spill are much contested. The people of
the most exposed community, Navajos, say they are sick. The government says they are not. But none can debate the fear, the nuclear uncanny, the little bit of hesitation before putting any local water or food
in the mouth. Maybe the most uncanny of facts about this spill is not
that it happened at exactly the same minute and on the same day of the
year as the Gadget's blast, but that it happened even as *Superman* was
still rocketing toward a $300 million box office.

Superman?

Yes.

July 9, 1945
(One Week Before the Gadget's Blast)

"Up it went, a great ball of fire about a mile in diameter, chang-ing colors as it kept shooting upward, from deep purple to orange, expanding, growing bigger, rising as it expanded, an elemental force freed from its bonds after being chained for billions of years. For a fleeting instant the color was unearthly green, such as one sees only in the corona of the sun during a total eclipse."

William Laurence will publish this description in one week after witnessing the Gadget's blast. But he's drafting it before the blast because he wants to get it right. All the sci-entists have clued him in on how it will look. They've done all the math. There's been talk the Bomb might light the atmosphere on fire. They for sure know there will be quite a show, but their equations say that on July 16 the world will

---

A year before the spill, Christopher Reeve had pranced around in his red tights and cape, shooting the climactic scene of the film only three miles from the United Nuclear Corporation's Church Rock mine, at a place that would forever after be known as Superman Canyon. The cli-max of the film's story happens after Lex Luthor has launched a nuke into the San Andreas Fault and Superman is trying to mitigate the dam-age by flying to the center of the earth and forcing up its molten core to plug the gap. But the earthquakes have already started and Lois Lane is caught in the quakes out in the desert along the fault line. She dies. So then, in one of the most iconic film scenes of all time, Superman con-torts his face into a devastating strokelike cry and flies around the world, against the direction of its revolutions, in a rage until he gets the world spinning backward and manages (despite the laws of basic physics) to re-verse time just enough to get back to the moment before Lois Lane dies.

Here's the uncanny part: all of the San Andreas Fault stuff was

not end, not on account of their Bomb. Laurence will be the only journalist allowed on-site for the Trinity test, has had mostly free rein for over a year to chronicle the Manhattan Project. Perhaps at this time, 1109 hours on July 9, Laurence sits in his room at the Los Alamos camp, sets aside his draft of the blast, and decides to do some official government work, begins revising a press release for the military to use after next week's test, one that will include no purple prose about elemental forces, one that will be a simple cover story to keep the existence of the Bomb secret. Then there is commotion out in the street. The soldiers and scientists have gathered. They stare up at the sky, up at a solar eclipse, many using the same welder's glass that will shade their eyes next week as they gawk at the first breath of the atomic age. The Los Alamos encampment is located at 35°84′N, 106°28′W, on top of a mesa, an extinct volcano. At this location the eclipse will reach its maximum at 1152:21 hours, when the moon will obscure 71.58 percent of the sun. Perhaps this eclipse is what gives Laurence the inspiration for his cosmic description of the Gadget's blast.

In other parts of the world, today's solar eclipse is total. The moon's shadow hits like the fine point of a dagger first

---

filmed not in California at the actual fault but at the canyon in New Mexico near Church Rock. So in July of 1979, even as that canyon was filling up with over a thousand tons of radioactive waste, tens of millions of people were in theaters watching that exact landscape get hit with a nuclear missile. Our stories of the Bomb, the superheroes we invented to deal with the fear of the Bomb, were already distracting us, were quite literally, in this case, putting us in a dark room and showing us a miraculously saved version of the landscape that was at that very moment flooded with the worst of our creations, the myth mapped over the actual and totally overshadowing it, because in the end Superman

in Idaho, then to Montana and northeast to Hudson Bay and across the North Atlantic to Greenland, then arcs back down through Norway, Sweden, and Finland before passing just seventy miles north of Leningrad in the Soviet Union. The citizens of Leningrad, if they look up at 1413 hours, will see the moon obstructing 98 percent of the sun. But they may not look up because they are still recovering, their heads still hanging from the 872-day Nazi siege that ended last year, still hanging from the weight of over 1.5 million dead, still focused on the trials of over two thousand of their friends and neighbors arrested for cannibalism during the hunger of war. But the Nazis surrendered two months ago, after Hitler's suicide. As the moon's shadow moves southeast past Moscow in the sixth year after our Second World War began, a third wave of mass suicide sweeps across the defeated Nazi regime. This is why we will sometimes call the solar eclipse of July 9, 1945, the Victory Eclipse, even though the war is not yet over. The moon's shadow finally peters out somewhere in Central Asia, just about three thousand miles east of Hiroshima, Japan.

Way back on May 28 in 585 B.C.E., another total eclipse of the sun occurred in the sixth year of a war. On that morning the moon's dark dagger of a shadow sticks into the Southern

---

saved the girl and everyone left the theater feeling triumphant. Never mind that Superman chooses to only rewind the world enough to save his girlfriend, never mind that he doesn't bother to rewind even just a few more minutes to stop the nuke-triggered earthquakes that are killing thousands, never mind that he doesn't bother to rewind enough to stop the nukes from launching, never mind that he doesn't bother to move back all the way in time to the days before the Gadget when there was not so much fear. Maybe the moral is that even Superman, with his ability to control the spin and tilt of the earth, with his ability to manipulate time, could never stop the human bend toward obliteration.

Pacific, then drags northeast over present-day Costa Rica and Haiti and over the Atlantic to France before swooping back down toward the westernmost protrusion of Asia, where a battle rages. The fifth-century B.C.E. historian Herodotus tells it this way:

> As, however, the balance had not inclined in favour of either nation, another combat took place in the sixth year, in the course of which, just as the battle was growing warm, day was on a sudden changed into night. This event had been foretold by Thales, the Milesian, who forewarned the Ionians of it, fixing for it the very year in which it actually took place. The Medes and Lydians, when they observed the change, ceased fighting, and were alike anxious to have terms of peace agreed on.

"Day was on a sudden changed into night," says Herodotus.

Isaac Asimov, in his book *The Search for the Elements*, credits this moment, when the prediction by Thales of Miletus is vindicated, as the beginning of science as we know it, the first time someone used observable facts to make a hypothesis about a cosmic event that then actually came to pass. That is, perhaps, a fairly singular pinpointing of these origins. But doesn't it feel good to believe that the very origins of science coincided with the end of a war? Isn't this where we have always hoped science would lead us, the commencement of peace? But then why might one eclipse have this effect and not another? If the sun were just a bit more obstructed by the moon on the afternoon of July 9, 1945, at Los Alamos, would that have made any difference? What if we could tilt the earth just a smidge so that the Gadget and its creators, exactly one week before Trinity, are in the eclipse's path of totality? Who among us has the power to alter the movement of our planet? But a week before Trinity there is already another bomb headed toward Japan, the Gadget's uranium counterpart, Little Boy, which requires no test, which will be dropped on Hiroshima anyway. Trinity is already just a formality. The science that maybe began with the Eclipse of Thales is now advanced enough to be confident that it can create the opposite of a total solar eclipse.

Night turned to day, says Henry Herrera.

Heaven came down.

"On that moment hung eternity. Time stood still. Space contracted to a pinpoint. It was as though the earth had opened and the skies had split. One felt as though he had been privileged to witness the Birth of the World." This is how William Laurence will finish off his description of the Gadget's blast next week. He will work hard to make it a beautiful piece of writing and an honest piece of writing, just as he will with all his future books encouraging our mass proliferation of nuclear armaments. But perhaps now, just after the eclipse, he heads back inside, sits back down at his desk to finish the lie that will be the cover-up disseminated in the days after Trinity. The document is modular and will tell the public what it needs to know in any scenario, regardless of the outcome of the test. The first paragraph is the only one that will be released to the public. It simply states that on July 16, 1945, an ammunitions magazine exploded on the Alamogordo Bombing and Gunnery Range and "there was no loss of life or injury to anyone."

A second paragraph, to be added in the event that something goes wrong, states, "Weather conditions affecting the content of gas shells exploded by the blast made it desirable to evacuate civilians." This paragraph will not be used.

Also never to be used is a third paragraph, prepared if something goes more than wrong, goes terribly wrong. This section contains only four words, followed by lots of haunting space for use by a future writer because the current writer does not expect to survive such a catastrophe. And in that way this brief, unused third paragraph of a press release—so much blank space—is the most honest description of the Gadget and its legacy that Laurence will ever write:

Among the dead were:
(names)

AFTER THE FALL

In the Year of Our Lord 2012

Aunt Yvonne says, *You caught me crying.* She's chopping onions. *Enchiladas as always,* she says, and pours over corn tortillas her big bags of homemade red sauce from chilies whose seeds are the kind without vandalized genes. *Heirloom, I guess you call them,* she says, meaning they are doctored neither to appease the weak nor punish the foolhardy. She wants to keep me busy eating so she can tell a story. She's my great-aunt, which means she has more stories and cooks better than a regular aunt. She tells this story: One time a spaceman floated down into the corral at the old family ranch. *I always wanted him to know how badly he scared us. We woke up one morning and those lights were just flashing and spinning and we jumped up and put on just enough clothes and running outside here was this balloon coming down in the corral! And then the spaceman in it—he got on the cover of* Time *magazine.* An heirloom is something handed down from generation to generation. The family ranch was sold when I was a kid, what was left of its thirteen hundred acres anyway, after the government gobbled it up using eminent domain until the ranch house was surrounded by a missile range. Look at a map and you can see this: a vast gray stretch in the gut of Southern New Mexico, the largest military installation in the United States, its eastern border below Highway 70 straight as an arrow save one notch, where the ranch house sits, where Great-Granddaddy sat on the porch with a rifle and said, *Y'all will have to go around.* And they surely went around until there was nothing left to ranch and no point in keeping a house where missiles and spacemen were falling. The ranch was sold but we have these stories and our heirloom chili, peppers that melt your body until you are nothing but the air you're sucking to cool off. These chilies make you float. And drift. *This was '59 or '60 or sometime in there,* Aunt Yvonne says. *The spaceman must have realized where he was because he kinda lifted up and moved out into the pasture. And here come spinning lights on cars and trucks and helicopters and all these men jump out. Cut right through our fence. Storm the pasture like you've never seen. Police and soldiers and reporters and everything else.* Weather balloons were always coming down on the ranch. She'd find a great wad of shiny fabric attached to a little metallic box. The box had a number to call. She'd call and the Army would answer and say thanks and then they'd come gather their balloon. And, of course, the missiles. Great-Granddaddy GB would call the Army and say, *You lose one?* And they'd say, *Yessir.* And he'd say, *Well, we caught one, here on the ranch.* This particular morning, in '59 or '60 or sometime in there, the balloon came down with a man. The man had on a space suit. Not the slick suits NASA would make famous but just a beat-up helmet and a pressure suit that looked like little more than a sleeping bag duct-taped around his body. His balloon crumpled in the pasture and then the storm of fence cutters were in a frenzy around him. *Your granddaddy just walked slowly out toward the commotion, said, "Every fence y'all cut you'll be fixing before I let this spaceman leave."* She guesses they fixed the fences. They usually did. I suck air and float. And drift. I will spend years scouring newspaper archives looking for the spaceman on the old family ranch. High-profile military balloon missions in these years called Manhigh and Excelsior were America's first real forays into space just before Kennedy's moon shot. I will consult Craig Ryan, who wrote all the books on these space balloons. He'll say, *We know that the first and second Excelsior flights originated near Truth or Consequences, and the third from Tularosa. I don't have a lot of information about precisely where those flights landed. But I do seem to recall Kittinger mentioning the White Sands Ranch.* Aunt Yvonne knows for sure it was Joe Kittinger. He was the test pilot who got on the cover of *Time* magazine by jumping out of the space balloons. He's well into his eighties now but is on the news again talking about another balloon project he's helping to organize, a multimillion-dollar commercial stunt called Space Dive. *I keep trying to call him when he's on the radio, just to see if he remembers, if he knows how badly he scared us,* she says. But the thing about the Excelsior project in 1959 and 1960 is that Kittinger didn't come down in his balloon. He jumped out from way up in the stratosphere. So maybe Aunt Yvonne has confused his parachute for a balloon. There is plenty of film of his last Excelsior jump, Joe speeding down from the stratosphere, then floating down toward the white sands below, landing in rings of creosote bush. He lands clearly in the vicinity of the ranch, boots touching desert that looks exactly like the ranch, but no buildings or landmarks are visible in the film to confirm the exact location.

Or maybe that spaceman falling to the ranch happened earlier than Aunt Yvonne remembers, when the test pilots didn't yet jump but rode the balloon's float all the way back to earth. I've found no footage of these. The point is, a lot of weird shit happened at the ranch, it being tucked into the dark soul of the military-industrial complex like it was. The White Sands Ranch. *Squeezed like a rabbit by a hungry snake,* Great-Granddaddy would say. *Then they slobbered all over and finished us off.* The ranch has a different name now, is not a ranch anymore but sometimes is a film location and often shows up in blockbusters about the postapocalypse. Aunt Yvonne says, *The point is, you can't even imagine how it shocked us. That man from the sky! Worse than the missiles, even.* We eat. We suck air. And drift. On these chilies, everything makes perfect nonsense. *It's a wonder the horses didn't kill themselves when they saw that spaceman. We had one good mare onetime, in the stall. Already had her sold too. She got frightened by a low-flying fighter or one or another of those sonic booms and she bucked. Kicked around in the stall till she broke her neck. Have you ever seen a horse break its own neck? Like it is crazy looking for something that shouldn't be there but saw it and so then—oh, Joshua, so terrible—the whole animal comes undone.*

SO LET ALL THE MARTIANS
COME HOME TO ROOST

In the Year of Our Lord 2013

He whimpers. And moans. He says, *Ow*. Or says, *Oh, well*. Says, *I will* or *Oh, life*. *Oh, love* or *Ah, Lord*. *Oh, well*. He hums from the very back of his mouth and then rolls the hum to his lips until a kind of whimper grows and a moan grows. A sadness that breathes and gasps exactly the way you want a lover to breathe and gasp and kind of whimper and moan. Blind Willie sings the loneliness that sounds a lot like the slow kinds of sex. "Dark Was the Night, Cold Was the Ground"—three minutes twenty-one seconds of viscous blues about our despondent Lord Jesus in a garden on Crucifixion Eve. Blind Willie sings it as a hymn in a makeshift recording studio in Dallas in December of 1927 with a penknife to the neck of his guitar, and he sings it as the NASA-approved expression of loneliness etched into golden records aboard our *Voyager* spacecrafts launched in 1977 to float forevermore interstellar, giving alien civilizations a taste of the human story, and he sings it to me poolside in the parking lot of

Americas Best Value Inn on the main drag of Roswell, New Mexico.

Pops is in a lounge chair across the pool with his peppered beard sparkling in the sun and his shades clipped on and his ball cap pulled low. His white T-shirt is threadbare from being stretched by his gut. His boots are off but his jeans are on. He's sunning his forearms. Madi Bear is splashing in the pool. She's maybe ten and already has a little bit of her grandpa's gut and a little bit of her uncle's gut and there's the three of our guts in the sun, bathing in the rays of our Lord of infinite love and scorn with the F-150 parked right by the pool, packed to the brim and the bed stacked to high heaven with all of dead Grandma's things, all the stuff that had our names stuck on with Post-it notes and plenty of stuff that had no names stuck on because she died and something's got to be done with it all. We're hauling our inheritance from her grave in Illinois to our house in Alamogordo, where Momma awaits our arrival, where all the stuff will get unpacked and sit around for a while before getting a new layer of Post-it notes, but we're in no rush to wallpaper the world with tiny wills. This is the Fourth of July and tonight's fireworks kick-start the UFO Festival. We sprang for the cheap room with a bed and a cot but we got the parking-lot swimming pool to ourselves. Just me and Pops and Madi Bear and Blind Willie on repeat, and on my lap is a book called *Flying Saucers: A Modern Myth of Things Seen in the Skies* by Dr. Carl Jung. Me and Madi Bear have resolved to unravel every mystery in the knot of alien existence. *Or nonexistence*, she would like to point out, even though I've assured her many times that aliens do exist even if they are just stories because stories also exist. She'd been to space camp earlier this summer and performed an alien autopsy but the corpse was just full of

Twizzlers. She didn't find that too satisfying so I got us a book. Blind Willie moans and Doc Jung writes, "In the history of religion there are not only sexual unions with gods, they are also eaten and drunk." Page 35 and everything's already more knotted than we guessed. Maybe aliens ain't a story for kids.

Oh, well, sings Blind Willie.

The whole town will trickle out to one spot from which to watch the fireworks at 9:15 p.m., but get there early, says our Americas Best Value Inn clerk, because by 8:00 p.m. the trickle becomes a bum-rush. Upon inquiring if, because fireworks happen high in the sky, there might be more than one place from which to watch them, we're told, *No, that's wrong. There is only one place you can watch them. Turn left at the corner of the Military Institute. Head toward the old airport. Just follow the cars.* Already there is a prescription for witnessing lights in the sky that I'm suspicious about. Madi Bear agrees. She says, *Let's just walk until we see them.*

Sand and gravel and we are in SNM again because we are walking in the glass of so many broken bottles too. The sidewalks cracked and crumbled and disappeared a ways back. *War zone,* says Madi Bear. Firecrackers all around and dogs and the streets littered with mortars of all sizes and kids of all sizes wearing no shirts in the junkyards of houses that should be condemned, adobe going back to dirt and no parents in sight and the kids running off as their fireworks explode on the ground, explode accidentally on the ground as the kids convulse with that kind of maniacal laugh-cry that is the one true trait setting us apart from apes. *Ah, Lord.* We have the capacity to be amused by our fears, and in this place on this night that's a beautiful thing. A whole bunch of handguns get shot at the sky. Some tumbleweeds burn. Then the big-ass taxpayer fireworks start and we pause right where we are on the street corner. Pops gets out a Phillies Blunt and leans against a stop sign. We gaze up and watch the explosions from right where we are because, as it turns out, when something is exploding in the sky, you can see it from a whole lot of different places on the ground. Pops gives me a Phillies Blunt too and Madi Bear swipes away some glass and pulls up some dust. Peonies and Palms and Horsetails and Crossettes and Salutes and all those Roman candles: things seen in the sky tonight.

This is the Summer of Snowden. The glow of Charlie Rose on television talking about the big government eyeball and the afterglow of fireworks on our faces as we shuffle around the cheap room at Americas Best Value Inn making excuses for why we shouldn't be the one on the cot. Pops says, *I'm too big.* Madi Bear says, *I'm too small.* I say our paranoia has turned inward. We are no longer scared about what's out there in the universe but terrified nothing can be kept inside. Google knows our thoughts and hands them over to the NSA. We Are Not Alone is a mantra that now has nothing to do with aliens. Madi Bear says, *Whatever,* and none of us give up our spot in the bed. Pops turns into a sack of snores before Charlie Rose figures out whether Snowden should die for shining a light in the big government eyeball. I drift off when talk turns to a murder trial and the likelihood that we'll all kill each other no matter what anyway forever amen. Madi Bear stays awake drawing aliens and having trouble sketching Doc Jung's version of a UFO: "It is difficult, if not impossible, to form any correct idea of these objects, because they behave not like bodies but like weightless thoughts." In the morning Madi Bear is still sitting there between me and Pops but looking a little green in the face like she stayed up so late drawing aliens she turned into one.

She couldn't sleep, she says, because between me and Pops she was bombarded all night long by a tremendous volley of farts. She'd tried covering her face with the blanket but the blanket smelled full of old farts and so she'd clung to the wall and turned green in the face. The world is so full of farts. Me and Pops agree to sleep on the floor for the rest of the festival but we also explain to Madi Bear how heat rises. There is no escape.

The mailbox in front of the civic center is painted up like R2-D2. That's a permanent situation. Also permanent are the Main Street lights shaped like alien heads and all the business signs with little green men painted on and the McDonald's that has outdone itself by remodeling the entire restaurant into a flying saucer. Inside the civic center chairs are set up for an audience of hundreds but we are only about thirty-five this morning. The family all wearing the same thick-rimmed glasses that we saw coming out of Starbucks looking like they were just exactly nerdy enough for a UFO festival are in fact here for the festival. The median age is fifty or sixty. And there's a lady with a butterfly clip in her hair and a guy with a safari hat and a guy in all neon green and there's a whole slew of crew cuts grown out into comb-overs—everybody has a good reason for being at the festival: Butterfly Clip is a general free-spirited sort and Safari Hat is on a serious quest/hunt and Neon Green wants to role-play with other lovable freaks and then there are the Crew Cuts into Comb-Overs who saw some weird shit during their military service and lately that weird shit's been running through their minds a lot and they can't think about much else anymore except trying to understand the weird shit and after many years of obsession and neglecting their high and tights they are here and mad as hell. There's one baby and it keeps looking at me. I'm here because it was on the way home from a funeral. But really I'm here because a long time ago I lost my religion and lately that's been feeling sort of lonesome. Don't tell anybody I told you that. I don't want people thinking I'm sad, or worse: on the prowl for transcendence. The banner behind the lectern advertises the upcoming Alien Chase and the upcoming Alien Costume Contest for Pets and Humans.

Stanton Friedman bills himself as the world's foremost UFOlogist (say *you fall a gist*). Stan the Man has the cadence of an evangelist with the nasal tone of an academic though neither of those descriptions capture how his ears and eyebrows seem shot into his face at amazingly congruent and sharply elfish angles. His head is huge, which makes it all the more remarkable when his eyes get crazy excited and swallow all his other features. Before we learn anything about the evidence for the existence of UFOs, we learn about the government's UFO lies. Stan the Man puts the words GOVERNMENT UFO LIES up on the big screen and tickles them with his laser pointer for effect. *It made me angry because I don't like being lied to,* he says. In this lecture and the next lecture and most all the lectures on UFOs, the talk will be only tangentially of the existence of extraterrestrial life and mostly all about the secrets our government keeps.

Something crashed in the desert near Roswell in July 1947. The local paper put *RAAF CAPTURES FLYING SAUCER ON RANCH* in the headline about the crash and locals talked about it for maybe a week. All manner of unbelievable military shit fell from the skies onto SNM ranches in those days, and most folks were just grateful when it wasn't an atomic bomb. So the crash was mostly forgotten until Stan the Man put himself on the case, starred in the 1979 documentary *UFOs Are Real!*, which claimed to blow the whistle about "the Cosmic Watergate." *UFOs Are Real!* uncovered government documents about more than one hundred UFO sightings in SNM, and put much emphasis on the 1947 crash in Roswell as the clearest evidence of extraterrestrial visitation. And so, in the eighties, as synthesized music took over the airwaves and Spielberg took over the big screens and personal computers invaded our homes, the Roswell Incident became a worldwide obsession. Roswell officially incorporated the International UFO Museum in 1991 and had a million visitors in its first decade. Under duress in the midnineties our government actually admitted to a cover-up at Roswell, said they'd lied about the wreckage being weather balloons because really they were Project Mogul, a fleet of atomic-bomb-detecting balloons they'd wanted to fly over the Soviet Union—but then they crashed in the desert near Roswell.

For Stan the Man the admission of a government cover-up was only an admission of the government's ability to carry out a cover-up and so still there are the stories of metal wreckage with unearthly properties of memory and stories of alien bodies pulled from the wreckage and stories of doctors poking and prodding those bodies with different medical devices over the last sixty-six years. Madi Bear says, *They're just full of candy.* I tell her not to talk during the lecture because I'm on the brink of an epiphany. *Patrionoia*: a word I invent that combines *patriotism* and *paranoia*. Patrionoia runs rampant in SNM. All the ranchers and illegal immigrants and atomic bomb downwinders and veterans and UFOlogists: all people whose love for America is outstripped only by their distrust of its government. Out in the parking lot is a Chevy Silverado with Stars-and-Stripes truck nuts hanging from a bumper stickered with the phrase LIES IN THE SKIES written in an airplane's chemtrails. These are otherwise reasonable people, many of them kin to me, who suffer an inability to reconcile the ideology of American exceptionalism they've internalized with the anxiety daily seeping up out of their pores. I love these patrionoiacs and I am of their breed more than I'd like to admit, but I understand—I think—that it makes no sense. For instance, so much of the belief in the existence of UFOs and extraterrestrial life relies on the belief that we have a government capable of keeping secrets. *Ouroboros* is the term for this kind of thing. A snake eating its tail. Doc Jung quotes Voltaire, who quotes Pascal, who quotes Empedocles, who looked up at the sky one night and said, *God is a circle whose center is everywhere and the circumference nowhere.* I want to stand up and yell, SNOWDEN, to remind all the patrionoiacs that our government is not as competent at covertness as their fear suggests. Pops sits to my left looking like a turtle slowly receding into his shell that is not a shell but the bulge of his gut. He ain't interested enough to be skeptical. He's never owned truck nuts.

Stan the Man says, *Somebody who showed up in 1947 would have looked at earthlings and said, "This is a primitive society engaged primarily in tribal warfare."* Whenever Stan the Man describes earthlings as idiots, which he does often, I tune in. Whenever he describes why the aliens came to Southern New Mexico, why SNM was their crashing spot— the advanced radar tests and the V-2 rocket tests and the atom bomb test—I feel some of that warped pride. Laugh-cry. If the aliens were looking for something interesting and nasty about earthlings, they were looking for it in SNM. Doc Jung writes, "We have here a golden opportunity to see how a legend is formed, and how in a difficult and dark time for humanity a miraculous tale grows up of an attempted intervention by extra-terrestrial 'heavenly' powers." Me and Madi Bear slap a high five after I say, *We live at the very epicenter of humanity's dark time.* But then she mulls that over and rescinds the high five by punching me in the shoulder. Well now, here's an absurd proposition, she must be thinking, that extraterrestrials are some kind of heavenly power.

In a few weeks I'll give Stan the Man a call to see if there is any news on the UFOlogist front. He'll repeat almost verbatim the lecture he's giving now. But also, when I press him, he'll respond to the question I keep asking—what the fuck is really going on with the alien situation? He'll breathe into the phone awhile and finally say, *What if there was an announcement tomorrow that the queen and the pope said some UFOs are alien spacecraft? Church attendance would go up. Young people would push for a new view of ourselves as earthlings. Right now nationalism is the only game in town. Tribal warfare. I've got a great-grandson. I'd like him to grow up in a world where we're not spending a trillion dollars on the military. Think about it: earthlings.*

Lunchtime and the guy at the table next to us in Peppers Grill & Bar is clearly out of it. He reaches for his full tea or his whole burger but never grabs either. Just reaches. Stops. Reaches for the other. Buries his hands under the table. Pulls out his wallet. Puts it back. Adjusts his white ball cap. His chips and salsa are untouched. Some of his fries are spilled out on the table. He is perpetually about to eat or has forgotten how to eat. Madi Bear says, *Stop staring.* Pops has the headphones in and decides that Blind Willie sounds constipated. Madi Bear doesn't know what to think of Stan the Man's lecture. She says it was like church but she doesn't know why. She says, *Okay,* when I suggest the commonality is some guy talking loudly about something she can't quite believe.

When we get back home to Alamogordo, she will deny having had such blasphemous thoughts and Momma will reprimand me for encouraging them. I will apologize. Madi Bear plugs into Blind Willie as she eats her chicken fingers. I want her to believe in something, but then, just as quickly, I want her to question that belief. Uncles only get so many opportunities to impart life lessons so I tell her to keep listening to Blind Willie until she figures out what he's singing. We linger in Peppers because they've got a misting system cooling our faces. Others have come and eaten and gone. Still there's the man in the white cap with his full tea and whole burger and mess of fries. The gray heels of his socks stick up over the backs of his shoes. He crosses his feet like a little kid. Uncrosses. Stares into the distance at nothing. Madi Bear takes out the headphones and says she doesn't like Blind Willie because he sounds sad and like he's been abducted. *I will* or *Oh, life. Oh, love* or *Ah, Lord. Oh, well.* There is no sense in bickering over government lies about UFOs if there are those among us who have actually been abducted by extra-terrestrials. In a booth farther back is a man in a pink shirt with a ginormous mustache. His wife wears around her neck and wrists and has dangling from her ears ten pounds of pol-ished turquoise rock. A woman behind me talks incessantly about the scam of refrigerated air. Are we not all sad and abducted? The man in the white cap is still stuck making up his mind.

I'm the only one pounding the pavement at 6:00 p.m. after the lectures have quit. The Alien Chase isn't for two days but I figured there'd be others out training. I want to have a good showing at the Alien Chase because it seems like the only proactive part of the festival. This is the 150th an-niversary of the Battle of Gettysburg, and on that battlefield they are reenacting the pivotal bloodshed with thousands upon thousands of men yelping and charging each other with bayonets. If we're serious about these aliens, we ought to have some kind of preenactment and the Alien Chase is the only thing on the schedule that sounds anything like war games. But tonight it's just me running through bulldog barks and minivan honks and lowrider rumbles until I'm back at Americas Best Value Inn. Pops is in the parking lot tightening the straps on our tower of inheritance. When we emptied Grandma's house, he snorted and guffawed every time something got put into his truck instead of the garbage. But once it was all piled in there, he lost sleep trying to get it packed and strapped just right for the thirteen-hundred-mile drive home. A truck driver has never cared for his haul so much. Morning, noon, and night—yanking on those straps and walking around the truck and yanking on the tarp at every rest stop and gas station and sometimes just pulled over on the side of the highway. Both of his parents are dead now. That's a messy fact of life he probably has no interest in try- ing to fathom, but tucking the tarp in all the right places and ratcheting the straps just so, that's a manageable task. Because he is dependable, he will unload the truck as soon as we get home to Momma, but I guess he'd feel more comfortable leaving it all packed up like that, ratcheting the straps every day until he dies and then just leaving me the keys to an F-150 packed beyond the brim and just right with a tarp over it all. Me and Madi Bear watch from the pool as he ratchets the sun down. Venus and Spica beside the moon and the moon itself and streaks of burning pebbles from the An- dromedids meteor shower: things seen in the sky tonight.

Early on the second morning Pops starts shopping the street vendors for an inflatable alien. Booths along two blocks of the main drag sell tamales and turkey legs, attempts at shitty carnival games, rides on tiny donkeys, and books preaching truth about aliens and Jesus. There are more vendors than shoppers. Over half the booths have inflatable aliens in stock but they all have the same three options: small and purple or medium and black or big and green. Pops goes from booth to booth anyway, says he's looking for the right one. Me and Madi Bear find a side door to the International UFO Museum and sneak in as protest against the exorbitant $20 entrance fee.

Today we wear our matching Billy the Kid T-shirts, gifts I got us a few years ago to celebrate both her participation in a Billy-the-Kid ballet at the local theater and my ability to sit through the whole performance. The shirts have a large picture of Billy that suggests he is left-handed because his Colt is holstered on that side, but he is not left-handed. The tintype original reversed the image. The shirts also have a lengthy biography of Billy and that's the reason I bought them instead of any of the other five hundred Billy the Kid shirts you can buy at most gas stations in SNM. How often do you come across a shirt that's also a biography? "No one really knows how Billy managed to acquire such legendary status," says the last paragraph of our T-shirts. "As an outlaw he had only a mediocre reputation; as a murderer he was outstretched by many. To this day he is a legend, regarded by some as a savior, by others as a juvenile delinquent." Why not both? I say. *We wore the wrong shirts,* says Madi Bear when we see so many other folks sporting the alien legend. Eventually she will become so concerned that we mixed up our legends that she'll demand we head back to Americas Best Value Inn so she can change. But this feels right to me, like Billy boy might prefer being mixed up with aliens to being mistaken for a delinquent savior, like all legends boil down to the same thing anyway: a nagging sense the story we're stuck living ain't the right one.

Pretty much everything there is to see at the International UFO Museum you can see from exactly wherever you happen to be standing in the International UFO Museum. I tell Madi Bear to stay near but she keeps ducking behind exhibits on account of embarrassment about our matching T-shirts. There's a decent crowd. All the celebrities of paranormal culture have set up book-signing tables. I linger around Stan the Man, who sits with his protégé Kathleen Marden, the 2012 UFOlogist of the Year. Together they wrote *Captured! The Betty and Barney Hill UFO Experience*, about the first-ever widely publicized claim of alien abduction. In 1961 Barney was a postman turned civil rights leader and Betty was a social worker and they were headed back to New Hampshire from Niagara Falls when Betty spotted streaks in the sky. Kathleen is the niece of Betty, the way Madi Bear is the niece of me. Stan the Man doesn't pay attention when I keep asking about Snowden but Kathleen tells me all about the times she's been wiretapped. She can hear them (government? aliens?) breathing on the line as she debates dishes for a potluck with her neighbor, so sometimes she'll just say, *Hello. I know you're there. Enjoy my bisque recipe.*

I'll keep in touch with Kathleen more than I do with Stan the Man but often she won't approve of my interest in her family. She has ten hours of uncut recordings of her aunt and uncle, Betty and Barney Hill, under hypnosis and trying to work through their abduction trauma. But Kathleen won't share. Some of the therapy sessions were published as transcripts in the book that first made Betty and Barney famous, *The Interrupted Journey*, but Kathleen will say that book left out much and got more wrong. She'll implore me to buy her book. She'll say I should place far more emphasis on the Hills' conscious recall of the abduction. Hypnosis just mixed things up, all the traumas from the past spilling out at once so that Barney's getting wounded in our Second World War slips into the abduction narrative and now there's the claim that he saw Nazis on the alien spacecraft. *Which he did not,* Kathleen will say. *And any of the hypnosis tapes posted online are illegal.* But that won't stop me from getting online and listening again and again to forty-five minutes of bootlegged Barney under a spell and getting grilled by a hypnotist.

I believe Betty is trying to make me think this is a flying saucer.

Was it light enough to see?

Just a light moving through the sky and I heard no noise. And I think, this is ridiculous. And, Betty, this is not a flying saucer. What are you doing that for? You want to believe in this thing and I don't. And I can't hear any sound. I want to hear a jet. Oh, I want to hear a jet so badly.

Why do you want to hear a jet?

Because Betty is making me mad. She is making me angry. Because she is saying, "Look at that. It's strange. It's not a plane." And I keep thinking, "It's got to be." And I want to hear a hum. I want to hear a motor.

You can remember everything now.

It's right over my right shoulder. God. What is it? I try to maintain control so Betty cannot tell I am scared. God, I am scared.

It's alright. Go on. It will not hurt you now.

I got to get my gun.

Then Barney screams.

You do not have to make any outcry, says the hypnotist.

But Barney wails.

Don't outcry.

And whimpers.

No outcry.

And moans.

Do not outcry.

Madi Bear darts out from behind the animatronic aliens at the center of the museum and says, *There's the man you were staring at.* He sits at a table with his name taped to the front: Travis Walton. His eyes are all bags and dark circles. A kid with a skateboard walks up to the table and says, *Are you the guy from that movie? I watched that movie. What's it like to get abducted?* Travis doesn't look up from the subatomic particles of the folding table he's been trying to stare through or rearrange with sheer willpower or extraterrestrial magic, but he pushes his book toward the kid and says, *It's all in there. Buy it.* But the kid walks off. The book, like the movie it inspired, is called *Fire in the Sky.*

Travis Walton on *Geraldo* in the nineties looks pretty out of it, sanitywise. D. B. Sweeney playing Travis in the movie adaptation of *Fire in the Sky* looks out of it too. Travis right now standing next to the projector playing old clips of himself in the movies and on *Geraldo* doesn't look a whole lot different. His mullet is red and seems dyed except that the color of his mustache matches exactly. Frances from Fort Worth leans over, almost falling out of her metal folding chair, and asks me why we are watching old clips of Travis when Travis is standing right there in the flesh. Frances is with me in the back row of the audience. She's at this lecture alone because her husband and son are boycotting the stupid alien festival to play a bunch of golf. I'm alone at the lecture because Madi Bear went with Pops to change out of the wrong legend and ride some miniature donkeys. So me and Frances from Fort Worth sit together. Her blouse is white and her pants are white and she keeps whispering in my ear. She wants Travis to talk about the poking and the prodding and what the alien eyes looked like and how their skin felt and what it was like to feel their breath (*Do they breathe?* she whispers) on his skin. She wants to know if he was really naked when his friends found him after he'd been missing for five days, but she doesn't laugh when I say he probably had on the same Western blazer he wore on *Geraldo*, that he's still wearing now. A lot of people suspect Travis is a faker because his abduction happened just two weeks after the first airing of *The UFO Incident*, a 1975 television movie based on *The Interrupted Journey*, starring James Earl Jones as our old friend, the original abductee, Barney Hill. On *Geraldo*, Travis says that's just a coincidence of time. Or maybe the aliens saw the movie too. Maybe the urge toward rebuttal after a Hollywood gloss is universal.

The clips end and Travis doesn't even introduce himself to us but just launches into the story he's told a billion times. Frances whispers some conjecture about how the story likely got him laid every day for the last thirty years, and I don't have the energy to work through all the scenarios that might result in a woman's running and screaming from Travis's motel room in any number of small towns that host these kinds of extraterrestrial conferences, or I'm overwhelmed by understanding all of the scenarios at once, but either way my face flinches like I'm about to register disgust but then, when I notice Frances from Fort Worth is totally sincere, I roll the whole flinch up into my eye and just wink at her, which will probably turn out to be a mistake. I don't think the problem is that Travis is unattractive or totally dull or otherwise unfuckable, but if what he says about the abduction is a conscious lie, then he's the kind of jerk that could send a woman running and screaming or, if it's an unconscious lie, then he's probably kind of ill and untreated and that could send a woman running and screaming or, if what he's saying about the abduction is true, then the aliens could come back in the middle of the night to tell him to pipe down on all his blabbering about the incident and that kind of postcoital visitation could send a woman running and screaming. But Frances is enamored of him, and lots of other ladies and gentlemen are snapping his photo. He doesn't shade his eyes from the flashes and I worry he'll seize into a flashback of the abduction, but that kind of evangelical dramatics doesn't show up at UFO festivals even though I hoped it might. Really it is all rather dull. Travis says he could only ever put together what happened to him when he underwent hypnosis. All of our best stories come from unconsciousness. I'm ready to be a little less conscious of this lecture so I put Blind Willie in the ear that doesn't already have Frances in it. *I will* or *Oh, well* or *Ah, Lord*. There are no definitive lyrics. Three totally different sentiments about getting it done or giving up or having faith and Blind Willie's figured out a way to say them all at once. And that's the only honest way to express any one of those feelings—all mixed up with the rest. Doc Jung writes, "Hence there would be nothing against the naive interpretation of the UFOs as 'souls.' Naturally they do not represent our modern conception of the soul, but rather an involuntary archetypal or mythological conception of an unconscious content, a *rotundum*, as the alchemists called it, that expresses the totality of the individual." Frances from Fort Worth puts her hand on my thigh. She wants to know what I'm listening to. *It's an outcry*, I say. She stares at me for a while. She declines when I try to pass her the headphones. She raises her hand, the one not on my thigh, and asks Travis if it's true that people who have been abducted will know other people who have been abducted just by looking them in the eyes.

The parking-lot pool of Americas Best Value Inn isn't supposed to be open after dark but we're there anyway, Madi Bear splashing around and me and Pops with a twelve-pack of Buds and our Phillies Blunts. He tells Madi Bear to climb on out of the pool because a storm might be rolling in but it's just overcast. Nothing: things seen in the sky tonight.

Five a.m. and I'm chugging Gatorade to clear out my system for the Alien Chase. Madi Bear won't wake up so Pops carries her to the truck and we drive our tower of inheritance to the starting line. By 6:00 a.m. over three hundred people have gathered, far and away the most attended event of the festival. Serious runners are stretching one another's quads and serious joggers are putting the finishing touches on their playlists and whole families are there complete with babies in strollers. I did not expect to actually chase actual aliens but I guess I expected more than this: it's just people. I sidle over to a group wearing T-shirts that say GONZALEZ FAMILY REUNION 2013, who all look like they are also regretting drinking and smoking and sleeping on a motel floor last night. They all laugh when my number gets called to line up with the serious runners doing the 10K. But really there is no line. Everyone just crowds toward a guy brandishing a bullhorn. I snug Blind Willie into my ears. Doc Jung writes, "If we try to define the psychological structure of the religious experience which saves, heals, and makes whole, the simplest formula we can find would seem to be the following: in a religious experience man comes face to face with a psychically overwhelming

Other." But it's just people. Three hundred of us in short shorts and tank tops, some with their faces painted green and one guy with a tinfoil hat and even the family with the thick-rimmed glasses but now with the added touch of sweatbands and wobbly antennae, everyone starting to jostle one another and a muscleman knocking over kids as he pushes his way to the front and everyone else picking the kids up off the ground and someone hoots from the back until all three hundred of us are hooting, all throbbing together in one outcry to get going chasing nothing but one another and on the edges of this melee Pops and Madi Bear blow hot air into a small purple alien as the guy on the bullhorn counts down from ten.

TRUTH OR CONSEQUENCES AT THE GATEWAY TO SPACE

In the Year of Our Lord 2013

They come from the north by helicopter, flying over scattered cattle, mesquite brush, yucca straining skyward. To the east is White Sands Missile Range. Farther: Roswell. Below is that old muddy snake, the Rio Grande. And just west is a town called Truth or Consequences. But the men on this cherry-red Bell 206 LongRanger are not sightseeing. They're headed to the middle of the desert where they plan to launch a bunch of spaceships.

December 2005. Rick Homans heads up the New Mexico Economic Development Department for Governor Bill Richardson. Homans sits shotgun in the LongRanger and behind him are three Brits, two top dogs in a company called Virgin Galactic and the godfather of all things Virgin, billionaire Richard Branson. The billionaire has recently licensed technology that won the $10 million Ansari X Prize in 2004 by taking the first privately built manned ship to an altitude above sixty-two miles, the internationally recognized boundary of space. Branson is confident that by 2007 Galactic will be making that trip daily.

As the chopper flies deeper into the desert, the men shout louder into their bulky headsets. Homans knows he might not get another chance to spitball with these men he considers some of the top branding minds in the world, so he has them brainstorming, a round-robin of hollering over the rotor noise to figure out a name for the place they're headed. And the billionaire finally says it: a new name that encapsulates all the ambition of the project, one that suggests a collective ownership—the hope that access to space will soon be available to anyone who desires it. The new name outshines the rather mundane Southwest Regional Spaceport, by which the project had been known for decades before Virgin Galactic flew into New Mexico. The new name is ingenuous and bold and plants a symbolic flag, a gesture fashioned in roughly the same spirit that Armstrong and Aldrin drove the Stars and Stripes into the surface of the moon thirty-six years earlier. More than a little bit of the old space race bleeds into the new one, even though the New Space Race is not about a cold war, but a commercial one. And so a British billionaire says it.

And so say we all: Spaceport America.

Eight years on and you've likely heard little or nothing about Spaceport America. All the talk is of Virgin Galactic, the self-proclaimed World's First Commercial Spaceline—since 2004 over seven hundred people have forked over at least $200,000 for a ticket and the promise of a two-hour spaceflight. The publicized passenger manifesto is a bona fide red carpet, a fantasy guest list, the irresistible front page of a supermarket tabloid: Mr. Lance Bass and Leo and Bieber and the cuddle-puddle of Brangelina. The Little Monsters scream that their idol Lady Gaga will be the first diva wailing heartbreak in space.

This is the promise the rich and famous have paid for: *WhiteKnightTwo*, the Galactic mother ship, will fly to fifty thousand feet with *SpaceShipTwo* strapped to its underbelly. *SpaceShipTwo* and the six ticket holders seated inside will then be released from the mother ship and rocket at up to 2,500 mph to suborbit, seventy miles high, where they will be weightless for a few minutes before gliding back down to earth, where they will sip champagne in the Astronaut Lounge and slap high fives the way only people who have been to space can slap high fives—reaching a little bit higher because every fiber of them now knows the magic of weightlessness. Three thousand wealthy tourists were supposed to have made this trip by 2012. That goal was not met in part because of problems with rocket development—a 2007 explosion killed three people at Galactic's test facilities in Mojave, California. One expects technological delays from a fledgling industry, but nearly every year Galactic promises to begin operations anyway. The last eight years of promises without a spaceflight recently culminated in Branson biographer Tom Bower calling the billionaire Virgin mogul an "overvalued aging sun lizard" whose Galactic company is "a total sham."

But the untold story is about New Mexico and its taxpayers, the people who paid for and built Spaceport America. The saga of their decade-old and nearly quarter-billion-dollar gamble on an aging sun lizard's quest to dominate the commercial space industry often gets buried by the big-media machine, relegated to a small paragraph or one sentence in favor of playing up the dream of space tourism or bashing the dream of space tourism or just gawking at Lady Gaga's breasts (she riffs on her Galactic gig in some revealing space suits for the March 2014 issue of *Harper's Bazaar*). But whether the dream will be realized or the dream will break or the dream will crash and burn or just stagnate, it will happen here in New Mexico, down the road from Truth or Consequences.

There's an ashtray for every barstool and the pool table is right in the doorway and beyond that there's lots of room for two-stepping or staggering. I'm at the Pine Knot Saloon in Truth or Consequences on an uncharacteristically frigid New Mexico day in late November. On my drive into town the local radio bemoaned Virgin Galactic's failure to begin operations from Spaceport America in 2013. Richard Branson would not, they said, don a Saint Nick getup and rocket to the edge of space with his kids on Christmas as he had hoped. Galactic would not fly for yet another year. Nobody at the Pine Knot seems too bothered by the news. A man lies on a bench beside a telephone booth, napping before his night shift. Three guys slowly orbit a billiards table. Everything in the saloon is pine and covered in a little bit of sweat from joy and a little bit of sweat from toil and there's that thick bar air from years of liquor-swelled dreams that don't quite break but just get stagnant and hang around.

You can buy booze lots of places in Truth or Consequences but the Pine Knot is the only real honky-tonk. Most nightlife is relegated to evening services at one of the town's nine churches. The sixty-four hundred residents here get by on an annual median income south of $22,000. The largest employers are Walmart and the public schools. Half the storefronts in the historic downtown are shuttered. Main Street stays pretty empty except for an Art Hop one day a month, when you can buy any kind of turquoise jewelry or Navajo rug or get your tarot read by Christopher the Bohemian Vagabond. Downtown's real treasure is its spas, fueled by countless natural hot springs rising from deep in the earth around the Rio Grande. If you've been to Truth or Consequences, it was likely for the spas, which are not the exquisite kind but the working-class kind, mostly just sheds around holes or steel tubs. For many years the name of this town was simply Hot Springs. Then Ralph Edwards held a contest in 1950 that required the winning town to rename itself after his popular radio show, *Truth or Consequences*. The age of advertising had begun and Hot Springs was ready to be rebranded. Though a handful of citizens moved out in protest, the name stuck. Now, six decades later, the town's identity is on the brink of another strange overhaul.

I'm hanging around the Pine Knot waiting to get a good look at Spaceport America. I'm sort of obsessed with it because I've lived most of my life just on the other side of the San Andres Mountains, grew up gazing at these desert skies, every far-off star blinking with the promise that there is more to life than this, whatever this is—the stars were hope and they were brightest in our desert. When I attended the 2007 X Prize Cup held near Alamogordo, I stood next to a mock-up of a Galactic spaceship and told a local news crew that I aimed to be the first-ever poet in space. The poetry thing hasn't worked out but here I am still wondering if I'll ever be able to wake up one morning in my own bed and then spend the afternoon weightless reciting sestinas. But tonight I'm stuck at the bar because the one road leading out to the spaceport is down to one lane and that one lane is frozen over. Well, alright. At least we're drinking.

Even though I've visited Spaceport America once before,

my experience of it wasn't matching the hype. The New Mexico tourism secretary, Monique Jacobson, had told me, *It can become an iconic destination like the Sydney Opera House or the Statue of Liberty.* Christine Anderson, executive director of New Mexico Spaceport Authority, also likened the building to the Sydney Opera House and told me, *It is an iconic jewel in the desert.* Richard Branson said at a 2011 spaceport dedication ceremony, *It could be one of the Seven Wonders.* I just want to look at the thing again, the way any of us want to look the future in the eye, to know for sure whether Spaceport America represents a paradigm shift for human travel or a boondoggle for the forty-second-poorest state in the nation or a carnival fad for the 1 percent or maybe a cathedral for a new kind of space-age spirituality.

When I ask the guys at the billiards table if this is, in fact, the closest bar to the spaceport, they respond with an incredulous *Huh?* I want to chat about how their honky-tonk is on the verge of a major boom in business, a major boom in tourism, a major boom in human consciousness—so many booms—but they don't want to hear any of it. They're aware of the spaceport's existence but don't know why I'd care to ask about it because, as they say again and again, not much is going on out there. Nobody's flying to space.

Or, almost nobody. Bonnie, who claims to have the permanent position of a sometimes employee at the Pine Knot, smokes Camel after Camel and tells me all about *the ashes of dead people that get launched into space over there.*

That old guy from Star Trek *and some astronauts,* she says. *They pay a bunch of money to just shoot their ashes in the air. Into space! And so we have to just . . . what? . . . breathe them in?* She ashes on the bar and the floor and in the air all around her big hair.

In the absence of Galactic operations, the only passengers who have lifted off from Spaceport America are the cremated remains of people whose families have paid UP Aerospace to launch their dead loved ones on a final joyride. UP Aerospace is one of a few small commercial space start-ups that have been operating at Spaceport America over the last eight years. Together those start-ups have conducted twenty launches. But these have been relatively small rockets at a vertical launchpad secondary to the prized Virgin Galactic terminal and they create a minuscule fraction of the revenue needed to operate the spaceport. UP Aerospace's first operation, the first-ever launch from Spaceport America, in 2006, malfunctioned well before it got suborbital, crashed, and spilled the ashes of a veterinarian in the desert. After that snafu, a company called Celestis took over sales of space burials for clients such as James Doohan (*that old guy from* Star Trek) and Gordon Cooper (one of America's first astronauts in Project Mercury). About their burials the company says, "Celestis missions are environmentally friendly in that no cremated remains are released into space." Bonnie assures me, though, that some of those ashes from Spaceport America's first tourist are still scattered out there in the desert.

Out there in the desert means eighteen thousand acres in the middle of the Jornada del Muerto, a stretch of mostly barren land, between the sharp San Andres Mountains and the rolling Caballo Mountains, that got its name from having killed so many Spanish settlers in the seventeenth century. Despite now being home to the World's First Purpose-Built Commercial Spaceport, that area is still pretty remote and difficult to access. First, you gotta get to Truth or Consequences (a road connecting the spaceport to the larger southern city of Las Cruces is still incomplete, being perpetually bulldozed). Then you gotta take a nearly hour-long bus ride along the one paved road that is sometimes down to that one lane. You could make the drive in your own vehicle but you'll be turned away at the gates by a security guard sitting in a shack with black plastic bags on the windows—only official vehicles allowed. Anyway, you should leave the driving on this road to the professionals or the seasoned locals. Besides having steep drop-offs and winding wildly like all canyon roads, this one is infamous for flash floods, and last year one of them took the life of an Arizona worker on his drive home from tiling the dome roof of the Spaceport Operations Center.

The ranchers Ben and Jain Cain were also once caught in a flash flood on this road, swept into the canyon. They were eventually rescued—hauled up, one at a time, in a harness dangling from a crane. Ben and Jain Cain's ranch, the Bar Cross, along with their daughter's adjacent ranch, makes up most all of the eighteen thousand acres of the spaceport. The Cains bought the Bar Cross for $120,000 after their previous ranch, Flat Land, was condemned in 1950 by the government, part of hundreds of ranches transformed into White Sands Missile Range after the so-called success of the Gadget in 1945. The Spaceport Authority has made much of the fact that they've entered into a co-use agreement with the Cains, that the commercial space industry has not come to SNM and stolen land the way many believe the federal government did after our Second World War. *The fact that Spaceport America sits on two working ranches is part of the spaceport's charm,* says Spaceport Authority executive Christine Anderson. *I always like to say it's the old frontier meets the new frontier. Sometimes there are cattle on our launchpads. But we have not lost a single cow!* As charming as the harmony of cows and rockets may be, Jain Cain, in her unpublished memoir, has a slightly different narrative about the co-use situation. She writes, "Ben and I signed a contract with Spaceport in 2008. The document gives them the right to install Spaceport America. We didn't have a choice. Ben didn't really want to give up what we had. He hated to give in. He loved solitude, but we turned around, did an about face, and opened our land to the world. Much of this ranch is leased federal and state land and, had we not gone along with it, we believe they would have condemned it."*

Maybe any argument over the land is moot because, as we all know, all the West, from way back, is stolen land. This was inadvertently and absurdly highlighted at the spaceport groundbreaking ceremony in July 2009, which Jain Cain

---

* Let me add a disclaimer as a personal note here: The Cains have long been friends of my ranching family. They were always in the same clubs: political, religious, business. The New Mexico Cattle Growers' Association named the Cains Ranchers of the Year in the 1994 issue of *Stockman*—a magazine that has featured many Olivers, including my great-granddaddy and his daddy before him. But the real bond between the families was that both ultimately lost ranches because of the creation of the White Sands Missile Range beginning in the 1940s—the federal government condemned their land and has been blowing up stuff on it ever since. But the post–Second World War swindling of ranchers in Southern New Mexico is a whole other story. This note is just to say that my family's bond with the Cains doesn't sway my thinking about the spaceport. Even if the New Mexico Spaceport Authority did pressure the Cains to cooperate, they were not totally swindled this time around. The land still belongs to their family, is still covered in their cattle, and they did not have to leave their homes. Word on the street in Truth or Consequences is that, this time around, the Cains are raking in six or seven figures for letting the frontiers of commercial aerospace percolate on their ranches.

recalls this way: "The ceremony honored the many eras that our land has seen. Actors dressed as conquistadors walked out of the desert and presented documents to Governor Bill Richardson, bequeathing the land the conquistadors once trod hundreds of years ago." This actually happened: wielding lances and helmets and corselets and the Cross of Burgundy and the Royal Standard flag (first flown over this country by a hopelessly confused explorer named Columbus), some dudes with goatees wandered out of the desert and handed Governor Bill Richardson and Billionaire Richard Branson a scroll that said (crassly summarized), "Have at it, boys! All our slaughtering of the natives might have been in vain had it not led to this transcendent moment—the possibility of Lady Gaga singing in suborbit!"

I first visited the scene of this incredible bequeathing in the summer of 2013, took a tour bus through the deadly canyon and the Bar Cross Ranch and passed the little Engle Church where Ben Cain played his fiddle for five decades and then, finally, our bus rumbled up to the spaceport. This was four years after construction on the main terminal began with the conquistadors' gift and two years after the lion's share of construction on the terminal was complete. Virgin Galactic had finally begun paying its million-dollars-a-year lease to New Mexico in January but only after insisting on a $7 million upgrade to the still-unused runway and new state legislation that limited liability for themselves and their chain of suppliers in case of an accident. But the real delay was in Galactic's being nowhere close to having their rocket motor perfected. So the place was built but empty. There was twelve thousand feet of pristine runway. There was the futuristic-looking terminal designed by the world-renowned architecture firm Foster + Partners, a strange building that fades up from the reddish desert in the shape of a horseshoe, grows from almost sand level on the south side into a three-story wall of glass that curves around the face of the building. That spherical glass wall looks north over the runway like the cornea of a giant eye blinking open out of the desert after about a billion years of sleep.

Back in October of 2011 Branson rappelled from the roof of the terminal with his kids and a team of similarly suspended ballet dancers and declared Spaceport America open for business. He christened the terminal the Gateway to Space and showered it with champagne. But two years later, when my tour group visited in the summer of 2013, the champagne was all dried up. The Gateway to Space was an amazing thing to encounter in the midst of all that open range but the facility had the eerie sense of one of the many ghost towns in the area, left over from the New Mexico mining boom of the late 1800s. The building was immaculate on the outside but the guts of it were hollow, unfinished—like the facade of a movie set. The only people there were three firefighters, who stayed busy washing their massive F-550 truck, which was already so shiny from lack of use I wondered if they weren't trying to scuff it up to give the monster a bit of character. On the runway, skid marks suggested that Virgin Galactic had begun moving its operation from its test facilities at the Mojave Air and Space Port in California to its purpose-built home in the New Mexico desert. But the burned rubber, a security guard said, was from Will Smith's private jet. The Fresh Prince had been there, just weeks prior, shooting promotional photos for his doomed blockbuster *After Earth*.

We planned rocket races. Like NASCAR. But with rocket planes. Former New Mexico governor Bill Richardson mentions this offhand over the phone from his office in Santa Fe. He was governor from 2003 to 2011 with a brief 2008 presidential run sandwiched between the two terms. Today he's just back from charity work in South Africa. I'm sitting on the ceramic-tile floor of my adobe room at the Pink Pelican motel in Truth or Consequences, killing time, still waiting for that November ice to melt off the one lane leading to the spaceport.

The Rocket Racing League, though it sounds cartoonishly implausible, is an actual business that had hoped to operate at Spaceport America. But they ran into financial trouble and failed to build any kind of worthwhile fan base after their single exhibition at the Tulsa International Airport in 2010. Despite these kinds of burnouts, it's hard not to feel absolutely confident about the future of the spaceport when talking to the guy still referred to by his entourage as the Gov. He's reflective now that he's not actively campaigning, a slow talker not because the words take time to formulate but because he wants to make sure they have time to settle in. We talk about his childhood dreams of playing pro baseball and his backup dreams of being an astronaut. We talk about our years of gazing up at the desert skies. More than once he says, *I consider the spaceport my legacy accomplishment.*

I liked the idea of New Mexico and space. I thought a spaceport fit in. The Gov says this like it was a decision he made on the fly, as nonchalant as a kid's backup dream of being an astronaut. Rick Homans incubated the spaceport project as secretary of economic development to entice Virgin Galactic to the state. But he confirms the Gov's gut decision. After a fifteen-minute presentation in 2004 about Galactic and a spaceport, the Gov simply looked at Homans and said, *Don't screw it up, Dickey. Get out.*

And from that moment on he never once wavered in his support for the project, Homans says. *I have huge admiration for him as a political figure, to make a decision like that and then stick with it.* But that confidence must have stemmed in part from the guarantee that New Mexico would be the exclusive home of Virgin Galactic. Branson's own story of that partnership, which he recently told to a crowd of businesspeople in the empty hangar of the Gateway to Space, is more epic: *The then governor [Richardson] said to me, "If you build me a spaceship, I'll build you a spaceport." And I replied, "Well, I guess if you'll build me a spaceport, then I'm gonna build you a spaceship." And then we shook hands.*

The idea existed long before the Richardson administration. In June of 1963, just a month after the final orbital flight of NASA's Mercury program, New Mexico governor Jack Campbell sent a letter to President John F. Kennedy that reads, "We in New Mexico believe the first inland aerospace port should be based here and earnestly solicit your acceptance of our views."

By 1979 a spaceport of sorts was actually operating in New Mexico. The White Sands Space Harbor was created to help NASA pilots train for landings. On March 30, 1982, the Space Shuttle *Columbia* landed there when its planned destination, Edwards Air Force Base, flooded. The Space Harbor is a mere fifty miles east of Spaceport America. Its thirty-five thousand feet of runways have not been operational since NASA ended the shuttle program in 2011. That brings the total amount of spacecraft runway in SNM not actively being used for space travel to almost nine miles.

In the late nineties, the current site of Spaceport America was in the running to become home of the VentureStar, a reusable space plane NASA contracted Lockheed Martin to build as a replacement for the Space Shuttle. But when that program was canceled in 2001, the plans for a Southwest Regional Spaceport languished until Virgin Galactic flew into town and the project got rebranded Spaceport America.

The difference between these other spaceport projects and the one that finally materialized was Galactic's commitment to operate exclusively in the state, with a primary focus not on scientific breakthroughs or explorations but on the unprecedented and undeniably sexy industry of space tourism. *I did a lot in the area of new job-creating initiatives and I wanted to bring international prestige to the state*, Richardson says. *Space tourism could do that.*

The Gov was famous for getting behind big-eyed projects. Some, such as the $300,000 he spent to convince the Mexican government to cosponsor an NFL franchise in the region, never panned out. Others, such as tax incentives to lure filmmakers to the state, have been incredibly successful. He says over 135 films have been produced in the state because of those incentives, everything from *Transformers* to *The Lone Ranger*. The producers of *Breaking Bad* cite those tax incentives as the primary reason they chose to base their production in New Mexico rather than California, and as a result, an entire cottage industry has sprung up around the fame brought to Albuquerque by Heisenberg and his blue meth.

But many in New Mexico fear space tourism has already proven itself a flop left over from the Richardson administration. One of the more outspoken critics of Spaceport America is Paul Gessing, president of the Rio Grande Foundation, a conservative think tank in New Mexico. *Politicians have these big dreams and frequently they sell people and give this rosy picture of "Oh, yeah, this is how we'll fix the poor economy,"* he tells me. *In reality space tourism is far more speculative and dubious than anyone actually knows. It's like building an airport before the Wright brothers had their first flight. That's what New Mexico did.*

Bobby Allen, a county commissioner in Truth or Consequences, told the *Santa Fe New Mexican* about the lack of return on his county's investment: *Over a period of ten years, we've been promised a lot of stuff. To date, we have seen none of it, not for the little people here in town.* The stuff they've been promised dates back to Rick Homans's fifteen-minute pitch to the Gov in 2004. Homans tells me the original vision was for New Mexico to be the center of not just space tourism but the whole commercial space industry. *You create research hubs that are focused on creating those technologies,* he says. *You become an innovation center. You have to do those things that are important and public to lay claim to being the epicenter of a new industry. That was our vision.*

But any informed observer will say the Mojave Air and Space Port in California is where all the breakthroughs are percolating. That facility recently released a promotional video calling themselves the Modern Day Kitty Hawk. They may well be right. Including Virgin Galactic, seventeen commercial space companies use nineteen rocket-launch sites at Mojave. *It is the center of aerospace entrepreneurial development,* says Galactic CEO George Whitesides. *There is nowhere else where you can design, build, install, and test space equipment all in the same place. Mojave is the only place in the world.* While Galactic still plans to fly their tourists from Spaceport America, the dream of New Mexico becoming the epicenter of a new industry never materialized.

So almost none of the thousands of high-quality jobs Spaceport America was supposed to create over the last decade have appeared. Galactic job offerings announced via Twitter in the final months of 2013 were for nearly fifty positions to be based in Mojave, ranging from jobs such as Systems Engineering Lead to Hydraulics Systems Engineer to Propulsion Test Manager. In that same period only nine jobs to be based at Spaceport America were advertised, and those jobs were not lucrative engineering gigs but decidedly more menial positions such as Warehouse Manager and Diesel Technician and Manager of Maintenance. For every one job based at the New Mexico spaceport, still another five are announced for Mojave.

Failing to attract a significant portion of the burgeoning commercial space industry, Spaceport America has been forced more and more to rely on the promise of their anchor tenant, Virgin Galactic, and that company's most immediate goal of providing an "unforgettable adventure" and "luxury life experience" for their ticket holders. But if the murmurings of boondoggle slowly arose over a decade as none of the high-quality jobs materialized to transform the economy, they have reached a crescendo as some New Mexicans realize that after all this time it may only be the 1 percenters who benefit from the state's investment. *What you have is one of the poorest states in the country and the taxpayers in this state subsidizing the business of a billionaire for the benefit of multimillionaires,* says Gessing.

The current CEO of Virgin Galactic, George Whitesides, often fields adversarial questions with this kind of classist bent. This one was fired at him in November at a National Association of Science Writers meeting in Gainesville, Florida: *With all the problems on earth, why are we creating amusement park rides in space for rich people?* Whitesides responded by pointing out that Galactic is a privately funded company.

You have a right to talk about your tax dollars, he said. *But these aren't your tax dollars.* Galactic is owned in part by Branson and in part by Aabar Investments, a company controlled by the government of Abu Dhabi. But Spaceport America is owned by New Mexico and its taxpayers.

Galactic's response to questions about the greater relevance of their venture, beyond just good times for rich folks, increasingly plays up the possibility of intercontinental point-to-point travel via suborbital spaceship. They say these early space tourism jaunts are a stopgap on the way to revolutionizing world travel. The idea is that you endured rich pricks lugging around brick cell phones in the eighties and nineties so that you could have an iPhone in your pocket today. So now you should allow the rich their space tourism so that tomorrow (maybe two decades by Galactic's estimate) you can travel across the world from London to Sydney in two hours or from Dubai to Vancouver in an hour and a half.

Superfast intercontinental travel seems to have been in the Galactic mind since the very beginning. As early as an October 2003 interview with Charlie Rose, you can hear Branson bemoaning the retirement of the Concorde supersonic airplanes and the inability of his Virgin Atlantic airline to purchase and continue operating those planes. Between the lines you see him formulating some kind of plan to replace the Concorde. Mostly he lashes out at his airline nemesis, British Airways, and scolds the British government for completely subsidizing the building of the Concorde airplanes without ensuring that it would benefit all the people of Britain. *As far as the British public is concerned,* Branson tells Charlie, *we, the British public, paid for the Concorde and not British Airways.* If you watch closely as Charlie waggles his stern inquisitional finger at Branson, you can almost see the word *boondoggle* forming on the mogul's lips.

But now the tables have turned and New Mexico's tax-payers are the ones with their money on the line for Branson. I asked Mark Butler, the Virgin Galactic manager in charge of operations at Spaceport America, if the company would continue to use the New Mexico spaceport should their business model shift toward intercontinental travel. He responded by e-mail with a succinct sidestep: "It is too early to say." That's undoubtedly true. But the concern for so long in New Mexico has been that the spaceport was too tied to Galactic, that if Galactic failed, the spaceport would go down with it. But here is a scenario in which Galactic could be too successful and leave New Mexico in that proverbial dust. As Paul Gessing points out, it's hard to imagine international travelers from New York or Los Angeles ever heading out to the remote Jornada del Muerto desert before rocketing off to Paris for dinner. And anyway, Galactic's *SpaceShipTwo* doesn't rocket off until fifty thousand feet. Until then it's strapped to *WhiteKnightTwo*, which operates much like any other airplane. Many runways at many airports in the world could conceivably be retrofitted for the flights. And even if Galactic's business model does not shift toward intercontinental travel anytime soon, they are currently building a spaceport in Abu Dhabi, this time with their own money and the money of the Abu Dhabi–controlled company that owns almost half of their company. Galactic is tight-lipped about the project, and despite repeated questions, I could get no one in the company to confirm anything other than that the spaceport project in Abu Dhabi was under way and they expected to have it completed in the next few years. I guess the oil-rich Galactic investors in Abu Dhabi will spare no expense to create a "luxury life experience" for their ticket holders that far surpasses anything New Mexico taxpayers can afford. The Pine Knot honky-tonk and all the hot-spring tubs in sheds, while charming, probably won't turn the heads of our Gagas and Leos and Brangelinas like the seven-star Emirates Palace in Abu Dhabi. The point is that while all of Spaceport America's eggs have been in the Galactic basket, Galactic has increasingly hedged its need for Spaceport America. This brings up all sorts of visions of the spaceport ten or fifteen years down the line, the creosote and cacti taking over again, just as abandoned as it was when I first visited.

One group of people could be the saviors of Spaceport America, if and when they show up. Christine Anderson, the current director of the New Mexico Spaceport Authority, calls them by this oxymoronic name: Terrestrial Space Tourists. She tells me the hope is to have a full 50 percent of spaceport revenue come from these old-fashioned tourists, not the few who can afford a ticket on *SpaceShipTwo*, but the many people like you and me who are expected to show up and gawk without ever leaving earth. *I think any commercial spaceport that wants to be self-sufficient needs to have a second source of revenue coming in*, she says. *In our case it is tourism. For Mojave [Air and Space Port] it is windmills. Just like most airports do not get all their money from airplane traffic; they get it from concessions.*

This sort of tourism has plenty of precedent. During the moon shot, a launch from Cape Canaveral, such as that of the *Saturn V* rocket and Apollo 11 shuttle on July 16, 1969, drew hundreds of thousands of people from all over the country to beaches and bridges and islands for miles in every direction. But that was a free-for-all picnic where the pilgrimage had a distinctly patriotic feel and everyone was at least guaranteed the fireworks show of a thirty-six-story behemoth of engineering blasting off with a force equivalent to a million pounds of TNT. Spaceport America is isolated, can't support such a flood of humanity, and won't offer such a brilliant spectacle. Galactic's technology isn't the fireworks of a million pounds of TNT—*SpaceShipTwo* ignites its rocket at fifty thousand feet, so any observers on the ground will only be watching the mother ship, *WhiteKnightTwo*, take off horizontally, much like any other plane.

So Christine Anderson has been hunting for a $21 million loan to help make the place more enticing to the much-needed Terrestrial Space Tourists. *Several years ago we had a company called IDEAS from Florida help us plan that whole Visitor Experience,* she says. *Many of the company employees are former Disney Imagineers.* We'll have a 3-D theater

---

* In a move reminiscent of those conquistador actors at the spaceport groundbreaking, the former Imagineers at IDEAS hired a Native American consultant for their design of the Visitor Experience. This guy, Larry Littlebird, has made his living as a Native American storyteller, both in the movies and freelance at high school assemblies and New Age spiritual retreats. Securing an interview with Littlebird for this story required months of permissions wrangling from the Spaceport Authority and IDEAS, including a condition that we not talk specifically about the Visitor Experience, which was particularly ridiculous because when Littlebird finally got the okay to talk to me, he said he'd never even been consulted about anything for the spaceport and that, so far as he knew, he was just a name on a website. Littlebird and I talked for hours and the whole conversation was a real mind trip, but none of it can be quoted here because I screwed up the recording of it and the fact-checkers don't believe that he said some of the things that he actually said, things concerning the long outwaiting of horses and rocket ships and a Pueblo prophecy about the second coming of an aging sun lizard.

*on-site and we'll have a restaurant and we'll have a little
observation deck that you can walk out to and watch as the
spaceships take off and land.* Anderson wanted to have all of
this ready so that its opening coincided with the first flights
of Virgin Galactic, which she hopes will begin by the end of
2014 and draw about two hundred thousand visitors annu-
ally. That number of expected Terrestrial Space Tourists has
been consistently revised downward over the last decade as
the spaceship launch delays have piled up and reality has set
in. Also likely to cut into this number is that for the time be-

---

The interview recording is not lost but is interrupted every five
minutes by a robot reading the First Amendment to the Constitution
of the United States of America: "Congress shall make no law respect-
ing an establishment of religion, or prohibiting the free exercise thereof;
or abridging the freedom of speech, or of the press; or the right of the
people peaceably to assemble, and to petition the Government for a
redress of grievances." Apparently this is a ploy to get you to pay $3.99
to upgrade to the Pro version of Android Call Recorder, the app I used
to record our long talk. The demo version of the app also records only
one side of the conversation. The First Amendment is read by the robot fifty-one times during the recording. Because so much of the interview is censored by the robot reading the First Amendment and all
the questions are lost, I cannot quote from it, but I can reconstruct it
based on my notes and the uncensored bits. So this is a reconstruction
I call:

Storylistening with Littlebird
Concerning the Long Outwaiting of Horses and Rocket Ships

Question:
Littlebird: *The most profound thing in Florida is Disney World. What
was going on with that human being that this Disney World came out of
his brain? Walt Disney is my hero.*

ing none of this Visitor Experience will actually be built—
Anderson recently shelved the ambitious plans to save money
in the wake of increasing boondoggle outrage. For the foreseeable future, the relatively small public gallery of the Gateway to Space will be the only area for visitors who have not
paid a quarter of a million dollars for a ticket.

Despite New Mexico's being at the end of a decade-long
limb for Galactic, the company has no specific plans to help
with the state's Terrestrial Space Tourism effort. Mark Butler, the Galactic manager at Spaceport America, told me,
The primary attraction of this tourism program is expected to

---

Q:

L: *He made the mouse move. He gave it a voice. It began to tell these
stories. Where did that come from? How was that expressed?*

Q:

L: *I'm going to tell you a story about a horse.*

Q:

L: *Everything is related, Joshua. All of these floating islands, these continents, they come from one great ancient floating island. Joshua, think
about the horse.*

Q:

L: *Our understanding of our place in this world comes from the return of
the horse to this continent. My people, my ancient people, on the one
great floating island . . . we knew that animal. We knew the horse when
it was still tiny. You know, three or four feet tall. Then it disappeared.
Gone overnight. That coincided with the separation of the great floating
islands, the breaking apart of the continents . . .*

Q:

L: *It makes for wonderful entertainment for the head.*

be Virgin Galactic operational spaceflights, so that is what our primary contribution will be.

Their focus is largely on that other group, the Rich Space Tourists.

One thing Terrestrial Space Tourists can still look forward to: a Welcome Center in Truth or Consequences. This building is slated for construction on land the New Mexico Spaceport Authority has already purchased on the outskirts of town, situated conveniently between a Walmart and a Holiday Inn. Bus rides to the spaceport will originate from

------

Q:

L: When the horse returned to this floating island, we were waiting for it, and when it returned, we recognized that animal by its spirit. Where is the spirit? Can you cut open my brain and find the spirit?

Q:

L: For me, as a tribal person, I see we are going further and further away from that which is of the spirit. Now a lot of tribal people across the Americas have stories of this connection, the recognition that occurs when the Spanish bring back the horse. Oh my gosh! These moments are like you're on a particular journey and then there is a signpost. The return of the horse is a signpost. And a big one. And what it means is that people that were separated in another time are coming together now. See? You are on the right journey. A signpost.

Q:

L: It's a different creature; it went away from here this little creature and it is returned magnificent. The spirit is growing in its presence in the world.

Q:

L: Yes, the horse was the first thing of this desert to really alter space and time. It's almost as if time is being taken away from us . . . a sense of timelessness . . .

here. *But we're also working on the mobile theater,* Anderson says. *You won't just be sitting on a bus for forty-five minutes, you're going to be in a digital experience learning about space and New Mexico.*[*]

When I first took the bus to the spaceport, there was no digital experience. I took notes on my iPad while our tour guide explained to us that we were getting a sneak peak at the future. His own notes were in a bulky three-ring binder—the standard tour-guide technology for the last seventy years. Slipped into one of the wrinkled plastic sheaths was an old photocopy of the earthrise, the famous photo

---

Q:

L: *Aging sun lizard?*

Q:

L: *But we must be storylisteners, Joshua. And so we are all prophets. When the Spaniard returns on the horse, this magnificent creature, we had listened and so knew already that the horse would come here again and so know the long outwaiting will end too. When this thing you say, aging sun lizard, returns riding the rocket, it will be so too. I'm seeing the prophetic nature of the return of the horse . . . What's going on with Galactic is a part of the story of what comes of this time of our long outwaiting.*

Q:

L: *Never good. Never bad. A prophet is only a storylistener. We all have prophetic ears, Joshua.*

Q:

L: *All lizards have ears. But no lizards vocalize—no sound comes from the lizard. Ears only, to hear beyond what's said. The lizard is the ideal prophet.*

[*] Eventually the money for building this Welcome Center will dry up too and the Spaceport Authority will take over the senior center in

from the 1968 mission of Apollo 8: from the Moon we see Earth floating in the dark distance of space like a little blue marble swirled all over with white clouds. This image is considered one of the most important photographs ever taken because it showed people on Earth, for the first time, a new global perspective. We are all on the marble together. But nobody ever mentions that a full half of Earth isn't visible in the photo, lost in shadow so that the little blue marble appears hacked in half.

When we talk about space tourism, particularly the suborbital kind that Galactic plans to conduct from Spaceport America, we're talking a lot about that blue marble—the view we can get of ourselves from way up there. This is how our spaceport out in the Jornada del Muerto begins to take on all sorts of spiritual dimensions.

The Overview Effect is a term coined by Frank White in 1987 to describe the experience of viewing Earth from space and the effect such an experience has on the viewer forever after. David Beaver, director of the Overview Institute, a group spawned from White's work, writes this about the view of Earth from space: "Nearly every astronaut has told of changes or reinforcements of attitudes, perspectives and motivations; deep effects on intellectual, emotional and even spiritual levels."

As Richard Branson says in a November 2009 Virgin

---

downtown Truth or Consequences, displacing the elderly citizens in favor of some space exhibits and a rather tacky G-Shock simulator—basically a glorified single-seat, 360-degree merry-go-round. The warnings for this simulator do not specifically exclude use by the elderly but the Spaceport Authority will never offer any members of the displaced senior center lifetime passes to ride the G-Shock.

Galactic promotional video, *This will be a trip like no other. It will give those that travel with us a unique and life-changing perspective of our planet.* Some version of this claim runs throughout all Branson's discussions of his space venture, and because of his persistent giddiness and his flowing golden locks that have faded to dirty white, he has a Gandalfish wizardry about him, a sense that his pitch for space tourism is mixed with more than a little bit of mysticism.

World View, another tourism company that has considered making a home at Spaceport America, plans to give people a taste of the Overview Effect via balloon ride. Their balloons carry a passenger capsule to only a third of the height of Galactic's spaceships, about twenty miles up, but they claim tourists will see the curvature of the earth and the twinkle-speckled black of space. The flickering piano and epiphanic strings of their promotional video's score play beneath slow-motion renderings of the blue marble. Despite their rides not technically getting to space, they're selling the same spiritual experience as Galactic, though theirs can be had for only $75,000. Another of these high-altitude balloon companies, this one based in Spain, even claims that its passenger experience will be superior to Galactic's because its space capsule provides enough room for passengers to meditate or do yoga.

Brian Binnie is one of the few who have experienced what Virgin Galactic is selling. In 2004 he piloted to an altitude of 69.6 miles the X Prize–winning *SpaceShipOne* that became the prototype for Virgin Galactic's current vehicle, *SpaceShipTwo*. Binnie describes Galactic's passenger experience this way:

Even though you're just, as a passenger, sitting there, you are fully engaged. Your senses are pegged. There's a lot of vibration. There's a lot of noise. There's a lot of g-forces on your body. For a minute and a half you're saturated by that. But at rocket motor shutdown it's as though somebody throws a switch and just like that the noise and the vibrations, the shaking, the shuddering, the shrieking and the shrilling of that rocket motor all disappears. And right with it you become weightless. And weightlessness means all the tension that was there is gone . . . You can drift to the nearest window and now you have this body sensation coupled in with that view. It's otherworldly.

David Beaver is wary of these selling points. He says, *It appears that the Overview Effect has either become marginalized by some of the more esoteric of the astronauts' experiences or minimized as simply thrilling or aesthetic experiences.* Beaver wants the view to be about social and political change, which he figures can't happen if it's sold as either religion or entertainment or some amoral combination of the two. He does say that, ultimately, we should have faith in Virgin Galactic and other commercial space companies because, like Stephen Hawking and Elon Musk, he believes the likelihood that we're destroying our home planet absolutely demands that we become an interplanetary species sooner rather than later.*

* Beaver was, at one time, in the running to design the Spaceport America Visitor Experience with his pal Douglas Trumbull. You've no doubt seen Trumbull's work. He's a Hollywood special effects guy who changed the whole industry with his work on *2001: A Space Odyssey* and *Close Encounters of the Third Kind* and *Blade Runner.* He's one of those guys who you almost never hear about, but whose vision for things, such as space stations and aliens and future cities, pretty much becomes the entire culture's vision because his art is great and he

Perhaps most telling was a story Beaver recounted to me about his buddy Frank White, the original champion of the Overview Effect, who recently flew to New York to meet with Branson. When Frank asked why Galactic never talks specifically about the Overview Effect, Branson responded, *I didn't want to encroach on your brand.* Frank laughed and told Branson that something so profound as the cosmic view of Earth should never be reduced to a brand. But the strategy of Galactic has largely been to use the transformative and spiritual aspects of space travel in service of their brand. *Galactic will put the Virgin brand on the map in a way money can't buy,* former president of Virgin Galactic Will Whitehorn told *Wired* magazine in 2005. *Every time someone mentions space travel, they'll mention Virgin.*

Galactic has also used the ingenious strategy of getting celebrities to pay them to endorse the brand by purchasing a ticket. Notice that even this essay began, with no small

---

keeps quiet while slipping it into other people's projects. Beaver and Trumbull pitched their Visitor Experience as a virtual reality simulation of the Overview Effect, which sounds cool unless you watch Trumbull's film *Brainstorm* starring Christopher Walken. *Brainstorm* is the only major film Trumbull directed, a lovably ambitious flop that proves he was born to be the magic ingredient in someone else's recipe. *Brainstorm* is about the mortal dangers of virtual reality—lots of murderous insanity ensues when the VR gets too real. The film uses the Wright brothers' Kitty Hawk as a backdrop for its climactic scene of Christopher Walken's VR-induced episode of violent insanity. Perhaps it was best that Trumbull and Beaver's VR Visitor Experience didn't get the spaceport contract, as the link to *Brainstorm* and violent VR-induced psychosis at Kitty Hawk might have been a bad omen for our spaceport that aims to be, they keep insisting, the modern-day Kitty Hawk. Plus,

amount of encouragement from its editors, by name-dropping the famous. So multiply this essay by the thousands of news articles and features that have used a similar hook for Galactic stories over the last decade, then add to that announcements of Lady Gaga scheduled to perform on a Galactic flight and add those photo spreads of her in revealing space suits and add announcements about tickets available to be purchased with Bitcoin and announcements about brand partnerships with Land Rover and announcements of a sweeping media deal with NBC that will include a flagship reality show called *Space Race* and announcements of live coverage of the inaugural Galactic flight to be shown across all NBCUniversal networks, a program that aims to rival Neil Armstrong's first steps on the moon in gluing wide eyes the world over to televisions (and now also monitors and tablets and smartphones, etc.). Well, alright. Now you understand how Galactic can maybe afford delays, how time just gives

---

I'll let you ponder all the possible societal fracturing implications of giving Rich Space Tourists the actual life-altering spiritual experience of the Overview Effect while sticking Terrestrial Space Tourists with some computer-generated facsimile playing on the scratched screen of a headset all sticky from the muck of spit and space ice cream dripping off thousands of grubby hands of the children of Terrestrial Space Tourists who are getting nothing spiritual out of the virtual reality video but are maybe getting primed for the relentless disappointments of impoverished life and maybe getting also the chance at a psychotic episode. Right now—on December 4, 2013—President Obama is live on TV saying, *Income inequality is the defining challenge of our time.* And he doesn't even know how close our spaceport came to ushering in a society of Overview Effect–enlightened 1 percenters presiding over the unenlightened masses all prone to psychosis from their shitty *Brainstorm*-inspired epiphany-simulation machine.

them more time to build an enormous brand in an unprecedented market before ever delivering a product.

*I'm leaving town soon, but by God, I'm still the mayor for a
few days,* John Mulcahy says. We meet during his last days
in office as mayor of Truth or Consequences, though he doesn't
seem to have an actual office, so we meet in a multipurpose
room attached to the civic center. The roof leaks and a
bucket is placed pretty close to under the leak and a maintenance man occasionally pops in to size up the rise of water.
The good news: the November ice is finally melting and the
road to the spaceport is likely passable. The bad news: this is
not the only leak in town.

Mulcahy talks mostly about the challenges he's faced trying to ease Truth or Consequences toward preparing for the
tourist boom promised by the spaceport. The problems are
big enough that they've contributed to his stepping down as
mayor in favor of heading up economic development in
Roswell, where there's already an entrenched cosmic brand.
The gist of the problems in Truth or Consequences, he says,
is that so much of the town is in disrepair and there's not
much money. *We're trying real hard to fix our blight,* Mulcahy
says. *We're painting. Fixing roads. And I don't mean spend a
bunch of money. I mean get out and clean up your yard. Put
the roof back on. Put the door on the front door. It's a poor community.* Because of the cold Mulcahy wore his cowhide work
gloves to our meeting, which he now twists into and out of
knots as he talks to me. *We've seen this coming. It didn't sneak
up on us.*

Sixty percent of the town is on a fixed income from Social
Security or welfare, according to the mayor. Most all of
the students at public schools are on a free lunch program.

Because the town is largely populated by senior citizens, the meal program at the senior center is one of the largest gatherings on any day. While nearby Elephant Butte Lake brings in around nine hundred thousand visitors a year, the campers and fishermen aren't exactly rolling in with big money, and what they do have goes to businesses around the lake, outside the city limits.

When I ask Christine Anderson how the New Mexico Spaceport Authority is working to help with economic development in Truth or Consequences, she says, *We meet with all the communities. But again, it's their job, not ours. We share our thoughts with them and our projections with them. But ultimately it's up to them.* The concern, as Mulcahy puts it, is that *a lot of players with very deep pockets* will roll into the community and transform the place into something unrecognizable, into some gold-plated playground that overshadows the town's unique culture. Galactic astronauts who purchase quarter-of-a-million-dollar tickets will want luxury accommodations. Michael Blum, a Galactic ticket holder and former PayPal executive, recently said to a crowd in Las Cruces, *I love the Hotel Encanto, but it's not up to the international standard that these people [Galactic astronauts and their entourages] are accustomed to.* The Hotel Encanto is likely the swankiest hotel in all of SNM. So Blum's remarks, while intended to urge locals toward luxury development, were also an indictment of their current way of life. For Mayor Mulcahy they were a warning about the dangers of deep pockets erasing the unique identity of Truth or Consequences. Even my room at the Pink Pelican motel might not survive. It doesn't meet Blum's international standard of luxury. It's too pink. Too crumbling adobe.

Across the street from my motel is its sister business,

the Pelican Spa, one of ten locally owned hot-spring spas in town. I soaked in a steel tub in a little room with one tiny window and a giant PVC spigot spewing steaming water like a fire hydrant. A nearby washing machine wobbled, and a family of five in the tub next door were having a contest about who could cackle the loudest. Blum might not have liked it. But it seemed pretty good to me. I could dip my head under the steaming water and the rumbling of the washing machine felt something like a rocket ride, and then when I surfaced, all the nearby laughter brought me back to earth. The hot springs flow from beneath Truth or Consequences at over 2 million gallons a day, pumped into baths all over downtown and even to the backyards of some houses. The geothermal waters come up at over a hundred degrees, spiked by the earth with minerals including gold and silver and mercury, a brew championed for centuries by locals as having vast healing properties. In the first half of the twentieth century, Hot Springs, New Mexico, was a major destination for those seeking a therapeutic experience, physical and spiritual, boasting as many as fifty medicinal spas for the old body-and-soul soak. So Mulcahy's call to *step up and say we're gonna manage this deal* is as much about seizing economic opportunity as it is about preserving the culture that, even without the spaceport, makes the place unique. It's a mysticism that dates all the way back to early Native American tribes, who used the hot springs and surrounding area as sacred ground—neutral in war and prized for healing battle wounds and prime for talks of peace. It's a mysticism that seems born to cradle, many centuries later, the launching point for that more spiritual notion of the Overview Effect where the blue marble becomes the only way we see ourselves, all calm and in it together.

When we talk to people about why they want to spend the money to go up to space, we hear a lot about that view when they look back at Earth. That it is weirdly an incredibly grounding experience, says the New Mexico tourism secretary Monique Jacobson. *We think that's actually what a trip to New Mexico can do for people, even if you're not able to go to space and look down at Earth, coming here can really ground you. The culture and adventures here are so unique—how you feel when you leave and how they're truly adventures that feed your soul.*

As part of Governor Susana Martinez's administration for the last three years, Jacobson has worked aggressively to rebrand the state, a skill she first honed with Gatorade and Quaker oatmeal. Her campaign is called New Mexico True and the slogan she repeats several times as we talk is *Adventure steeped in culture.* Indeed, much of the tourism campaign for New Mexico is about recreational activities alongside Native American and Hispanic culture. The New Mexico True brand largely ignores the presence of the aerospace industry, suggesting maybe that aerospace is not True to New Mexico. But Jacobson thinks this can change and says she does have plans to create a Space Trail that will originate at Spaceport America and direct Terrestrial Space Tourists to related sites around the state via touch-screen kiosks.

Currently the New Mexico tourism website features nothing about Spaceport America, though film locations and ghost towns and the state's penchant for green-chili cheeseburgers are featured. The True brand is taking its time going Galactic, either because they (like everyone else) are waiting for Galactic's first flight or because current governor Martinez was a bit annoyed at inheriting the old Gov's troubled legacy project or because they are mindful of not letting Galactic overshadow traditional New Mexican culture. That last bit is likely the case, so a tussle surrounds Spaceport America, a battle to be the defining brand.

Even the New Mexico Spaceport Authority has gotten into the branding game in the last year, sporting a new logo that looks like the *Star Trek* insignia dipped in the Stars and Stripes and tipped on its side. The logo is on T-shirts and hats and looms large in the tiny Operations Center adjacent to the Gateway to Space. All three of these brands, Virgin Galactic and Spaceport America and New Mexico True, need to coexist for the spaceport to succeed. The Overview Effect (the real potential for political and social change), because it is not a brand, may get lost in all that marketing. And anyway, at this point Galactic's brand undeniably dominates. Consider the very architecture of the building. The spaceport is not just any mythological eyeball rising out of the desert. The Gateway to Space, when all lit up, is designed to resemble the Virgin Galactic logo: a blue iris painstakingly modeled after Richard Branson's own eye. From a descending *Space-ShipTwo*, after you've seen the holy curve of Earth, you'll get to glide quietly down into the big eye of a billionaire.

The November ice finally melts off the road and runs into the dam. The bus rumbles through the canyon and over a few cattle guards, and the water in Elephant Butte Lake is rising for the first time in years. After soaking at the Pink Pelican and drinking at the Pine Knot I'm finally headed to the spaceport again. As we steer around stray cattle, Spaceport America peeks out of the red desert horizon. We get closer and it finally blinks open, three stories of glass gleaming in the sun. Looking directly at it requires a hard wince.

I wonder what it might be like to sit inside, just before

rocketing to space. I think of Dr. Pat Hynes, director of the New Mexico Space Grant Consortium and a Galactic ticket holder, who told me of sitting in the third floor of the Gateway to Space, which will become the Astronaut Lounge, complete with a champagne bar. She was there one afternoon, meeting with the UK spaceport delegation, when everyone stopped to watch as a thunderstorm rolled into the valley, the whole of the storm visible because of the open desert horizon and the massively panoramic windows looking north over the runway. That view from inside the Astronaut Lounge must be great, a stark precursor to what Galactic ticket holders will see from above.

But most of us, the Terrestrial Space Tourists, will be gazing at the building as I am, from the outside. We will get the same panorama of New Mexico landscape but it will be a reflection on the windows' exteriors, the curvature of those three stories of glass, like a sphere, throwing the mirrored image of the desert back at us. That perspective is strange, the opposite of the Overview Effect and kind of sidelong, so the world is not growing smaller and more whole in the distance but is magnified all around you and your own reflection is enveloped in it, a kind of fish-eye perspective that forces you to see yourself as tiny in the emptiness it reflects. It is beautiful, that perspective. But also, because of that same curvature and the way it warps your body's reflection, it's more than a little bit like a giant fun-house mirror.

BEFORE THE FALL

THE VIOLENCE OF THE WIND AND THE EDDIES AND AT THE SAME TIME THE CONSCIOUSNESS OF THE TEMERITY

•

In the Year of Our Lord 2012

Start the cameras and our guardian angel will take care of ya is the final thing we hear over the communications radio from Joe in Ground Control. This is a high-tech affair but the radio cracking and beeping into our stream is anachronistic, as if our daredevil in a hulking space suit with so many bells and whistles and gizmos ought to be able to get messages sent straight to his brain—straight to our brains— as he stands on the ledge of a gondola, a shiny space capsule, a fiberglass teardrop floating twenty-four miles above Earth. And angels—those winged anachronisms—what use are they up here? No good angel has ever fallen. And so the nerves kick in. Our daredevil's heart beats three times per second, and fifteen cameras inside and outside the teardrop record thirty frames per second each in glorious 4K HD. And still there are more cameras. *Start the cameras . . .* says Joe in Ground Control, and he means the body cameras, the one on the chest and two on the waist and one on each thigh: a view from our daredevil's chest up past the dark visor of his eight-pound helmet and the view down the left leg of his puffy white pressure suit and the view from his back as if we have saddled him like a horse. Giddyup. All of time has passed since a fall was experienced so much, so far and wide. But this will be a literal fall in which gravity will work on flesh as on object, a fall we have just begun to believe is really going to happen because Joe in Ground Control has invoked *our guardian angel* and we feel the tickle of nerves as we stand here, floating twenty-four miles high. Our daredevil is the one in the pressure suit but make no mistake: the fall will be ours. We can see it all. We are 8 million people: 16 million eyes drowning in a Net stream of the teardrop's cameras and our daredevil is not yet falling but just standing on the ledge. We are on the ledge. See the blackness around us? Look at great big Earth below and the fragile polyethylene balloon above—fabric thinner than a strand of human hair—which has slowly expanded over the last two and a half hours as it rose and its helium that is now too dense in the light air of the stratosphere to carry our thirty-two-hundred-pound teardrop any higher. Feel the breath inside the helmet. See the fog on the visor. Feel the heart beat inside the suit, inside the restraining mesh and gas membrane and thermal liner, inside the flesh-and-bone cage. In the weeks leading up to this moment the news reported again and again about the possibility of "his blood boiling, brain bursting, and eyeballs popping out." During the fall he will catch up with and push through his own sound waves and experience vibrations that could, sinew by sinew, tear his body apart. He had to be told twice to unbuckle his seat belt. Told four times to disconnect his oxygen. But Joe says the magic words only once: *Start the cameras.* We look down. We will fall. Joe has invoked *our guardian angel* and now there is no choice.

Because there is always a fall at the beginning of things. With falling there is immediately an engaging story. From where? To where? What flight aborted? What mistakes? What banishment and why? What injuries now needing to be overcome? What loved ones now gnashing with grief? What dreams on which we rose so high? This is why falling is our prime mover of a metaphor, why our big religions use it to describe the beginning of human history. The fall makes for a good start to the story. The way it's told most, we fell from where we were supposed to be and now we suffer until we can get back. But then falling might also be an escape. From here on the ledge looking down it's a matter of whether we're better off down there.

When we click through the excess of video in the coming weeks, we will know that this ledge moment lasts less than a minute, a mere fifty seconds before the fall. But in this moment we linger to the point of paralysis. We swell the hesitance because still the only important question is unanswered, the question anyone always asks on a ledge: Why? Or, what's the point?

Our daredevil and his team mostly avoid calling this mission a fall. They say *jump* or *dive* or, if the word must be used (and it must because they seek world records for highest and longest free fall) they say *free fall*, but try to make clear that falling is only one part of the mission and that, on the whole, it will be a *controlled descent*.

They say again and again, *This is no stunt.*

Everything is under control. Everything happens for a reason.

They call it the Mission to the Edge of Space and the Space Dive and the Supersonic Jump, though none of those are totally accurate. Traditionally we've drawn a line in the air at sixty-two miles and labeled everything beyond it with that eloquently ambiguous term *space*. But Earth's atmosphere roams as far as five hundred miles beyond its surface. The International Space Station orbits at two hundred forty-nine miles. American pilots earn their astronaut wings flying as low as fifty miles. We cruise at around six miles with our tray tables down and our economy seats reclined at a maddening 106-degree angle. Anything above twelve miles will start to rip at unprotected sinew. So the twenty-four-mile height of our floating teardrop is somewhere between here and there, smack-dab in the middle of a place called the stratosphere. Our birds don't come this high. Our storms rarely storm this high. But this is not that fabled far-off *space*. This is a kind of skyward purgatory where we are not home or totally away from home. And if our daredevil goes supersonic, it will not be because he is jumping but because he is falling. But say Fall from Somewhere Less Than Halfway to Space and nobody pays attention. So: Space Dive.

And: *This is not a stunt.*

The mission team in Ground Control is nearly two hundred people including experts in aviation engineering, skydiving, ballooning, meteorology, and medical science. The director of the medical team for the mission is Dr. Jonathan Clark, a former NASA crew surgeon. Clark's wife, Dr. Laurel Clark, was among the seven astronauts killed when the Space Shuttle *Columbia* broke up on reentry and showered West Texas with debris in 2003. For sixteen days, orbiting Earth at over two hundred miles, Laurel helped complete nearly eighty experiments in zero gravity on Space Shuttle *Columbia*. She studied the lick of flames, saw silkworms morph to moths and cancer cells morph to more cancer cells, gasped as roses bloomed without any gravity to pull at their petals, and stared hard at sand *trying to understand how sand moves,* she said, *and where to build homes on an Earth that shakes.* But she never made it home. Her husband became obsessed with spacecraft emergency escape. He helped NASA write a report declaring that what the *Columbia* crew endured—loss of air pressure and an explosion at thirty-eight miles high— was absolutely unsurvivable. Dr. Clark has never liked the odds of *unsurvivable.* He wants space travelers to have a last resort, even though some of us already consider space travel itself the last resort for when Earth is too hot for flowers or shakes too much for homes.

Who will want to escape when we are all already escaping?

And what is it like to pore over all that grim research and then have to explain, in words that come one after another, all the ways your astronaut wife passed through the sky fire and returned again to just the chaos grains of star stuff from which we all came?

But Dr. Clark is pragmatic about the realities of space travel in the here and now. He wants something useful to come from his wife's death, and in this way his pragmatism about the Mission to the Edge of Space becomes kind of heart-wrenching. And in this way he is the most convincing of anyone on the mission team when he talks about *egress,* the word they throw around when questioned about the point of sending a man via balloon to fall from the strato-sphere. *We are pioneers,* they say, *in the future of space egress.*

Egress has long been the name for any kind of ejection or escape system in aviation, but the word has the rather casual Latin origins of *gradi* (to step) and *ex-* (out). *Just stepping out for some air. Just a small egress, darling.* The word's most common usage these days is as a legal term about one's lawful right to exit one's own property. So here on the ledge, twenty-four miles above Earth, we are involved in a rather casual exercise of our right to survive, a right to easily come and go from a place we feel we own, a place that is not exactly home but is not exactly away from home: the stratospheric heavens. Dr. Clark says, *The ultimate reason I am here is to validate that crews can survive stratospheric bailouts . . . We're accumulating a huge amount of data that can further that effort.* And we think of Laurel and how she never had the chance to bail out with her space roses and licking flames and all her questions about sand. And we think of how all humans have been perplexed by sand for all of time—how one grain of sand added to one grain of sand does not make a heap, and one grain of sand added to that still does not make a heap and so on and so on, but a child on the beach with a handful of sand running through her fingers will have notions of the infinite. In language philosophy they call it the problem of vagueness—our words, such as *heap* and *egress* and *space*, are unstable, not defined enough. But Laurel was not studying language. And with sand it's a problem of accumulation. *We're accumulating a huge amount of data,* says Dr. Clark. When will we accumulate enough to have a heap, to have notions of the infinite as the grains of it run through our fingers?

Joe in Ground Control also wants this to be more than a stunt. He is the famous Joe Kittinger, the living heritage of the Space Dive, the guy who first did all this ballooning and falling for the U.S. Air Force five decades ago. In 1957, Joe piloted a balloon to almost ninety-seven thousand feet as part of the U.S. Air Force's Excelsior program. In 1959 and 1960 they added falling to the experiments, wanted to know if man could fall from that high and live, and Joe did. His gondola was more basket than space capsule and there weren't so many cameras, just three spring-wound film machines with hot-water bladders duct-taped to their sides to fend off freezing. In 1960 he set the record for world's highest skydive at over nineteen miles but never bothered to fill out the official-world-record paperwork because skydiving is a sport and he was not falling nineteen miles for sport. He was a military man, and they were testing a parachute and the parachute worked and that was the only thing he figured fit for the history books. The drogue chute, they called it, a little parachute that would deploy before the main chute in any egress system, a chute not to slow a falling man down but just to keep a falling man from spinning out of control, from having his brain mushed by the spins. Our daredevil has a drogue parachute but no plans to use it. Our daredevil has filled out the official-world-record paperwork, and use of a drogue chute would be considered a crutch, a lifesaving measure that would eliminate his bid for world records. For the record, we risk spinning out of control.

Ever since Joe's military balloon experiments, these high-altitude dives have been all about records. In 1962 a Soviet suited up and chased the record and died. He cracked the visor of his helmet on the way out of his gondola's hatch and the liquids in his body vaporized. In 1966 a former truck driver and iguana salesman from New Jersey decided to suit up and try the fall but didn't make it out of his gondola before something went awry with his visor. He remained inside for the entirety of the fall but his blood turned to vapor anyway and he died after four months in a coma. Our daredevil has been anxious about his visor too. During the ascent he worried it was frosting up too much, that the heater for the visor was broken and that, just like the Soviet and the iguana salesman before him, the need to see would be his undoing. But now our daredevil is mostly calm because he's worked with a sports psychologist to become one with his twenty-eight-pound space suit. The suit has made him claustrophobic ever since he first tried it on, got riled into an angry panic, and was nearly booted from the mission. *Fighting against my own mind* is what he calls coping with being enveloped by the state-of-the-art suit-beast. Breathing exercises and visualizations of utopias and all manner of whispering under the breath as cognitive therapy were used to keep our daredevil's mind from rejecting the suit-beast. The thing is shiny white and tailor-made and looks like an artist's immaculate rendition of a space suit. Back in 1960, Joe was suited up too but his pressure suit looked more like a standard-issue Army sleeping bag just wrapped around and duct-taped to his body. Joe sported actual red duct tape on his ankles, calves, thighs, and back. He carried the weight of the over-hundred-pound suit like a turtle, hunched and moving slowly, legs wide for stability. Despite the bulk and the red tape and the dull green color, Joe's suit seems cleaner, purer because there was no consideration of aesthetics in its creation. The duct tape did not look tacky but vital with a hint of desperation. Nothing on the suit was meant to do anything other than preserve Joe's life.

Our daredevil's suit-beast has no desperation tape but is covered with other colorful things: the logo of a Swiss watchmaker and the logo of a communications company and the logo of an aerospace company and no less than ten iterations of the logo of a billion-dollar energy-drink corporation. Back in 1960, Joe didn't even think to patch a little American flag onto his suit. Now, down in Ground Control, Joe wears on his polo and his jacket the logo of the billion-dollar energy-drink corporation (BDED Corp) that we will not name because we too want this to be more than a stunt. But we know BDED Corp well and have, at this very moment, one of their slim cans in our hands, hoping to get a little buzz of vivacity to accompany our experience of the fall. In Iowa City and Baton Rouge and Los Angeles and Paris and Istanbul and Vienna and Cairo, we sip our BDED Corp juice and lock in to our Net stream and join our daredevil on the ledge of the teardrop. We tell ourselves consumption does not make us complicit but here we are. We tell ourselves there is no way to be complacent when hopped up on glucose and caffeine and taurine, that we will know straightaway and be jazzed to act if we suspect some farce is afoot. We sip and gulp and look down.

BDED Corp's logo is a couple of hot bulls locking horns in front of a yellow sphere that is maybe the sun and maybe the reason the bulls are red-hot, or their heat is meant to be metaphorical because bulls, by definition, still have their balls and are meant to use them. This is, we guess, the kind of vivacity BDED Corp wants us to believe is (barely) contained in their can and rumors of actual bull semen in the formulation have persisted for years. The logo covers our daredevil's otherwise pristine suit and helmet and mars the slick silver fiberglass of the teardrop space capsule too. The logos, we know, have no bearing on the preservation of life but are all over everything just like Joe's duct tape and trying to appear just as vital.

BDED Corp will never disclose exactly how much of the

bill they've footed to slap their logos everywhere, to be the primary funder and sponsor of the mission—somewhere in the vicinity of $30 million over four years. They routinely spend a third of their profits on marketing, largely in sponsorship of death-defying feats such as cliff diving, BASE jumping, rock climbing, freeskiing, mountain biking, auto racing, air racing, extreme wingsuit flying, and now space diving. And it's not just sponsorship but often the total creation of these events, from athlete selection to film production. BDED Corp is now as much a media empire as it is an ED corp. Any little documentary or Net clip about death-defying or otherwise extreme feats that we've recently seen was likely created, produced, sponsored, and distributed by the corp that annually courses over five hundred tons of caffeine (and probably not any bull semen) through our veins.

Six people have died participating in BDED Corp–funded stunts in the last few years, including a fourteen-year-old motorcycle racer run down by a competitor and Ueli Gegenschatz, who, after jumping from the Sunrise Tower in Zurich, floated to his death beneath the giant BDED Corp logo screenprinted on the underside of his parachute. After Ueli's death, German communications professor and media theorist Norbert Bolz said BDED Corp *has developed a marketing strategy that is, in a sense, without any competition, because no one else dares to elevate dangerous living to a program.*

Why? Or, what's the point?

BDED Corp has again and again said that their Space Dive is not a stunt, that we are not on the ledge of this teardrop twenty-four miles above Earth on account of advertising gimmicks, that their mission, their very existence as a modern global corporation, includes the imperative to "transcend human limits—a core extension of the company's values."

A 2010 complaint in Los Angeles Superior Court claimed BDED Corp stole the idea of the Space Dive from a party promoter who pitched it to the company years ago as "marriage of daredevil, record-breaking 'stuntsmanship' and cutting-edge technology." The promoter claimed the stunt would get any corporate sponsor up to $625 million worth of advertising.

As far back as August 1938 a guy by the name of Dunkel, who billed himself as a "veteran stunt balloonist," landed on the cover of *Popular Science Monthly* boasting he could fall from the stratosphere after being carried there in a "bomb-shaped gondola" tethered to a giant balloon. The 1938 article begins, "One of the most daring and fantastic stunts ever attempted—a twenty-one-mile parachute leap—is now being planned by a Cleveland, Ohio, dare-devil." Dunkel estimated the stunt would cost $100,000. He planned to carry scientific equipment in the gondola, but clearly science was subordinate to the feat itself. He didn't have any corporate sponsors lined up. He kept saying *stunt*. But then we got worked up into our Second World War and the Bomb overshadowed the bomb-shaped gondola and so Dunkel never fell. But maybe he was right not to shy away from the word *stunt*. Maybe the problem with our daredevil, the thing making us so uneasy up here on the ledge of the teardrop, is that he is not enough like the daredevils we have known and loved.

With our old pal Evel Knievel there was never any reason to ask *Why?* when he jumped a motorcycle over a twenty-foot-long box of rattlesnakes or fourteen Greyhound buses or 141 feet of fancy fountain at Caesars Palace Hotel & Casino, the 450-pound Triumph Bonneville rumbling between Evel's legs as they (man and machine) sailed between two forty-foot geysers spurting their good-luck welcome to suckers from every corner of the world. Presiding over everything at that particular stunt was a clone of *The Winged Victory of Samothrace*, the ancient Greek statue now housed in the Louvre. The clone of *Winged Victory* still perches on the Strip and guards the casino fountain and we snap selfies with her while stumbling around with our yards of margarita, but forty-five years ago, during Evel's stunt, she kept her back turned to him and his Triumph, her marble head gone and her marble arms gone but her marble wings intact, a broken angel, a bit of foreshadowing about the price Evel would pay for trying to fly through those palace geysers, but also, in the precise sculpting of her rippling toga and the flight-strained feathers of her wings, a reminder that even twenty-three hundred years ago we humans had a sense of the overlap between violent action and absolute paralysis— the way right now we're totally motionless on the ledge of a fiberglass teardrop in the stratosphere as the first part of an epic fall.

Looking back at his whole life, in an interview published in *Maxim* just two weeks before his death, Evel pondered the ledge question: *You can't ask a guy like me why. I wanted to fly through the air. I was a daredevil, a performer. I loved the thrill, the money, the whole macho thing. All those things made me Evel Knievel. Sure, I was scared. You gotta be an ass not to be scared. But I beat the hell out of death.*

Some years earlier Evel said, *Being a hero in the United States of America is the shortest-lived profession that anybody could hope to participate in. Or hope not to participate in.*

Another corporation is reaping the advertising benefits of this great fall: a camera company whose slogan is Be a Hero. We'll avoid this corp's name out of fairness and because still we hope the Space Dive is not a stunt. This corp makes small cameras that get strapped to all sorts of athletes and animals and professionals and porn stars and average joes and janes, cameras made small to share points of view that have never been shared before, that most of us would never otherwise experience. Their innovation is in the small size of the camera and the consumer-friendly price point and the ease of sharing what the camera captures: every imaginable point of view. In this way the cameras are a sort of empathy system, a way to get us to quite literally see the point of view of another, of all the others when the cameras inevitably get small enough and cheap enough, a Digital Empathy Imaging System of Mankind. So, these little cameras—DEISM, we'll call them—are strapped all over our daredevil and his teardrop and they are the magic portals by which we are on the ledge too.

Here we are.

Deism is a word we remember from our high school studies of the Enlightenment. In that context the word is about belief in something akin to a god—a creator—but one known not through divine revelations such as the Bible or Koran or any amount of miracles or angels, just a sense of god understood through paying attention, looking around, and seeing. This is more or less what our little cameras—the DEISM—are about in their best iterations. Be a Hero is the slogan of DEISM Corp and their aim is to put every experience forever in the most present tense. With DEISM we get to see the world from the POV of a dog and see the world from the POV of a squirrel's nut and see the world from the POV of a fireman saving a cat. We get to see the world from the POV of a whole lot of people fucking in a whole lot of interesting ways. And we get to stand on the step of a fiberglass teardrop and hear Joe invoke a guardian angel that Deist theology more or less repudiates. Well, alright. We will get to fall.

FULL POV is the title of the Net video BDED Corp will eventually release that contains all the DEISM views of the fall, all at once. They mean that it is uncut recordings of our daredevil's point of view, the points of views of all cameras on his body, throughout the fall. But the video's title maybe also means *FULL* to describe the amount of POV rather than just the recording's length, as if first-person or third-person POV can never be enough, that there is somewhere, somehow a FULL POV that is maybe every possible angle, that disregards physics and even time and gives us the most complete possible view of a scene from past and present and future, such that we feel not that we are just a single point viewing a scene but that we have fully inhabited every possibility of the scene, a kind of collective omniscience— the FULL POV of DEISM. Have we ever had a medium with such lofty aspirations? What you are reading now is called an essay.

In sixteen months, DEISM Corp will get a thirty-second spot during the Super Bowl. And not just any spot, perhaps the most coveted commercial spot of all, just before the start of the halftime extravaganza. They will use the spot to showcase their video of our daredevil on the ledge. In the moment that spot airs we will become not just the 8 million of the Net stream and the tens of millions who will have replayed the thousands of Net videos of the fall, but also the

116 million watching and waiting for the Super Bowl half-time show. DEISM Corp will edit out Joe's talk of guardian angels and leave only talk of what we put our faith in now: *Start the cameras*, says Joe, and then we are on the ledge and when the commercial ends with our daredevil falling toward Earth we'll be transported to the fifty-yard line of MetLife Stadium and a chorus of children holding hands and singing beneath a downpour of hangdog fireworks at the start of the halftime extravaganza for Super Bowl XLVIII. The kids will sing a pop song: "Billionaire." They will sing about being blinded by their names lit up bright on marquees around the world. They will sing: *Oh, I . . . I swear the world better prepare. Prepare!* And then *PREPARE* once more as they raise their little hands triumphantly, but this time the word will be accompanied by an offstage angelic chorus rising a few octaves higher than even the kids can manage. But the kids won't finish the verse that everyone knows concludes with the kicker that gives the song its name: *For when I'm a billionaire.* That would be over the line, we know, to have children singing with an angelic chorus about the unfettered pursuit of gross wealth. But, fame? The aspiration of frivolous riches will be left unsung and we'll have only the moment of the children belting about fame while behind them the pixels of a giant LED American flag flash in an approximation of the ripple of Old Glory's fabric in wind.

In 2014, BDED Corp will settle a lawsuit claiming that their slogan Gives You Wings constitutes false advertising. There is no known instance of BDED Corp formulations ever giving anyone wings and in fact right now we are experiencing BDED Corp's Space Dive, which relies entirely on not having wings. You will not get wings from any of their ED formulations including Original, Total Zero, Red, Blue,

Orange, Silver, Cherry, Lime, or F1, the Formula One race car flavor (unclear if it's meant to be the flavor of a race car or licking a race car or just drinking the octane gasoline). As part of the settlement, the slogan will continue to be used and BDED Corp will give its customers up to thirteen American dollars each just to shut up about how drinking their product does not literally give them wings in a naturally growing or gene-altering or artificial/mechanical implantation way. But already lawsuits are pending in which drinkers claim the BDED Corp juice is physically unsafe. BDED Corp says that no more than five 250 milliliter cans should be consumed per day, though technically a caffeine overdose would not occur until consumption of the hundred and twentieth can. The lawsuits include cases of alleged blindness and full-on heart attacks resulting in deaths of avid drinkers. Maybe the BDED Corp juice really does try to live up to its slogan and maybe the human heart just cannot bear the burden of growing wings, and when the juice is gulped, there begins a rearrangement of nerves and the slight shift and elongation of ligaments in the shoulder but as soon as the human heart gets a notion that it might be a party to the growing of wings, it just fucking explodes. We are not meant to fly. We are the falling sort.

The hoopla in recent days makes much of BDED Corp's fall happening on the sixty-fifth anniversary of Chuck Yeager becoming the first human to break the sound barrier. He did it in an X-1 rocket plane. Our daredevil will do it with just his body and the suit-beast and us. But nobody mentions Eilmer the Flying Monk, who, just about exactly one thousand years ago today, took to a tower of Malmesbury Abbey in Wiltshire with wings of willow strapped to his hands and feet. He gets the First Man in Flight award from many of

our detectives of hidden history, but what Eilmer really did
was have himself a good old-fashioned fall. If we were all to
stand around watching Eilmer as he stood on the ledge of
the abbey's tower in the year of our Lord 1012, or better yet,
if we were to somehow get DEISM's FULL POV of the stunt
way back in the year of our Lord 1012, we would see the cool
wind tousling the hairy halo part of Eilmer's pious tonsure and
the cool wind making the bald part of his pious tonsure all
bumpy like a goose's ass, see each ripple in the fabric of his
gray frock that is covered in no logo save the wooden crucifix dangling from his neck, see bound to his ankles and
wrists with desperation twine the dried branches of willow
now finished with all their weeping and formed like wings
complete with hinges to flap and chicken feathers to flutter.
In DEISM's FULL POV of Eilmer's crowning moment we
would hear on the wind from neighboring Winchester
Abbey the sound of four hundred pipes and seventy men
squashing the twenty-six giant bellows to force air through
the pipes to make the world moan and wobble. A bishop
named Aelfeg has recently installed at Winchester Cathedral
the world's largest pipe organ and the echoing melodies of
its powerful exaltations of the Lord daily grinds at Eilmer,
who cannot stand to have his church overshadowed by the
fancy, newfangled tech of a neighboring abbey. Or maybe
Eilmer has just noticed how his monk pals have begun to
depict the ascension of Christ in their art, the Messiah no
longer carried to the heavens by angels as their paintings
had shown for centuries, but now, as one historian puts it,
"The Anglo-Saxons of Eilmer's days were beginning to show
Christ almost jet-propelled, zooming heavenward so fast
that only his feet appear at the top of the picture, while the
garments of his astounded disciples flutter in the air currents

produced by his rocketing ascent." So in Eilmer there is envy of technology and envy of divinity, a suspicion that there must be some sweet spot in their overlap. But also we know Eilmer likely read the Roman historian Tranquillus, who relates the death of a daredevil who donned wings to entertain Nero during a lull in gladiatorial bouts but, because of a technical malfunction, fell from the sky and crashed near the imperial couch and "bespattered the emperor with his blood." Maybe Eilmer was just enamored of an old stunt. And what words did he have on his lips, who of his pals down in Ground Control invoked *our guardian angel* and what prayer—that oldest of wireless communications—did our monk pray?

Maybe there has always only been the ledge question.

"What with the violence of the wind and the eddies and at the same time his consciousness of the temerity of the attempt," related one of Eilmer's monk pals about his winged stunt, "he faltered and fell, breaking and crippling both his legs." And so Eilmer never flew or fell again. And so Eilmer hobbled forever after.

Here on the ledge of the teardrop in the year of our Lord 2012, we have risen above the violence of the winds and risen above the eddies but Lord please let us never rise above the consciousness of the temerity. Existence has always been a foolhardy thing. Look around. Look down. Best to do it out of sheer audaciousness then. No glut for fame or advertising dollars. The record will be broken in two years anyway. Another man in a space suit will rise higher by eight thousand feet, without any capsule at all, just dangling from a balloon by a tether until he's higher than our daredevil, until he cuts the tether with explosive charges and falls without any

fanfare or worldwide Net stream, with hardly anyone notic-
ing at all.

Joe says, *Start the cameras*, and now our daredevil is ready
to say his piece for posterity.

Our daredevil says, *The whole world is watching now.*

About 14 percent of the world's population, 530 million
people, watched the Apollo moon landing in 1969, when
Neil Armstrong uttered his famous space words for posterity.
A couple of cricket matches between India and Pakistan
have hit nearly 1 billion viewers. In this moment, through
the magic of DEISM, 8 million of us are with our daredevil
on the ledge. If we include all of us who will watch the Super
Bowl spot and all of us who will plug into the *FULL POV*,
maybe 200 million of us will experience this fall, less than
3 percent of the world's population. So when our daredevil
says, *The whole world is watching now*, he isn't quite right.
But then he says, *I wish you could see what I can see.* Well,
alright. We've been here the whole time. We see what you
see. We see exactly what's down there.

Five decades ago, when Joe did his falling, the day had
so much cloud cover that from nineteen miles up it looked
like he could have been falling to anywhere. In some ways
that makes the footage of Joe's jump more universal than
our daredevil's: Joe could be anywhere, could be anyone
falling without flags or corporate logos and with his legs
kicking the way any of our legs would kick as we plummeted
through thick white blankets of cirrocumulus. But today the
skies are clear and below us is a specific place.

Look: at the apex of the curvature of the earth is a white
splotch, 275 miles of gypsum dunes. In the midst of that
gypsum is a runway where the Space Shuttle *Columbia*

once landed. Almost directly below is Roswell and the air-strip where Joe sits in Ground Control with the mission team and reporters and our daredevil's mother, who wears a souvenir-type green plastic alien ring on her finger. There are the Sacramento Mountains and the town of Alamogordo, and White Sands National Monument is the brightest spot on the world. Everything that is visible from the ledge of our teardrop is the blackness of space or a place called Southern New Mexico. There's the Malpais lava flow running along the Jornada del Muerto. And the edge of our view on the north side is almost exactly the 34th parallel, which cuts New Mexico in half.

When our daredevil begins his fall, he will start to spin uncontrollably, and in BDED Corp's DEISM FULL POV we will spin round and round with our daredevil and see SNM shook up below us, everything swirling around us, the Guadalupe Mountains and Carlsbad Caverns and a little bit of the top of Mexico and round toward the Texas Pan-handle, spinning from the Chihuahuan Desert and the gyp-sum sands where the Space Shuttle *Columbia* landed in 1983 and around to the Great Plains where the Space Shuttle *Columbia* broke apart and showered down in 2003 with the flames and silkworms and cancer cells and roses and astro-naut Laurel Clark with all her questions about sand. We will spin around and around like this until our daredevil fights his arms into the delta position and gains control of his speeding flesh and suit-beast and locks on three splotches of brown heaps: the Mescalero Sands, our landing zone. We will see so much in FULL POV and still it will not be enough to get notions of the infinite.

FULL POV will not show us that at the core of the

Mescalero Sands is shinnery oak. That more than two hundred years ago, before American settlers and cattle, it wouldn't have been dunes at all but would have still been prairie land, before the grasses were grazed to nothing and mesquite shrubs spread everywhere and started collecting sand. The dune fields we'll fall toward are a consequence of American progress but FULL POV cannot show us that. FULL POV cannot show us the red-eyed, inch-and-a-half-long insects beneath the sand, cicada nymphs feeding on rootlets for thirteen or seventeen years before their cyclic emergence as swarms of full-grown cicadas dying—literally dying—for just a few weeks out of the sand, in flight. Where are we in the cicada cycle now? Will we fall through a swarm of 10 million bugs rising from the dunes? Or have they just burrowed, every female dropping six hundred eggs that will hatch and dig deeper and suck on roots for another seventeen years until the next man falls from space? They bioturbate, these bugs, burrowing into the dunes, a meter down into the soil that is only a hundred or three hundred years old and another meter down through aeolian sands that are five thousand or six thousand years old. Then they rise up in swarms. Between the cicadas burrowing and rising in swarms and the ants colonizing and the badgers digging after their prey, more than thirty-seven tons of sand per acre per century is brought to the surface from below. So what is on the surface is mostly ancient, sand from the time of humans first learning to churn earth with the invention of the plow. This is where our daredevil's feet will touch down after he falls from the stratosphere: on sand formed as humans worked through the invention of written language in Sumer, the very beginning, scholars say, of *recorded history*. This is where we will land:

on sand from the very time of creation as pinpointed by the Mayan calendar that runs back 5,126 years and, our worried ones say, runs out in just a few weeks at the end of the year of our Lord 2012. Already some among us are prepping for the end-time with underground shelters and pilgrimages and suicide pacts. So many of us want to escape. Why? Or, what's the point?

Our daredevil is on the ledge and has something to say. His heart slows. *The whole world is watching now. I wish you could see what I can see.* Oh, but we can, daredevil. We see what you see and more. *Sometimes you have to get up really high to see how small you are. I'm coming home now.*

Somewhere, in an interview or a documentary, we have seen Dr. Clark cry about his dead astronaut wife, Laurel. Or maybe it is a manufactured memory but it is here in our minds on the ledge of the teardrop: him pulling his glasses from his face and wiping his eyes, smearing the tears across his cheeks as if he were trying to wipe from the sky over the Great Plains the trails of fiery star stuff as the Space Shuttle *Columbia* explodes. We all want a chance at egress, an opportunity to escape. We all just want to go home, to find a way to come home again, to perfect an escape technology, sure, but also to have the adventure, ever more temerarious, just to get that feeling of coming home again. And so maybe despite all the absurdity of BDED and DEISM, our daredevil hits upon some words for posterity that are even more sincere than Armstrong's *giant leap for mankind.* Our daredevil says, *I'm coming home.* Then he jumps—we jump in a way that is just a step from the ledge, not a dive at all, just a nudge of the self from the ledge of the teardrop in the stratosphere. The crew calls it a *bunny hop* or a *step-off* or maybe

it is that original kind of egress—just stepping out, darling—
but Joe in Ground Control says, *Jumper away!* He means the
fall has started.

See us hurtling?

There we are. Fallen.

Welcome home.

RAGGEDY, RAGGEDY WABBITMAN

His name is George Bradley Oliver but all of his friends and family call him GB and Lord knows more than enough of his male progeny will be called GB but he doesn't yet have any friends in this territory and his progeny still linger back in Texas. He's got big plans to start a proper business: he's entertaining the thought of himself as Mister Oliver—the name all big and written in his head like those swirly vines, the way words are always just too fancy for themselves at the top of newspapers and on business signs. He's fifty-six now and everything has been downhill since he was a teen shooting from the losing side of a civil war. Nobody asks much these days, but when they do, he stands up straight and says, *Company K, Jake Thompson Guards, Nineteenth Mississippi Infantry. Mustered without qualm and first thing in Itawamba and Tishomingo Counties.* But even now, through his tremendous collection of whiskers, he says it like a kid playing soldier, like a skittish private, like the froth of someone else's boiling hate. But he believed the hate and held it dear for many years and that succeeded in nothing but making him destitute. He's out of the South now and in the West and worrying mostly about his own. He's got a promise to his wife and five kids back in Cooper, Texas, says he will not cut a hair on his head or shave a hair on his face until he has $500 in the bank for a better life in this New Mexico Territory. But his try at a pool hall in Roswell fizzled out and his try at a sandwich shop in Eddy went belly-up and now the word for what he is getting to look like is *bushy*. Several years' worth of bushy. And bushy is exactly how the letters of the name George are written in his head and why he's got the urge to switch over to the sleek vines of Mister Oliver. But there are not currently a whole lot of people lining up to address him in any way at all except for these children milling around and they're not addressing him so much as they are pointing and yelling at him and calling him *Wabbitman*. He's got a baker's dozen of them jackrabbits hanging in the tree, dripping blood. Cutting the heads off for draining ain't necessary unless the suckers are huge. And some in this territory get that way, if you believe the rags. And George does. He has a whole box of scraps from the rags as a kind of motivation to make a business out of these giant pests. But the ones he has now are just alright, sizewise, the throats slit if a bullet didn't finish the job—heads dangling a tad more than any god intended, the already-long ears stretching earthward, their lateral eyes coming round so just one is looking at you, then the other, then the other again. The kids get a big laugh out of the dangling. *Raggedy, raggedy Wabbitman! Ye rabbits so raggedy, Wabbitman!*

There's not a whole ton of blood in jackrabbits and these have already been dead a few hours, already dragged a few miles. The blood is not a torrential situation but it is pooling in the crooks of the tree's exposed roots. The tree is only a sapling so the branches bow from the weight of the dangling bodies, bow and sort of bounce. The tree is without leaves because it is January so there is just the gray of the branches and the dirt white of the hides and the pooling red and the death pallor of winter in a desert. But don't you know if you stand and stare long enough at the night sky, you will see stars twinkling slowly and, even though they are far apart, they seem to breathe the twinkle into one another until the whole sky undulates sluggishly, coming to life as one big glimmering monster? Yessir. George suspects that is the exact sense the fancy folks gazing out the lobby window are getting as they look on at the slow, asynchronous drips of blood from his baker's dozen of jackrabbits hanging from the bowed branches of a young cottonwood out front of Hotel Alamogordo. He's performing a kind of advertisement. The blood drips. The tree breathes. Mister Oliver's jackrabbit business is one of the great wonders of the universe. Y'all better step out and see.

Around Hotel Alamogordo's front is a wide veranda where men sit in armchairs or lean on posts to smoke their pipes and take the air and gaze past George for fifty miles, admiring in the mountains the snow-covered form of the Sleeping Lady. George is especially conscious of looking busy when he smells the pipes, hears the door open. But mostly the men smoke inside, and all the women in their cerise silk gowns outshining even gay New York, they never stray from their mingling.

The reason for the party is the city.

Alamogordo has been up and running for all of six months since the railroad arrived and now, at the beginning of 1899, the hotel is raised and decorated and staring down a whole new century. "The linen shines with whiteness, the covers are light and warm while the mattresses are soft and the springs first class," writes one El Paso newspaperman. But George sleeps on the dirt in a tent. Kids go to school a few days a month in a big tent with a white sand floor. There are only a few actual buildings: the lumber mill, train depot, and now the hotel on the wide dirt road they're calling downtown. A shiny new street sign says NEW YORK AVENUE. Some frame houses are scattered around, little more than shacks. The big distinction in town is between tents with white gypsum floors and tents with just plain brown dirt. The fancier tents and the big public ones, like the school, have got themselves wagonloads of sand from the blindingly white dunes of gypsum west of town and covered their floors with those crystal grains to keep the dust down and to give a sense of Alamogordo as "the chief jewel in the rich crown of southern New Mexico territory," as the rags keep saying, keep talking it up trying to get the town to boom. For now it is just a dusty collection of tents, and the first of its inhabitants to go insane will no doubt be Mr. Green, the street sprinkler, the man charged with keeping the dirt out of people's lungs by driving his carriage of spewing barrels around and around and around. Any desert street sprinkler is born to lose. People will hate him because the dust is infinite but the water he's using to wage the futile fight isn't. Mr. Green will slit his own throat soon enough, bleed out right into the fledgling community's main water supply, and for at least a hundred years there'll be whispers about the town's haunted waters. *Another sip closer to madness*, they'll say.

And the new crown jewel of SNM has other nicks, too. The school tent doubles as the Justice Court. When the gamblers and brawlers and drunks are brought to the tent, the students are ushered out. Their education amounts to fleeing when sinners show up, learning to pray for more and more sinners so as to avoid any education at all. These are the little monsters yelling, *Wabbitman*. Maybe George is one of those they've prayed for.

There are plenty of places to gamble but only one place to drink: the Club House Saloon. *This will not be a whiskey town*, says the founder. But prohibition didn't work so well for his last town—all the whorehouses and saloons posted up a mile away and started their own town and that's the one where everybody stayed. That's where George made and lost a few small fortunes playing cards. So far he has managed to refrain from sitting down at any poker game in this new town. But way back in the corners of his brain he knows he could do better—win the whole $500 for his family—in a town where card games ain't only at the saloon. Gambling's less of a gamble when you ain't swimming in gin. It's a science, even. George has done the math. Three years and fifteen thousand jackrabbits. Or one good string of cards. Such a strange little town, Alamogordo. The word itself is a jawbreaker for some, who roll it around in their mouths as though it were a red-hot potato: a lumber town in the middle of the desert, a railroad town lacking water, all these white sand floors and sober poker players.

The railroad offices and mill and most of the shops will be gone by 1907 and the population will drop from a bustling four thousand and rising in that year to a sad twelve hundred lingerers and will grow ever more ghostly until the next big gadget comes along and starts a new industry—not a thing to move people, this time, but a thing to blow them up, burn them, poison their blood. George will not work for the railroad, will not work at the mill. The Olivers will employ themselves in this new territory. He's decided that will be the goddamned truth of the matter. He bites into the leg of a strung-up rabbit, makes a space between the meat and the skin and digs his finger in.

They're hares, really, but what does that matter? Better to know what's useful: breeding season is April to August and by now the little suckers are everywhere. Hares ain't hiders. They run. Well, first they do a whole lot of sitting, grass or fiddleneck in the mouth and chewing, eyes darting exactly opposite directions. At the crack of the gun they leap straight up, then manage to go three different directions on their way down, hitting the earth hardly at all before disappearing beyond a zigzag of dust. The local rags call this "elusive" and put "Elusive" in the headline and reprint the myth on the front page when news of rustling or manslaughter is slow:

Deming Headlight (Deming, NM), 12 APR 1898
The jackrabbit is awkward, appears to be lame in every joint, holds up one foot as though it pained him and altogether creates the belief that he is a dilapidated wreck of an ungainly animate thing. The settler is surprised that he cannot grab him. The settler's dog also is confident that he can quickly make an end of the rabbit. He bristles, runs leisurely toward the rabbit, doubles his speed, doubles it again, triples that, quadruples the whole, when, lo, the rabbit disappears. There is some flying grass, a vanishing streak of light, a twinkling of two prodded feet extended forward, and he is gone. The dog sits on his haunches and concludes that it was a dream and that he did not see a rabbit at all.

They might be a dream sure enough if there weren't so goddamn many of them, a thousand appearing for every one that dissolves. Anybody with enough shots or a scattergun could fill a tree, though most just do it for the shooting, never collecting anything of the kill but the scream.

That scream: "No way to account for such an ungodly squelch," say the rags.

George has it stuck in his ears, high-pitched but coarser and louder than the cottontail's, almost the wails of a newborn human if that baby were suckled on peyote and its head were a tiny kettle boiling over, psychotic steam screeching out the spout of its little mouth. When a pest-control brigade gets raised, if you listen past the boom of guns, you will hear so many screams, the kettle yell, the earth sprung with leaks and the ancient angry ghosts spewing out. They're just little rabbits though. Nothing nightmarish in how they tend to mate up and stay in pairs. Four ears straight up out of the reed grass. When you get one, there's another nearby, not yet ready to run. Don't you know that "Two birds, one stone" is a warning about love? But maybe them rabbits know nothing of love. Maybe somebody ought to tell them so they don't die twice as fast. Maybe, for all their ears, they wouldn't listen.

The females are larger than the males and give just a bit more meat and hide, but one too many times George has cut open a female and paused at the unchewed yellow petals of fiddleneck or groundsel flowering out of her gut around a fetus. Now he's got a game, to make it more like hunting, to avoid the babies and the flowers: he looks for just one set of mangled ears popping up out of the grass. Ears is where males get bit in fights over ladies. Jagged ears means a loser, a loner, one that will not be missed. He tears the skin down from the hanging leg to the belly and rips back up the other leg. Nobody will notice but he takes pride knowing his tree is hung with nothing but jagged ears, even if it is poor business sense.

Back in the seventies there'd been some trouble with George's brother in Mississippi. Jesse was a gospel preacher. Jesse died. Something was amiss in the death and a sort of war started up in the Baptist rags, some defending Jesse and others printing that he "shot himself through the heart with a pocket pistol, while in bed with his wife—a terrible end to a perverted wrecked life." That's the exact horseshit the papers printed. The first part is totally true. The second part is just plain mean-spirited. What makes a man pull back the sheets, put his hand on his wife's shoulder, cock a peashooter, and back himself into the arms of darkness? Did the ears of Jesse's wife peek up over the grass of life when that bullet hit his heart? How much did it kill her too?

George rips at rabbit skin.

Jesse's defenders claim insanity led to the unfortunate deed. Insanity caused by sunstroke. And here is George in a desert chasing rabbits all day in the sun, wondering when he will lie by his wife again.

Jesse hated Baptists because they didn't interpret the Bible literally. *The word is the word and there is nothing else,* Jesse would say. This is the doctrine of the Church of Christ and George's progeny will all more or less fall in line with that doctrine. But George knows how words only mix things up. Back in Roswell there was a miner who liked to drunkenly spin his gun on the bar and holler, *Come down, ye bald-headed Jesus Christ with your Waterbury clock and your buckeye mower, and get on with getting me back to darkness!* The old miner had Jesus Christ crossed with the grim reaper but George never said nothing because it was one of them drunken blunders with the air of truth.

Jesse's tombstone says HE LOVED THE BIBLE. The inscription goes on about FAITH LOVE PRAYER and TRUTH but doesn't mention any god, or son of god, for that matter. This love for the Book was the main thing. The perfect Book. This is what has been in the family from way back. The divine word. The binding of all them words into a thing you can hold. A Book. Make the Book disappear and there you are holding your hands out in front of you, just slightly open like begging any god for anything.

So then George avoids churches mostly. Avoids most reading too, except for the rags. He does not want to go insane like his brother. He does not all that much believe in sunstroke. He can spell Mister Oliver just fine and that's plenty to write and the rags is all he needs to read. He saves the clippings about jackrabbits. He's not making a scrapbook. Just a trunk of scraps to have something to show for all his pondering, a trunk of dreams into which his progeny will throw all their scraps of aspirations and accomplishments and angers and fears, the trunk filling up through the generations until it overflows on the lap of George's great-great-great-grandson, who will never get even a sliver of all that experience into his book. But this is 1899 and books are on their way out anyway. Everyone loves the big stage plays and right now *Ben-Hur* is sweeping the nation with its live-action chariot races. Everyone loves the photograph and these days there is even the moving image. These days there's one moving image sweeping the nation, a Western, a fifty-second joint from the Edison Company being shown in Mister Thomas Edison's Kinetoscope parlors but your eyes can only gander at its grandeur if you subject yourself to the highway robbery of five whole cents. The moving image was captured up north in this territory at the Isleta Indian School, shows Pueblo children paraded out of a school building. They bound down the steps and then circle around right back up the steps and into the school again, not a single one of them holding a book.

The Trans-Mississippi and International Exposition in Omaha just wrapped up in November 1898—an exhibition to showcase the development of the West. Geronimo was there after many decades of warring, capture, escape, and recapture. The rags bill him as the most murderous man in American history but he was not in Omaha as a murderer: "He sells the buttons off his coat and the hat off his head— he has brought a good supply of each and sews new buttons during rest breaks. He sells autographs and photographs of himself. He is the famous Mister Geronimo." Everyone's a businessman now. Everyone's got their photographs. What will Mister Oliver ever sign? There's a whole cottage industry in the Southwest of altering photographs of jackrabbits, making hares look like giant game or showing them saddled for roundups or bucking off a cowboy. Postcards. He will buy one and send it to his family and sign it with great big swoops of ink like vines. He will let them know he is truly a part of the mythmaking out here in the West. He will send them some of his scraps from the rags for proof.

The Rustler (Cerrillos, NM) 11 DEC 1891

One of yesterday's hunters killed a jackrabbit so large that he would not bring it home, as he had to carry it about three miles before the camp was reached. Hereafter fish stories must stand aside when rabbit stories come on the carpet.

At Belen within the past year, it is on record that a tenderfoot huntsman arrived there and sallied forth to see and kill his first jackrabbit, and actually shot and killed a burro, thinking that it was the game for which he had been looking. After killing the slow going little beast he rushed to town greatly excited and asked for help to bring in his game, stating that he had killed a jackrabbit bigger than two could carry.

The jackrabbit is dark meat and will cook like beef and is perfect for a stew because stew is just fire and water and general refuse. Or maybe potpie. George wishes he had the flour for potpie. What he doesn't sell, he'll eat burned on a stick. Inside the fancy hotel a table is set and the people seated. At the head: the mayor of El Paso. At the foot: the proprietor of Hotel Alamogordo. This is a wedding feast. The railroad has married these great cities. The menu:

> Cream of Celery Soup
> Broiled Salmon
> Roast Turkey, New England Style
> Filet de Boeuf, a la Champignons
> Salami of Game, a la Chasseur
> Macaroni and Cheese, Bechamel
> Roman Punch, Alamogordo
> Lobster Salad
> Mince and Pumpkin Pie

George bites at another leg. Rips. Some hunters will just cut into the back of the hide and rip in both directions like a strongman contest. But George likes the show of doing it without a knife, biting through the hide at the legs, then ripping and rolling the hide into a little handhold around the midsection, like a ring of fur around the rabbit's belly. He gets them all like this, half skinned from their feet to their bellies, their top halves still like regular rabbits except for being strung up. And this is why he hangs them: to grab the handhold of fur at eye level and get momentum. One by one he grabs the ring of hide and hops a little and holds on as he's coming down, lands on his knees, and the violent pull tears the rest of the hide from the rabbit. The violent pull even brings the head off with it. And the violent pull—if the rabbit was put together right—rips out all the guts too and George ends up on his knees holding over his head a dripping bag of inverted hide full of hare insides. This impresses the kids and they yell, *Grisly, grisly Wabbitman. Ye rabbits so grisly, Wabbitman.* Some of the older kids beg for the trick of squeezing the guts out through the ass but the Wabbitman does not take requests. And his method, however brute, preserves the hides.

White Oaks Eagle (White Oaks, NM) 30 DEC 1897
To Be Rounded Up for Their Fur, Used in Making Fine Hats

New York parties have advertisements in many western-Kansas newspapers offering three cents each for cured jackrabbit skins, culls and pieces three cents a pound, and common cottontail skins five and a half cents per pound. The New York parties want the fur for making hats, and as they represent European hatmakers, it is stated that the traffic in rabbit furs has been transferred from Australia to the United States. Skilled rabbit hunters in western Kansas can make good wages killing jackrabbits, and in the vicinity of Dodge City sportsmen are preparing for several grand roundups. Frequently the people of western Kansas have surrounded a large section of country, driven the rabbits to the center, and slaughtered them by the thousand. The only disposition made of the pests was to ship them to Chicago and New York for food for the poor. The hunters did not realize that rabbit hair entered largely into the manufacture of fine hats.

In a day or two the fancy people at the wedding feast will take the train up the mountain to Cloudcroft, the shiny new Baldwin Engine 101 and the winding rail built on trestles circling the mountain hundreds of feet off the ground, "one of the greatest pieces of engineering skill in railroad annals," say the rags. Cloudcroft already has snow and the fancy people will surely want a decent hat. Fifty good jackrabbits will make a blanket. Their hide is an inch thicker than wool. Three or four will make a decent hat, depending on the bloat of the head. George sizes up the bloats of the heads through the window of the hotel.

His pile of hides grows.

The feast ends and a Mexican orchestra tightens their strings, warms up with a bunch of plucking. George cracks the sinewy front arms at their joints and tosses the feet to the kids for luck. The cerise gowns float. George cuts along the spine, deep and quick, and like a stick along a picket fence his knife plays the little ribs. The men hit the veranda with more tobacco smoke. The bloat of their heads grows and George quickens his skinning pace.

The pelvic bone is a puzzle best not pondered too much. It is too difficult to cut around, so as soon as he sees the ball joint of the hip, he grabs high on the leg and breaks it from the torso. He leaves the tiny calf muscle on as he cuts off the rear feet. The meat of the hind legs is the meat that matters. These are the big legs, the ones used to run.

The gentlemen and their ladies, done feasting, done dancing, walk out of Hotel Alamogordo and past George and glance at his tree but just barely. His rabbits are now all reduced to piles, front quarters and hindquarters and back-straps and inverted hides full of heads and guts. Piles of scraps like the trunk of dreams torn from the rags but these will not last.

The first photograph George ever saw: a man standing next to a pile of bison skulls collected to be ground down for fertilizer. Not a pile but a mountain, the skulls towering twenty, thirty feet above the man's hat, and the base of the mountain of skulls stretching some hundreds of feet, beyond the bounds of the photograph. Dead bison. Dead Indians. And the photograph means something else too but George can't quite put his finger on it. Maybe he's killing things out of lonesomeness.

George's piles of rabbit will never grow into even the tiniest hill. Well, alright. He pulls a lucky foot from the pile, feels one good string of cards coming on. He will go on being called George and never have a floor of white sand. All the jackrab-bits will disappear. A century from now the landscape won't have them. The grass will be gnawed to nothing by thousands of cattle. Then will come the creosote, tarbush, yucca, mes-quite, and juniper, all rough and thorny and unappetizing to a rabbit. Then will come George's family, not on the backs of jackrabbits but on the one good string of cards he's about to play. And all the other families will come too, ranchers and miners and soldiers. George feels it all coming on as he walks to the Club House Saloon. Just a few drinks and one good string of cards. All the jackrabbit screams and the train steam and the whir-hack of the sawmill and the Mexican band serenading the wedding party to a close. When you're feeling lucky, everything always sounds like a prelude. Scientists will come and a bomb will come. All the soldiers will come. There will come a Border Patrol, their ATVs will come and their SUVs will come to roam the roads and trails all night, hunting more people who are trying to come with their own trunks of dreams. There will be such feverish patrolling, so much pointless driving back and forth and all around trying to make an imaginary boundary real. The roadkill will pile up, will attain the mountainous proportions George saw in that photograph of bison skulls. In a hundred years the tires of the Border Patrol will have all but wiped out the white-sided jackrabbit. They will go the way of the bison and it will mean something else too. George grips the lucky foot like it's the last one on earth. The thirst rises inside him, the hope that chance is a real antidote to fate. He steps into the Club House Saloon and throws back the first whiskey and throws his coins onto the table and thinks no more of the rabbits, their blood soaking into the dust and soaking to the roots of the little tree, Alamogordo born finally for good.

LIVING ROOM

THE INSTANTANEOUS ART OF NEVER FORGETTING

•

In the Year of Our Lord 2010

Spectral Glow

Kate got crashed-up in an eastbound Toyota Camry. Johnny overdosed on drugs in the bathtub of his trailer. She was on her way to kill herself by driving her car off the steep face of a cliff near Cloudcroft when she lost control of her vehicle on the sinuous road and veered into an oncoming SUV. Johnny took a heap of pills when she never returned from speeding furiously up the mountain on account of their most recent lovers' quarrel. They were engaged to be married.

I'm not sure I ever met Kate or Johnny, though we all lived in Alamogordo. Johnny was much older, already out of the Army and divorced and into a second career as a mental health technician, but Kate was just twenty-one and maybe still naïve about life's knack for fracturing our narrative of it—the belief, at that hell-bent age, that we will never have the need to break and begin again. She was my age, a high school classmate of mine, but I have no memory of her.

A few months after the deaths, when I was home again after college failed to make me immediately rich or even employable, Kate's mother arranged for me to have Kate's old television. She'd heard through the grapevine that I was poor and back in town and she invited me to her home. Pictures of Kate in fancy frames were on the dresser where the TV had been. I didn't recognize her as anyone I'd known, but I smiled and accepted hugs and carried the heavy TV from the girl's bedroom as her mother walked after me, apologizing for having lost the remote control.

Now the TV takes up an entire corner of my living room, an older set with imposing bulk that generates thick gravity—crashed-up Kate's TV with my furniture in its orbit, every piece arranged to accommodate its spectral glow, the terrible chill of twinkle-twinkle when you're old enough to know the facts: despite the light, that little star is long since dead.

I think of Kate most every day. I think of how I must have seen her in the halls, at the dances, sitting on the hoods and gates of beat-up Fords at the Sonic Drive-In. I think of her stretched out on her bed, clicking the remote control at her dresser, wondering why these days she can only ever see old pictures of herself in fancy frames.

Your TV is in my living room, Kate.

Bodies in the Rubble

Mark Twain invented a board game, a means of memory improvement he patented in 1885—Mark Twain's Memory-Builder: A Game for Acquiring and Retaining All Sorts of

Facts and Dates. Unfortunately, the game's rules proved too convoluted for people to follow—too in-depth to memorize or learn. The game never sold.

Twain had a lifelong fascination with memory: "When I was younger I could remember anything, whether it had happened or not; but my faculties are decaying now and soon I shall be so I cannot remember any but the things that never happened. It is sad to go to pieces like this . . ."

In 1887, in the midst of a funk born of his board game's unequivocal flop, Twain enrolled as a student at Magnificent Professor Loisette's School of Memory in New York, lured to the shyster's conservatory by a promise scrawled on the sign above the door: THE INSTANTANEOUS ART OF NEVER FORGETTING. Twain had not been in a proper school since age eleven. He was fifty-two when he became a student at that back-alley brick house on the griftier side of New York City. He must have swallowed oceans of pride to sit again, as the legend he'd become, in the cramped desks of another man's classroom—a wonky board game and now the pupil of a charlatan.

In the fifth century B.C.E., Greek poet Simonides of Ceos jump-started the art of memory by devising a technique, eventually dubbed the Memory Palace, in which things to be recalled are placed in an orderly way throughout a familiar physical space, the mind's instinctive map of that space, so that knowing a list of words or numbers becomes as effortless as knowing your route home from work or the floor plan of your home—the arrangement of a living room. Simonides figured this out, Cicero tells us, while digging for the crushed bodies of friends in the rubble of a collapsed dining hall (faulty architecture, too much aesthetic grandeur); the mangled flesh was unidentifiable but Simonides had given a lecture at the banquet just before the collapse and found himself able to identify every corpse because he recalled exactly where everyone had been seated. He'd stared out at the gathered faces of friends and effortlessly—unconsciously— memorized on account of organization within a physical space. A groundbreaking but endlessly unsettling discovery: human engagement with memory is, at its origins, about death—so many bodies in the rubble.

Twain's own memory game relied on the Memory Palace, the spatial philosophy of memorization, but instead of buried bodies, Twain used a series of pegs spread throughout his front yard in unique patterns, each peg marked to represent something to be cemented in the head. "In this way," he says, "knowledge could be situated in space and compartmentalized so that the steps in learning would be actual paces." Originally, the game was intended to help his daughters memorize the dates of ascension for European monarchs, but Twain became obsessed and the game expanded to include awarding points for recalling even miscellaneous facts. From the official rulebook: "Miscellaneous Facts are facts which do not depend upon dates for their value . . . anything that is worth remembering, is admissible, and you can score for it."

Twain had not merely stumbled upon an early incarnation of trivia. He was already up to something much more desperate; hear the first notes of grave urgency in his game's final instruction: "Waste no opportunity to tell all you know."

Twain did not mean for us to sit around until identification was the only thing we could do with bodies in the rubble. He was aiming for us to furiously dig through bodies for one that is still alive, to go through the telling of "all you know" until you find that one truth worth the most points, the gasping memory at the bottom of the pile that you don't even recall inviting to the banquet.

Living Room

My memory palace: crashed-up Kate's TV with Granddaddy's trunk as a makeshift stand. A mirror above the TV acquired from a neighbor who got it from an acquaintance who skipped town after trouble with the law. A pleather Barca-lounger by the door, a Goodwill thrift-store find, a classic chair where men sat and smoked pipes, where cousins on holiday curled up two and three at a time, a chair that sat in some other house for thirty years—first as a trophy piece, then as Dad's chair, then as Dad's old chair, then as the chair there wasn't room for anymore. Soon I'll pass it on to an ex-con, who'll say it sleeps better than a lethal-injection table, but for now I wear my story into it. Two handsaws, handed down from Granddaddy—one big, one small, both rusty and dull—hang above the one large window in the room; they are rusty from the sweat of Granddaddy's palace toils. The smaller saw hangs from the same nail as a gas mask from our Second World War, acquired from a dead music teacher's estate. Life-size cardboard skeletons hang around the room, five of them—Halloween decorations displayed but never stored away. Against the far wall is a futon bought for twenty bucks from a trailer-park grandma whose grandkids *never pissed on it too much. Take this blanket,* she said, *cover up them stains.* The blanket is green and smells pissed on too. There are always bugs in my living room. None of the doors or windows fit snugly in the century-old adobe walls that are pockmarked and mapped with continents of mud patches. The vigas that run the length of the ceiling are freshly painted but the spruce is full of nicks and holes and splinters from time and weight and maybe bullets because this living room was once a motel pit stop for Billy the Kid and his pals and all the copycat cowboys with guns and whiskey and hooting and hollering if there were whores but I bet mostly there was loneliness within these walls. The vigas dominate my living room, a dozen tree trunks resting atop the mud walls, *fluke gallows* they call them, because amid domestic spats maybe vigas seem a good place to hang oneself. But the ceiling sits right on the beams; there is no way to get a rope over them. They're also called *standing deads*, which is the term for a tree that, in a forest fire, loses enough branches and bark to die but doesn't get burned to the core. If the fire moves fast, many trees are left perfectly stripped, ready to cut down, to crown a living room as fluke gallows.

Centered in front of Kate's TV is my red leather couch, a double recliner love seat bought at the Salvation Army thrift store. One side reclines perfectly but the other kicks out arbitrarily, like an unbroken horse angry at being corralled or saddled. I've got bruises on my shins from the angry bucking but the couch is the nicest piece of furniture I own—genuine red leather with no visible tears or stains. Everything is a bit classier with it in the room—the handsaws are shabby chic, the gas mask is historical high fashion, the skeletons are audacious in a time when popular décor strives for minimalism. Even the bugs seem more appropriate, attracted by the great, wild stallion of a love seat.

While jimmying with the reclining mechanism at the store, I found a Werther's candy, only slightly sucked, buried deep inside the love seat. I made a scene of the discovery and got ten bucks knocked off the price even though my shrieks were largely born of awe about the candy's immaculate preservation rather than disgust about its presence. Later I mention the discount to my girlfriend, Elle, as she digs her foot into the cushions to make room for me between her legs. She shudders and slides out from beneath me. *We're not fucking on a couch where some old man died,* she says.

Elle's right. We should pause to mourn the man who'd owned this sofa before—the grandfather who experienced the confusion of nodding off during the evening news only to wake and find the Werther's candy he'd begun the long process of savoring had disappeared, not in his mouth or stuck to his chest or anywhere visible on the red leather surface, not even in the shallow regions of the cushions' crevices his arthritic hands could still explore. The candy was there and he knew it must be there but for him the candy might as well have never existed at all. The grandpa died, the candy never found; I bought the couch and it became my wild red stallion of the living room, and if we could just get past the slightly sucked Werther's candy and the infectious loom of mortality, then my wild beast might go a long way toward getting me laid. But there are things to consider when your furniture is used: so many stories accompany what I own—the hand-me-down things I use to make a home— that I'm amazed there is any room to live in the pressing crowd of secondhand specters, the rich and awful memories that are mine but not mine, the memories I may never have but am now living with, in this intimate space, the chilling tangle of others' lives as Elle leaves me paralyzed on the couch, turned to stone by a writhing bouquet of half-known yarns like serpents still slithering from Medusa's severed dome, and Elle's shudder, the brittle sensation that spooked her away, that's the gossamer crackling of shed skins, the static on crashed-up Kate's television, the slough of so many head snakes crumbling to dust as I shift and sink into the worn cushions of my wild red stallion.

In the ceiling I've installed—bolted to the fluke gallows—a top-of-the-line LED disco light and a thirteen-hundred-watt fog machine that, once warm, pumps twenty thousand cubic feet per minute of dense white glycol vapor. These are the only things I've bought brand-new, the only possessions of which I am the original owner. When I turn them on, everything else in my living room disappears.

War and Interior Design

My granddaddy didn't eat Werther's candy. He sucked on peppermints, sometimes. I was seven and he was seventy and we'd play cribbage on a board that was an exact replica of the aircraft carrier he'd been stationed on as a Navy pilot during our Second World War. We'd play serious-as-war cribbage and suck on peppermints in his living room—a living room that was never rearranged after the day he and Grand-mommy first moved in. Not permanently, anyway. And everything in that living room only ever belonged to them.

The baby grand piano takes up most of the room. A long couch on the far wall has a floral pattern modeled after flowers that never existed or only existed in the 1950s. Two rocking chairs are placed where they can never really get rocking, one in the corner by the couch and the other in the nook of the piano. Granddaddy's easy chair is directly in front of a wood-paneled television that only receives, despite the giant antennas on the roof, four shitty channels. The easy chair has on its left arm what appear to be some of the first electronic buttons ever manufactured, buttons that promise a customizable back massage, which means only that you can slightly vary the speed at which it boisterously shakes your bones. The television always had to be louder than the seizing chair and the phone had to ring louder than the television and Granddaddy had to talk louder than everything else. Except when we played cribbage. Then everything was off. Everything was silent because cribbage, as Granddaddy would say, is not just a board game: it is a counting game. Counting is thinking and thinking requires silence. Well, alright. Everything would be quiet and I'd be counting and thinking and Granddaddy would take the long silence as a cue, every time. He'd jump out of his chair and start in: *Them Japs didn't know what they got themselves into, alright?* I'd say alright and sit back. He grinned a lot when he was telling stories. He didn't have a single straight tooth in his mouth. That went a long way toward his credibility.

First he'd swing the couch around so it was in line with the piano. Then he'd push the piano toward the hallway. *Everything that's not something is ocean, alright?* His hands were always the planes: F4U Corsairs. They'd take off from the USS *Floral Pattern Couch* and head for the piano. The piano was always the Japs. He was always bombing the piano. Every now and then he'd drop a bomb on the easy chair and I'd run to hit the boisterous massage button for dramatic effect. He'd move every piece of furniture in the room to set the scene for a battle. He'd walk around real slow, from his chair to the couch to the piano and back again. He'd stop at the bookshelves when the brutal tale of war demanded heartfelt sobriety, put one hand on the shelf of Bibles like he was landing his plane for a quick sermon. This whole adventure would unfold for a few minutes until Grand-mommy noticed: *Aren't you playing cribbage?* Then he'd go back to his chair, back to his peppermint, back to counting and thinking while Grandmommy moved all the objects in her living room back to the heavy dust outlines they were always in the business of etching into the space around them.

I hated cribbage. I loved the aircraft-carrier game board because it might get swept up in Granddaddy's story, but I could never make sense of the game—how the plugs were supposed to fit in the holes. I could never pick up on the patterns. I only ever played because there was always the chance a war would occur: Granddaddy in command of the furniture, the living room coming to life.

Said Mark Twain

"Any lecture of mine ought to be a running narrative-plank, with square holes in it, six inches apart, all the length of it; & then in my mental shop I ought to have plugs (half marked 'serious' & the others marked 'humorous') to select from & jam into these holes according to the temper of the audience."

Said Others

Tennessee Williams says something about memories having music—every recollection precisely, beautifully scored. Someone else likens memory to a sack. A great big sack. No, wait. It was a purse. Whoever it was said that memory is like a purse—if it gets full, it won't shut and everything will fall out. "Take heed of a gluttonous curiosity to feed on many things, lest the greediness of the appetite of thy memory spoil the digestion thereof." That's something. And then there's Clive Wearing. Clive Wearing is best known for saying, *What the hell is going on here?*

Statuesque

I haven't told Elle the story of my TV, of crashed-up Kate. Elle has a slight aversion to secondhand items—or doesn't revel in them as I do. She is not like me, not a ragtag amalgamation of arbitrary acquisitions and fragments of stories. She is cut from a single slab of fine-grained marble, hips and cheeks and collarbone, hammered into elegant contours that are smooth against my face; she smells of chisel on stone, earthy sparks, fierce and ancient, the promise of something— anything—immutable. Elle has lost a father to suicide and a second father to cancer and lost to some other cancer the grandfather who raised her more than either father ever did and still she is statuesque. She holds herself together by never holding on to anything, especially loss.

Elle buys new things often and tosses old things often; she does not get attached to or worry about the narrative of an object and she absolutely does not tolerate clutter. Because she loves me, she endures my décor but she keeps the living room tidy. If an item is not an official and permanent part of the living room, then she is trying to store (or throw) it away. Her tidiness should not bother me but I'm often infuriated by her fastidiousness.

During Simonides's lifetime, Greek artists began using marble from quarries on the isle of Paros to sculpt their gods because its translucency was reminiscent of human skin, because over time it became more resistant to fracturing, because they thought it might always hold together. Now we know that holding, the handling of that sculpted marble, is what ruins it most: the corrosive oils of our skin. Eventually Elle and I will cease to hold on to each other, forced to break and begin again after too much holding, but for now I lap up her promise; me and Simonides's pals without any notion of aesthetic grandeur's tendency to crumble.

I like my things out and spread around where I can see them and trip over them and remember that they still exist, all at once, in my living room. Elle's greatest fear is that others will have to clean up after her if she ever suddenly dies, that she will be found broken apart in a disheveled living room like the corroded pieces of a forgotten goddess some archaeologist will never quite fit together.

I do not tell Elle of crashed-up Kate's TV because I cannot remember Kate and because I fear it is a story in too many pieces.

Forgotten Ear

Clive Wearing got some kind of brain herpes and as a result he forgot that he had the ability to remember. I first learned about Clive when the famed neuroscientist Oliver Sacks wrote about him in *The New Yorker*, an article published a month before Kate died in the eastbound Toyota Camry.

Clive can't make new memories, can't remember much after 1967 except for his wife, Deborah, whom he married three months before he got the disease in the eighties. Deborah is an amazing woman—still married to Clive after two decades of his drawing blanks except for one thing: her.

Every time he sees Deborah he believes it is for the first time in a long time: he shouts joyously, hops exuberantly, grins from ear to forgotten ear and kisses all over her face. He doesn't remember anything about her or anything specific about their relationship; he doesn't know her at all except for the joyous feeling that arises from deep within at every glance. I can't help but smile as I watch film of this ecstatic greeting happen over and over, but then I frown and think of Kate and Johnny. Why is the most interesting, most memorable love always this tragic kind of love?

Clive's short-term memory lasts a maximum of thirty seconds. Ask him a question and he'll only get halfway through the answer before he trails off and forgets you've asked him anything at all. Seeing this is odd because he's retained his intelligence—he speaks multiple languages and can compute complex math. He still plays music brilliantly. Before the amnesia he was a prominent conductor and pianist and one of the leading musicologists in the world. Also, he's British, so to experience him seems initially like a Monty Python skit. You're sure you're being put on—his vocabulary is immense and his extensive academic knowledge (though briefly accessed) is evident and his tone is the epitome of British condescension and, my god, the way his fingers stalk and speed and pounce around the keys of a piano. But take a look at any one of his thousands of diary entries since the disease ravaged his brain and you'll understand the severity of his condition—every page of every notebook has the same line written over and over, crossed out over and over, superseded by its slightly varied self over and over: "I've just woken up after a long sleep, I've just now woken up, this time I have really become conscious for the first time." He can't ever get to the second line of his diary entry for the day because his brain resets several times a minute. Oliver Sacks offers this grim diagnosis: "He no longer has any inner narrative."

The only time this amnesia doesn't interfere with his life is when he's playing music or conducting an orchestra. Everything about Clive changes when he begins to conduct. All of his parts click into place so that he has actual posture and no longer seems tossed together and his face loses the droop caused by the relentless strangeness of things. He conducts with an intensity that suggests he understands that melody is the only thing he understands. Only in music is Clive able to perform as flawlessly as he did before the disease. And only in his love for his wife is he able to perform better. As Deborah tells Sacks in a letter quoted at the end of his article: *Clive's at-homeness in music and in his love for me are where he transcends amnesia and finds continuum—not the linear fusion of moment after moment . . .*

Static

I'm staring at the television: the gossamer crackling. Even when it's off, I stare, pondering the horrific way the TV came to anchor my living room.

Kate had threatened to kill herself several times before but never really tried—cried wolf—which leads me to believe that when she crashed into that SUV on the mountain, she was truly afraid for her life, first sad with regret for saying things to Johnny she never meant and then genuinely afraid for her life. The *Alamogordo Daily News* reports, "She was not wearing a seatbelt and police do not know the reason she drove her Camry into another vehicle." That doesn't sound like an accident; *drove* implies such intent, dark and re-morseless. But her obituary refutes the darkness, or at least the intent: "Kate, 21, passed away Sunday . . . in a motor vehicle accident."

I care whether she really meant to die because I am now the owner of her TV. I care whether she really meant to die because of something I should have mentioned before: I have the scraps Kate kept of me. Maybe she had a crush, a high school infatuation, but I never knew, didn't recognize her in the fancy frames when I claimed the TV and don't, for the life of me, know the girl with dark hair and a bright grin and milky skin in the head shots from our yearbooks or the glow-ing photo from her obituary. I didn't know her name when, shortly after she died, I got a stack of things from her mother: newspaper clippings, theater programs, snapshots—all pic-tures of me or snippets of things about me that might have been in my scrapbook. But they're not in my scrapbook. I don't have a scrapbook. These were things Kate kept—not a lot, not so many that it was an obsession, but just enough to be significant, to be passed along after death. I received the collection of papers without explanation as if they were per-sonal belongings I'd lent Kate years ago, as if I should have anticipated their return all along, as if the whole lot of them weren't unabashedly incriminating evidence about my role, however indirect, in the girl's demise.

So the TV wasn't the first thing. The scraps came first. Then Kate's mother invited me to take the TV. I accepted the scraps and later I said yes to the TV because I wanted a TV and because maybe I felt guilty; if I can't remember the girl who made a point to hold on to pieces of me, maybe the least I can do is care for her old set. I didn't know I'd begin searching the static. I didn't know I'd turn on the TV just to have the static keep me company—or to keep the static company, the impossible patterns in the crackling: dark hair and milky skin. Where Elle is statuesque, Kate is soft, amorphous, a feather bed to sink into, be consumed by, a cloud to vanish inside. In a few years Elle will move on to another lover and our time together will be tucked into the annals of relationships, fixed in the fattest section, titled "Wrecked," which comes right after the second-fattest section, titled "Doomed," but with Kate things are forever undefined, just beyond my grasp, and that is a closeness I will learn to treasure; clouds, unlike statues, will never shatter. I hit the TV's power switch. The crackling shrinks like a blizzard drifting into the far night, and with a sudden flash-pop that reaches from the TV to steal away everything in the room to nothingness, the static disappears.

Mirrors, Held Close Together

Kate and Johnny both struggled with mental illness. They met, I'm told, through therapy at the local clinic. I'm also told that when Johnny got to the hospital and learned Kate was dead, he took to the parking lot and smashed—hammered— his head repeatedly against an ambulance until he was finally restrained by force. Then, just weeks later, he was found comatose in the bathtub with so many pills in his blood.

I don't understand mental illness, none of us do, but our scientists are trying hard, as a start, to understand the brain. Sometimes I make the mistake of obsessing over the candied summaries of brain studies I pick up in the news. Consider these:

1. When a monkey watches another monkey use a hammer, the watching monkey's neurons fire in the same pattern as the hammering monkey's neurons—neurons firing in the exact same pattern in both monkeys: mirror neurons. Humans have mirror neurons in abundance. This is how we empathize, the scientists hypothesize, the hard wiring for our intangible connections with one another—the brain's ability to mimic another's pattern of neuron activity, just by watching.

2. Researchers at UCLA used clips of Homer Simpson to track the memory-making neurons of epileptics after surgery. When they asked patients to recall a clip they'd watched, the researchers realized they could predict which clip the patient would choose based on the activity in the brain. The experiment's conclusion: "Spontaneous memories arise through the activity of the very same neurons that fired when the memory was first being made." Your brain does the exact same thing when you watch Homer Simpson strangle his kid and when you remember Homer Simpson strangling his kid. One researcher described memory as "resurrection of neuronal activity"—as far as your brain is concerned, the original event happens all over again.

So why aren't we always experiencing other monkeys' memories? Because when the hammering monkey is remembering being watched as he hammered, his brain is doing the exact thing it was doing when he was actually being watched as he hammered: "resurrection of neuronal activity." But . . . if the watching monkey's neurons mimicked those of the hammering monkey's brain during the original act of hammering, wouldn't that neuronal activity include not just the hammering but also the sense of being watched? So can we conclude that when the watching monkey recalls the hammering, he is recalling the event as if he were the monkey with the hammer, the monkey being watched as he hammered? What have I not factored into this equation? Consciousness?

Humans have a unique awareness that our lives are stories that begin when we're born and end when we die, says Antonio Damasio, a neuroscientist and one of the world's leading experts on consciousness. *And because we know we're going to die, we are not satisfied with merely surviving day to day. We want our personal story to mean something.* To me Damasio has always sounded like a prophet: *You're constantly rearranging the narrative of your life.* Amen. I feel stuck in the infinite rough draft and I can't remember any of the previous drafts. *When you tell your story to yourself, or to someone else, it's going to be told not on the basis necessarily of the time course, but rather on the basis of how it was valued by you . . . You're assigning value naturally as life unfolds and that's this very important element for the construction of one's narrative.*

But then when you're dead, someone else assigns the value, edits the final draft. From Kate's obituary: "She was a volunteer candy striper . . . she volunteered as a Big Sister . . . helped with the local American Cancer Society Relay for Life . . . worked providing care for the elderly. . . . would often purchase personal items for them with her own money, read to them on her time off, and make them small crafts to cheer them up . . . often provided meals, clothes, and other personal essentials to the homeless and donated her time each Thanksgiving preparing and delivering meals to local people in need."

Johnny's obituary is much the same, citing the Military Outstanding Volunteer Service Medal as one of about a dozen military commendations he received: "He was employed as a mental health technician and respite provider. He was committed to the welfare of those he served. During the Thanksgiving holiday, Johnny and his fiancée, Kate, donated their time to help deliver meals to people who were homebound and in need."

My generation, the one straddling X and Y, the blur of kids that melts the music-video phase into the reality-show phase of MTV, we tend to understand volunteerism as a necessary sacrifice for creating a quality résumé. We'll help out so long as we know some other monkey is watching the performance. But Kate and Johnny seem to have helped others without ulterior motives. They had an excess of empathy, maybe a fountain of mirror neurons not totally overtaken by the selfishness of consciousness. In this way they were odd— mentally ill, maybe—remembering themselves as hammering monkeys, which is to say they saw great pain in the world and felt that pain and fought that pain as if it were their own. If humans are special because of an excess of mirror neurons, then I guess Kate and Johnny overflowed with mirror neurons; they felt the hunger of a homeless child and were compelled to act again and again. But when the mirrors in their brains caught each other's glimmer and got to sparking all at once, they opened up an infinite reflection of emotion—she was joyful and he felt her joy and she felt his joy, or she was sad or afraid or mad and he felt her madness and she felt his madness, and the crescendo knew no end just as mirrors will always, when you hold them close, create an infinite tunnel to nowhere. And if this all sounds sort of precious, it is. I'm assigning value to the story of Kate and Johnny based on what I want my life to mean. I want it to be a love story.

Peach Sherbet

When Granddaddy died, he left behind Grandmommy and two freezers full of peach sherbet ice cream. His memory had begun to falter in that last year but the sherbet, of all things, did not melt away. For five decades, on special occasions, Granddaddy bought Grandmommy a gallon of her favorite ice cream. She rarely ate ice cream but the occasional peach sherbet made her happy. After his stroke, Granddaddy would hobble around the grocery store, up and down the aisles with no recollection of the necessities he'd come to buy. Then he'd spot the sherbet. Holding just the ice cream in his arms, against his chest like an infant because his hands were too arthritic to get a grip, he'd grin his big goofy grin until he got home and found the freezer already full of peach sherbet. Maybe once a week he did this, hammering another pink carton into a freezer already packed full of pink cartons. He could remember little until he remembered he was in love and then that memory was all-consuming—so much sherbet. Now that he is gone Grandmommy eats more ice cream, spoons away the stockpile, feels, nearly every evening, the need to enjoy a bowl.

The Gas Mask

I find my antique gas mask endlessly entertaining and I often try to involve Elle in the fun. *What if there was some*

Russian aggression, baby? What if this is the only gas mask and the world is destroyed except for us? I want her to say, *Oh, baby. You should put on that mask and rock my apocalypsed world.* I want her to say, *Put that mask on me and put a baby in me and repopulate the earth with your exceptional seed.* But she just stares at me and says, *A gas mask won't do shit if it's a nuclear bomb. We'll both die. Our skin will burn off, baby.*

I reluctantly hang the mask back on my living room wall. The crinkly rubber hose that connects to the filter hangs down beside the window like the trunk of an infant elephant I've hunted and stuffed and mounted because I'm monstrous. Elle says I deliberately do odd things because I'm bored, but I guess the problem is my fear that none of this will be worth remembering, that it won't have value in my narrative. Elle says I just want an interesting story. Yeah, that's how the brain works, baby.

The guy who originally owned the gas mask was a high school music teacher, conductor of teenage noisemakers. Momma found the mask while digging through the trash as the man's distraught daughter emptied his storage unit; he'd died in a nursing home after years of dementia-induced confabulation.

The gas mask was dusty but in otherwise pristine condition, like something he'd sent away for during the escalation of the Cold War because he was paranoid and *Reader's Digest* was offering a mail-order special. But he stuck the package in storage and let it gather dust for decades because it represented fear. I wonder what story the old man might confabulate if he were still alive and I could remind him of the gas mask after so many years. I wonder if, like Clive Wearing, the only thing still functioning in the old conductor would be music. I wonder if he'd grab the mask and put it on and begin conducting his band—*This is how we win the war, boys!*—all of his parts clicking into place and the droop of his face invisible behind the mask, the hose flopping out from his head as he slams his fist to the downbeat—*BOOM! BOOM! BOOM!*—the wrinkly geezer all gas-masked and flailing out a frenzied, fraught, fucked-up understanding of himself as someone surely rooted in a meaningful narrative.

Pink Skirt

Several weeks passed between the day Kate's mother offered me the old TV and the day I went to pick it up. During these weeks I often worried about the conversation we might have, if Kate's name might come up and if we might talk about Kate and how I would tell this woman who only gave a damn about me because Kate held on to a few scraps, *Your daughter was less than insignificant in my life. I have no memory of her. Thanks for the boob tube.*

Kate's mom was exceedingly gracious when I arrived and was not interested in grilling me about her daughter. She was just happy to do something nice for someone. Kate's obituary, which I assume her mother helped write: "Kate felt that her purpose in life was to help others."

I held the heavy TV in my arms and was on my way out the door but hesitated because I felt a bit like a criminal, someone taking something he didn't deserve. I turned to Kate's mom and said, *Kate was real nice.* I paused. And for some reason I will never be able to explain, I continued, *I remember she liked to dance on the beach in pink skirts even when it was windy and cold.* Kate's mom put her hand on my shoulder and quietly said, *Alright*, and I loaded the TV into my truck and drove away.

Said the Psychologists

"Patients who confabulate are not deliberately attempting to deceive anyone. Some psychiatrists still assume that confabulation is an amnesic patient's way of filling in lost details to save face. However, they really believe with conviction that what they're saying is absolutely true.

"In fact, we may all confabulate routinely as we try to rationalize decisions or justify opinions. Why do you love me? Why did you buy that outfit? Why did you choose that career? The intriguing possibility is that we simply do not have access to all of the unconscious information on which we base our decisions, so we create fictions upon which to rationalize them.

"Nevertheless, it is an unsettling thought that perhaps all our conscious mind ever does is dream up stories in an attempt to make sense of our world. The possibility is left open that in the most extreme case all of the people may confabulate all of the time."

Use but Little Moisture

Mark Twain received three patents in his lifetime, the memory board game in 1885 and two others before that. The first, in 1871, was a patent for a belt to be worn on the bottoms of shirts rather than the tops of pants. He called it Improvement in Adjustable and Detachable Straps for Garments. He hated suspenders and wanted to rid the world of suspenders and this was his warpath, the shirt belt—a new way to hold yourself together. All of Twain's patents were born of this infinite struggle to hold one's self together.

His second patent came in 1872—Mark Twain's Patent Scrapbook. This was nothing more than a blank book with moisture-activated adhesive all over the pages. Hard-core memory hounds could simply lick the blank page of their book and stick a scrap of their life into its proper place among all the other important scraps. The inventive thing here was the elimination of glue. Memories could be saved anywhere you could salivate. "Use but little moisture," Twain warns. "And only on the gummed lines." The many options when ordering your Mark Twain's Patent Scrapbook included anything from a pocket-size of forty-eight pages for fifteen cents to a full-size, centerfold-ready two-hundred-page behemoth (made of three-quarters Russian cloth) for the hefty sum of five bucks.

For all of Mark Twain's great writings and all of his wild popularity, he died knowing the scrapbook was his bestseller, accounting for nearly 25 percent of his book sales while he was alive—nothing but an empty journal with blank pages meant to be spat upon and filled with scraps and the only words are the initial warning: "Use but little moisture." And what if the book that sold best during Twain's lifetime wasn't also his greatest satire: the whole country slinging drool in a mad attempt to never forget.

By all accounts Twain himself was a prodigious scrapbooker, compiling hundreds during his world travels. But only a few years after his Patent Scrapbook success he began to fret and toil over the intricacies of his memory board game. He grew weary of stuffing his pockets with scraps, grew dry-mouthed from spitting and licking, grew anxious about relegating memories to a single spot where they would grow brittle, as loogies always do, and disintegrate. He longed for a way to get those miscellaneous facts into his head, a way to stuff the slobbery book into the skull and have "all you know" at any time accessible as you recount the narrative of your life, accessible and interchangeable (the value of things always changing as the story evolves) and in the end the stickiness of "but little moisture" proves not too delicate or ineffective but too firm a connection for scraps, too rigid when the story must still unfold.

Mine of Her

Shortly after I received Kate's scraps I started collecting my own and now I have two piles: hers of me and mine of her. Three years after the Toyota never returned from the mountain, mine is a pile still growing. I have twelve pictures of Kate and two pictures of her fiancé, Johnny, in his military fatigues. I have pages and pages of notes about Kate in her eastbound Toyota Camry and Johnny in the bathtub. I have obituaries and copies of guest books from the funeral homes. I have blogs written by her friends. I have a newspaper article from the year Kate was born about a superachieving candy striper who volunteered 750 hours in just two years. This is totally irrelevant except that Kate was once named outstanding candy striper of the year and so I keep it around, hoping it fits. How do you get to know a person you can't remember, can't ever meet? The article about the super candy striper says her duties at the hospital included "installing and removing televisions."

I've printed files and documents and web pages and set
them around the living room—articles on the coffee table
and notes on the windowsill and obituaries on my wild red
stallion. I've spread my piecemeal knowledge of Kate throughout a physical space—my living room beneath the fluke gallows. Now I wait for the collapse, hope to recognize bodies
in the rubble.

When reading about the car wreck, I realize I know the
people who were in the SUV she hit: parents of a guy my
sister dated in high school. When reading the guest book from
Kate's funeral, I recognize more than half of the names. A
high school girlfriend of mine writes this heartfelt note for
the funeral: "She will always live in my memory as the girl
who played on the beach in her new pink skirt even though
it was so windy and cold." I did not witness this moment. The
girlfriend never told me about this moment. There is no way
I knew she was friends with Kate because . . . I never knew
Kate. But this—the pink skirt—is my memory of Kate and it
does not feel stolen or fabricated; it arises from deep inside
me. I see Kate and the pink skirt dancing around her knees
and the cold sea. The wind gives me goose bumps as she
twirls in the sand. This is not my memory but it is real inside
me and it has value in my story and I can't say I feel bad for
claiming it as my own, for digging furiously with the belief
that I can do something to make it breathe again.

Handling Sin

In the articles about Kate's death I have circled one name
several times—Sergeant Tingwall. Sergeant Tingwall was
the state trooper who said he could never know the reason

"she drove her Camry into another vehicle." This is the closest any officer comes to publicly saying *suicide* in the days
after Kate's death. Most town officials dance around the
word, but only because Kate's intent goes a long way toward
establishing who'll foot the bill for the damages caused by
her wreck, the expensive cleanup. But Tingwall's succinct
statement is a Rorschach test. Some days I read it and wonder if Kate's final moments were criminal. Some days I'm
happy she died with agency. Some days I hate that I know
she didn't. Sometimes I wonder if we do ourselves a disser-
vice by caring about the dead at all.

Just over a year after investigating Kate's crash, Sergeant
Tingwall died when his helicopter wrecked into a mountain
as he was trying to save a stranded hiker. His obituary shows
up on a law enforcement memorial website and the first reply
to the post is a succinct but ominous "I remember you . . . ,"
which makes me think the first guy to respond to Tingwall's
memorial is some perp with a sour memory of being collared
a few years back. A memorial is at once a recognition of loss
and a celebration of life. *I remember you* can be a compliment
or a threat. Memory saves people and drives them mad and I
suspect we've forgotten what it was really meant to accomplish. The first recorded use of the word *memory*, as we use
it now, is in a fourteenth-century text written by the monk
Robert Mannyng titled *Handling Sin*; Mannyng describes
his book as "illustrating the vices and weaknesses of men."

Requiem Opus

We walk in after a long night at El Patio Cantina and straightaway Elle tidies up the living room, gathers my scraps of

Kate: stacks articles on the windowsill, slides pictures into yearbooks, moves annotated obituaries from the couch. I tell her there's an easier way to clean; I warm up the fog machine. I hug and kiss to stop her destruction of my scattered palace. I grab the gas mask and fall on the couch and grin. *Do you smell something toxic, baby?* The wild beast bucks as I sprawl. The insects get to buzzing.

Soon Elle and I will move to a new living room and things will not be the same. She will be in charge of the décor and things will not be the same.

Take off the mask. Don't be a child. Elle reaches behind me to get at scraps that have slipped between the cushions of the love seat. I rip them away. She gathers faster and raises her voice: *It's never about me. It's always on some couch or about some story and it's not really ever about me.* She waves the paper when she says *story.* She has never asked about Kate but she knows enough to indict the scraps. I follow Elle around the living room and snatch up the loose papers. I put them in places she cannot easily reach—stuck in the frame of the mirror, folded over the handle of the saw, tossed behind the TV. She jumps and grabs at the mounted saw but comes down with a floppy leg ripped from a cardboard skeleton. She swings the leg, she punches, she reaches out to rake the skin of my face but I'm fully masked so I just back up and laugh. *Baby.* My pants are around my ankles. I have no shirt belt, no way to hold myself together. I trip—crash into the tile mask-first. Elle drops a handful of scraps, drops the cardboard femur, and slams the bathroom door. The crooked vigas that run the length of my ceiling are the character of this room, the long brown fingers of the hands that built it, the Gothic spine of the beast it has become. There's a growl. The Barcalounger is upset without its family. The futon is loud with piss. The ripped skeleton screams. There's static on TV. Goddamn, Kate. I don't guess forgetting is the problem. I don't guess you died because there was something you couldn't remember. You are an inexplicable urge I will always have. Elle will become that longing too, the loss of something I can't quit feeling. The bugs collide and the fog machine pumps glycol and the hanging handsaws squeal. I stand on the coffee table with handfuls of scraps and wad them and throw them everywhere at all the noise of the room but it doesn't stop. I throw them into corners where I will never come across them again, and when I'm out of scraps, I still feel the need to flail so I begin to conduct. I'm on my toes and my hand is as high as I can reach and I'm slamming it down to make a beat of the noise and jerking it up again—*Boom! Boom! Boom!* The futon explodes into crescendos. The Barcalounger lingers in dense countermelody. The vigas wobble deep and drop. I cue the saws with my left hand for high-pitched tremolos, the mirror with my right hand to echo it all. Something shatters. Elle is out of the bathroom and throwing glass against the wall. I fling my wrist at her as if I've conducted what she's done. It is unforgettable. Another glass hits the wall and becomes a thousand decibel shards. Elle and I are launching glasses and smashing up the walls. Scraps and shards. The symphony devolves into cacophonous regret—fades. In a moment there is only the sound of my mask-muffled breathing. Elle wipes a strand of damp hair from her face. We sit, very close to each other. The fog comes entirely. For one moment, there is no story but ours. Then she grabs a broom and I get to my knees with the dustpan. We sweep away the rubble.

THINGS MOST SURELY BELIEVED

In the Year of Our Lord 2011

You Fucking Dust Devil

I drop down into an arroyo thinking that may ease the tide of desert flying at my face, but down here any reduced wind is countered tenfold by the greater frequency and size of debris caught up in the storm, no longer just an infinite spray of sand but now also weeds and newspaper and plastic bags getting swept up and launched down the chute where I'm stuck because climbing banks in a sandstorm ain't the same as stumbling down them and anyway I'm dragging along dead-drunk Old Man Sam. The sting of a New Mexico sandstorm finds every nook of your skin. You never knew you had so much skin or that it had the capacity to feel so much. It burns a little, an allover paper cut where the pain never drives to the core, a place you can at least own it, bury it in your gut. Sandstorm pain crawls all over just on the outside so it never feels like it belongs to you, the pain of all the dirt in the world and you got to be aware of it, wear it all because the pain knows settling inside you would be a waste: you are already dead there. Nothing can change that kind of numb so it just blows over and blows on. A lonely thing to be dragging Old Man Sam through the arroyo in a sandstorm. The whole scene is an embarrassment for us both except there's no forgetting how every now and then Sam gets his feet planted under him and shoves me off and holds steady while yelling into the wind, *I am not done being reformed by pain, you fucking dust devil!* And this strikes me as the most hopeful thing I've heard in a while, the thing I'll find myself often reciting under my breath when those proverbial tough times come calling once again. Finally upon my ears: honest-to-god poetry. But mostly the scene is graceless like so many other stumbles homeward launched from a barstool at El Patio. Sam is dead drunk again and I'm half dead drunk, dragging him home because he has promised in his drunkenness to finally give me a scrapbook from his stint working at the penitentiary in Santa Fe. He said he'd kept a lot of shit from those days because he had big plans to make that shit a book. Some weeks ago we were at El Patio drinking as always and he asked what I was working on these days because he'd heard a lot of us hanging around Mesilla were claiming to be writers and I said, *Something about the last man executed by New Mexico. I mean the previous and the final. Before we quit executing.* And Sam said, *But we are the forever-killing kind.* Then he nodded a bunch and slapped the bar to emphasize the profundity of the statement and said, *But you mean that shitbag Terry Clark? I used to always take my lunch-break nap on his lethal-injection table.*

Art

Nineteen eighty-seven. The Penitentiary of New Mexico in
Santa Fe. Terry Clark sits in his cell tracing the outline of his
small plastic dinner plate onto a blank piece of paper. He is
careful. Meticulous. He has time. He has only just been sentenced to death. These days executions are about patience.
He finishes tracing and sets the plate beneath the small grate
in the door through which his dinner was passed an hour
ago. He ponders. In the top left portion of the circle he draws
a bird. A dove that is rudimentary—strangely impressionis-
tic. Terry has a steady hand and despite the amateur technique his bird is confident. He knows animals—was a ranch
hand down by Roswell before this mess. He moves to the
center of the circle. Stops. Examines his hands. Draws. Terry's
is the hand on bottom, palm up, fingers outstretched, a
small dark attempt at a shadow on the slightly deformed outline of the back side. God's is the hand on top, reaching
down, fingers outstretched, the outline steady but marred by
a giant black attempt at a shadow on the palm. Terry holds
the drawing at arm's length. Stares hard for a long time.
Grabs his Bible and, using it as a straightedge, slowly engulfs
the picture in a geometrically perfect crucifix and Star of
David. He examines the finished product. The drawing is
odd the way any attempt to capture the Holy Spirit must be
odd—naïve or ignorant. Terry prints his name and the date,
small in the bottom right corner, and slides the finished art
into his Bible. He will show it off the next time the prison
chaplain, Brother Maxey, comes to visit. *Lord, I've been
changed. Angels in heaven done sign my name. With the holy
ghost in me now, those angels done sign my name.*

Blow to the Head

At trial Terry Clark blamed it all on a blow to the head, a ranch-hand injury from a few weeks before the crime. Plus post-traumatic stress from his time in Vietnam. Back then they weren't always calling it a disorder. Just stress. Terry claimed he reached the breaking point when, lowered by helicopter onto a refugee boat, he held a dying Vietnamese girl in his arms while fighting off pirates. Then, years later, working as a carpenter at the ranch in Roswell, a blow to the head. Al Maxey, despite having become good friends with Terry while ministering to him on death row, doesn't hesitate to dismiss these claims: *Terry never saw combat.*

Maxey knows combat. He was a Black Beret in Vietnam. A door gunner in a Navy helicopter. The Gulf of Tonkin. Mekong Delta. The fighting HAL-3 Seawolves. Imagine *Apocalypse Now*. The sky of choppers. The river battles and big explosions. The strobe of war and the dirty faces of boys in its glow, their expressions melting or hardening or not changing one iota after making another kill. This was Petty Officer Maxey. He saw extensive combat and suffered more than a few blows to the head. But he became a preacher in the Church of Christ, the very church in which I was raised, the big aluminum warehouse of a chapel on Cuba Avenue in Alamogordo. My preacher: Brother Maxey, tall and lanky and always with those colorful ties, that thick mustache, hanging on to the pulpit Wednesday nights and twice on Sundays and, once in a while, working as a prison chaplain, ministering on death row, befriending a killer the papers spent fifteen years calling the most hated man in New Mexico.

Brother Maxey is adamant that the lingering fog of war

had nothing to do with it. Or, at least not the killing part:
*What really got Terry was the ports. The Philippines. Japan.
Hong Kong. Two or three days of pure debauchery. Not like
anything you could imagine. Sexually and drinking and everything. Young girls. Those clubs in the Philippines and every
sailor with a wad of cash burning a hole in his pocket.* Brother
Maxey says it matter-of-factly: *Terry got hooked on little
girls.*

Brother Maxey and Terry were on the same WestPac tours
in the Navy during Vietnam. They figured this out shooting
the shit through the food slot in the door of the cell, a murderer and his state-sanctioned chaplain finding common
ground in their past as servicemen in the state-sanctioned
killing corporation. Imagine showing up at the cages where
we house the worst of our kind and finding someone with so
many of the same experiences as you, another man who as a
boy walked the same ships and ran the same drills and wore
the same clothes and visited all the same wild ports along
with you and tens of thousands of other American sailors.
We were all headed down the same road, Brother Maxey says.
But I guess I pulled out of it.

That nod toward a history of sin lingers in the air of the
office at the warehouse chapel where we're chatting. Usually
confessions flow in the other direction. I want to ask Brother
Maxey to describe in further detail all of his transgressions
but I'll never do that, partly because I suspect he will only
evangelize, witness only to get me spilling my sins, and partly
because the older I get the less I believe in sin like he taught
it to me. We humans are obliged to be good and fair to each
other, generous even, but some otherworldly hellfire as punishment for not apologizing to a carpenter who was crucified
two millennia ago, that's a notion that increasingly strikes

me as preposterous. Plus, as a writer, the Greatest Story Ever Told! sounds like nothing more than a challenge.

The silence breaks when Brother Maxey starts in on the story about baptizing Terry on death row back in 1987. *He was washed of sin. No longer blamed the head injury. Took responsibility and repented. Accepted Jesus as his Lord and Savior.* Brother Maxey believes he helped the killer save his soul, first with baptism and then through acceptance of just punishment. But then that also means Brother Maxey helped to kill a friend.

I've known Brother Maxey since almost before I can remember, sat through hundreds if not thousands of his sermons, dropped tithes from my paper-route money into his collection baskets, played guitar with his son in a hard-core-as-Jesus-gets Christian punk band. Brother Maxey was there when I gave my first sermon before I could even see over the pulpit, had to stand on a crate and even then pushed myself up on the pulpit to loom higher over the congregation, on tiptoes hollering about hellfire and most of my weight on my arms so I started shaking, which I'm sure was the most effective part of the sermon. I spent a lot of Sunday mornings envying Brother Maxey, feeling called to the pulpit myself, knowing I could probably work the congregation up into a frenzy as Brother Maxey never did. I was born into blood that flowed through preachers way back and in all the tributaries. There's hardly been a Church of Christ west of the Mississippi since 1850 that didn't have a Wheeler or an Oliver or some other farther-flung branch of my family tree banging on the pulpit at one time or another. This seemed for many years just the way things would go: I'd grow into another branch banging on the pulpit. But then I ate all the psychedelics and read a few books other than the Bible and went off to college in California, where my Granddaddy said there was nothing but fruits and nuts. When I came back to New Mexico, it was with the same blood but a different brain. This is the first time I've entered the warehouse chapel and visited Brother Maxey in years. He must know I've given up the faith, that I'm only here because I've experienced some great awakening and have begun to question if it was really all that glorious a decade ago when our congregation sat in the hard pews of the warehouse and sang "Amazing Grace" in honor of Terry Clark just after he was executed.

An Account of Jailhouse Immersion

I really didn't want to put him in a garbage can so I rigged up a laundry cart with a large plastic bag. The cart was plenty big enough to fit in. We placed the bag inside and filled it with water. He had a towel to dry off with.

You could see he was excited. I was joyful too.

The cart looked full enough. It was leaking here and there, but it didn't matter. Just as long as it does the job, I said to myself. He climbed into the cart. Then I said I baptize you for the remission of sins (as I started putting him under) in the name of the Father, of the Son and of the Holy Ghost. He went under, but his knee-caps were sticking out of the water—I tried to push them down but to no avail. I pulled him up and helped him out of the laundry cart. He said Well, did it work? Of course my answer was No. I could see the disappointment written all over his face. He said Well, I guess we will have to try again tomorrow. I saw the hurt in him. I didn't want to let him down.

I suggested we get one of those 50 gallon garbage cans and wash it out. And the excitement was back. We washed a can—filled it with water. The water got past the halfway mark and I said: That should be more than enough. He said No. Go higher. I want to be sure.

He climbed into the can and as soon as he got in, the water overflowed. I said I now baptize you for the remission of sins—in the name of the Father and of the Son and of the Holy Ghost. He went down into the can, and yes, the water was flowing over! This time his back was sticking out. I pushed down on it but it did not move. I pushed down much harder and, yes, he went down fully into the water and was covered completely. Praise the Lord! I started pulling on him so he would come up. He came up and stood and asked Well, did it work? This time I was happy to say Yes! Welcome to the Lord's church, brother. I gave him a hug before he even dried off. He was so happy. You should have seen his face! As we were mopping I said Look at all these sins all over the place! Come on, let's get 'em all mopped up and dump 'em down the drain!

Sane and Ready for Heaven

November 5, 2001. The Penitentiary of New Mexico in Santa Fe. Dinnertime. This is not quite Terry's last meal but it is the one where he exercises these last freedoms: fried jumbo shrimp, fried okra, french fries, vanilla ice cream and peach cobbler. He has been on death row for fifteen years and still has years more of appeals but has volunteered to go ahead and get the poison in his veins tomorrow night. He has found Jesus. He believes in a thing called grace. When his lawyers and groups such as Amnesty International tried to stop the execution on his behalf, claiming he was mentally unstable—suicidal—Terry wrote to the judge, wrote to the state's Supreme Court, insisted he was sane and ready for heaven.

At his sentencing all those years ago he'd flung a kind of conundrum at the jury: *If you come back with a verdict of death, then I'll just have to live with that.* But now he will live with death for only twenty-four hours more. He will have breakfast tomorrow morning, technically his last meal, but it will be the standard prison fare: soggy eggs and potatoes and green chili. He will decline lunch and die on a mostly empty stomach at 7:12 p.m., the first man executed by New Mexico in nearly forty-two years. With his not-quite-last meal Terry gets two packs of Camel cigarettes from the warden, who often lets him smoke despite the prison's ban on tobacco. *Terry is a good guy these days,* all the prison staff often said to one another.

This shrimp isn't bad for prison food, Terry says. He shares the symbolic supper with Brother Maxey, who chuckles often as they eat. Though the moment is grave, it is always cause for celebration when a man repents. And here is one willing to repent to the death, a sincerity the likes of which most preachers never see. Brother Maxey laughs with only his face and even then just his mouth and even then there's that mustache hiding his lips, the same long push broom he's cultivated since his days in the Navy.

I wasn't sure I even wanted a last meal.

Well, I'm glad you got the shrimp.

I knew I'd break down and get the peach cobbler, I guess.

The concrete death-house cell is small. The meal is large. The quiet loud as Terry scrapes around with his plasticware. Brother Maxey waits for Terry to speak. And waits. And then: *The shrimp don't seem important as spending the time with you in study and prayer.* Terry works up the nerve to ask if the congregation down in Alamogordo will sing "Amazing Grace" for him once he's gone. Brother Maxey can think of no better tribute. They gather the food back into the serving dishes.

It's sure a lot. A lot of food here.

Terry bangs on the cell door twice. Waits for it to crack. Hands the dishes through. *You boys enjoy,* Terry says behind the grub. *Them guards always have an appetite.*

They're real linebacker sorts, aren't they?

Brother Maxey will tell me these guards sobbed when Terry died: *Everyone who knew him at the end knew he was changed.* They sit together on the concrete bench. Concrete was chosen by the State of New Mexico out of cheapness but maybe also, however unconsciously, for its aesthetic value: the gravel and impenetrable-seeming sand, the fly-ash-and-slag cement. Concrete takes time to cure, a decade or more to reach full strength. Steel would be the impenetrable alternative. But nobody escapes the death house. This one was built for Terry, has been waiting for him for fifteen years, the concrete hardening imperceptibly as he learns the lesson of grace, slowly convincing himself to die. Bibles are the only possessions allowed in the tiny death-house cell and now that the food is gone, Terry and Brother Maxey can't help but have those books, at all times, in their laps. And they can't help but be knee-to-knee and face-to-face. And they can't help but hold hands.

Bone Graffiti

The notebook is called "In Prison." I know it's called "In Prison" because a cutout from a newspaper headline is glued to the front cover and that's what it says: "In Prison." The scraps inside are from Old Man Sam's time spent both as a prison employee and a prisoner. The title is a pun. Sam was a library associate for the penitentiary in Santa Fe. His Corrections Department ID is here along with all kinds of correspondence with different inmates. And Sam's sketch of a bare-breasted woman and a receipt for $3,000 bail from some mix-up back in San Jose and the Christmas cards Sam drew for inmates in the mideighties and the evidence tag for Sam's Colt .25 pistol that he once whipped out during a spat at El Patio Cantina and a document called "Instructions for How to Survive in Mexican Prison." Sam's real name, it turns out, is not Sam. Sam is the name of a murderer who once helped Old Man Sam get out of prison in Juárez and that's why he uses it now. A tribute. There's one page from one chapter in a book about a prison riot that Old Man Sam will never finish writing: "The glorious sun brown days of Indian summer had passed. Now the wind blew from the north and the mountain peaks above Santa Fe were capped with snow. As usual, getting up in the morning was a bitch. Too cowardly to negotiate the cold wood hallway to the bathroom, I stood on the bed and pissed out the window."

Old Man Sam is full of stories. Out front of El Patio is a wooden post with one chomp's worth of bite marks sunk almost full tooth into the pine. Sam did a little too much of that Mexican cocaine cut with everything under the kitchen sink and couldn't resist the feeling in his jaw that urged him to gnaw. Or he couldn't help his gape as he flew mouth-first when his motorcycle hit a spot of missing bricks in the plaza road. Or he was trained in a circus freak show and his talent was hanging from things by his chompers. Sam has a new story each time he tries to impress a lady by fitting his teeth into the post. Says it's his bone graffiti. He's hunched from falling off a roof and breaking his back. Says there's graffiti all up and down his spine too.

In my living room is a Barcalounger I've decided to pass along to Sam because he says his graffitied spine sleeps bet-ter at a slight recline. I load it up in the truck and drive it to his house and move it to a bunch of different spots in his living room while he watches. He cannot lift much anymore. Once we get it vibing with the feng shui, he plops down, tells me how much better it feels than a lethal-injection table. At first I don't believe there's any way a librarian snagged the execution chamber for siestas. But the timeline fits. And Sam's rare consistency on the matter makes it, in my mind, likely.

New Mexico started building a death house specifically for Terry Clark shortly after he was sentenced in 1987. He was the only man on death row because at the end of 1986 the outgoing governor commuted all death sentences to life in prison. Terry pled guilty in 1986 on the belief that, if he re-ceived a death sentence, it would be commuted too. But the judge in the case took his time with the sentencing, lolly-gagged until there was a new governor in 1987 who believed in eye for an eye. So Terry was alone on death row. Then they started pouring the concrete. Terry wrote to his lawyer in 1989, "They're building a new death house up here and I'm not really interested in breaking it in." This was the be-ginning of years of vacillation on Terry's part. Wanting to fight to live. Then sane and ready for heaven. Then back again. And back again. The death house sat unused and

largely unfinished for many years. Terry could see it from
the rec yard, where he was allowed to loiter for an hour a
day. Old Man Sam was in there snoring.

Even as Sam carries on about the cold hard table and
scratchy sheets and the shiny buckles of the restraints and
the way the table's arm extensions don't quite rise to ninety
degrees—*To keep it from looking like a crucifixion*, he says—
he hands me a stack of papers. They are administrative forms
from the penitentiary and daily roll calls from the North
Unit, where Terry Clark was housed. On a roll call from
September 1995 there's a note: Terry is out for exercise in the
rec yard and someone needs to contact the Catholic Church
for him.

Terry's death sentence was once briefly overturned on a
legal technicality—from September 7, 1994, to March 18, 1996,
he lived without execution looming. That he still sought religious counseling in this period where it seemed he might
escape death and someday get out on parole seems some evidence that his conversion was genuine. More and more I
think the reason I'm compelled to keep poking at this story is
to somehow prove that Terry didn't change, that the world is
black-and-white, that there is no slippage between Good and
Evil. That's an easier world to navigate. As Sam sits in the
Barcalounger miming twitches from an IV feeding poison
into his veins, he says, *Oh, no. You didn't know? That's when
Clark was asking to get married.*

A *Leper to These People Lord*

My first phone conversation with Terry Clark's death-row
fiancée lasts three hours. There is much sobbing on her end.

Jean Ortiz says she hasn't hardly thought about all this in a decade. She sets the phone down so many times, *to get more crying towels*, she says, that by the end of our conversation I imagine her perched atop a nest of them. *He made me swear to never look back. I don't know why I'm talking to you.*

Before calling Jean I spent many hours at the microfilm machine in the library reading up on her. She first got involved with this mess just days after Terry was arrested for the rape and murder of nine-year-old Dena Lynn Gore. Terry committed the crime while out on $50,000 bond as he appealed a conviction for the 1984 kidnapping and rape of six-year-old Donita Welch. At the time he was also a suspect in at least three other incidents of sexual predation in Roswell. But no charges had been brought in those three cases and the bond release was granted after his conviction for rape, in part, because the only evidence was the testimony of the victim; the court was hearing arguments about whether the six-year-old witness understood the difference between a truth and a lie.

Jean Ortiz was one of the first to team up with Jayne Willis and Betty Williams Lehrman, two other Roswell residents, to spearhead a years-long campaign to change the laws that allowed convicted rapists to go free on bond during appeals. Their campaign was successful largely because Colleen Gore, the mother of Dena Lynn, joined the efforts and testified several times before the state legislature, explaining to them the obvious: that her daughter's death could have been avoided if only convicted rapists weren't immediately set free. During these trips to lobby the legislature in Santa Fe, Jean Ortiz and Colleen Gore traveled together, ate together, cried together. They shared the same goddamn motel room.

We were friends, says Jean. *Now she'll say she hardly knew me. But that's a lie.*

Jean is a traitor in the worst way, Jayne Willis told *The Albuquerque Tribune* after Terry's execution. *She stabbed Colleen Gore and her family in the back.*

On May 17, 1994, eight years after Dena Lynn's murder and six years after the women from Roswell succeeded in passing the Dena Lynn Gore Law to keep convicted rapists from going free on bond during appeals, Jean wrote her first letter to Terry Clark. *I just wanted to know why he wasn't dead yet,* she says. But then he started writing back. *He wasn't monstrous or anything. He was sincere. In fact, he was sweet.* Then she began to visit him on death row.

We fell in love, says Jean from atop her nest of crying towels.

Back in 1996 she testified on Terry's behalf in his resentencing hearing: *We haven't had an engagement party, but we'd like to get married someday if they'd ever give us permission. I love Terry as a best friend and a man . . . I believe he loves me.*

On March 17, 1996, the *Roswell Daily Record* printed the headline "Woman Who Protested Murder Wants to Wed Clark." The headline was maybe their most shocking since 1947's "RAAF Capture Flying Saucer on Ranch." Jean Ortiz seemed the least likely person to wed a child rapist and murderer, if anyone at all can be said to be predisposed toward that sort of thing. Besides being an advocate for the Dena Lynn Gore Law and a friend of Dena Lynn's mother, Jean was Roswell's director of ChildFund International, was often on the evening news or in the papers raising money and organizing events aimed at finding and punishing people exactly like Terry Clark. She was a prodigious writer of letters to the editor, complaining about the salaries of city employees or announcing a new stop sign erected on her street or warning people to be on the lookout for intoxicated hot-air balloonists. She was what you might call an engaged citizen. Though, in retrospect, she also seems the kind of citizen my granddaddy would say sits down in a fire so people can see her better.

After our phone conversation, Jean sends me a flurry of e-mails. If she ever had any reticence about sharing her story, it quickly evaporated. Her e-mails are long, full of digressions and emojis. She spends much time defending her actions, asserting often, without my ever asking, that she was not a publicity hound. I mostly believe her. She gave only one interview immediately following Terry's execution. In it she says Terry just wanted to be left alone, by both the media and his lawyers, be allowed to make his own decisions about ending his life. So then I'm surprised when I arrive at this paragraph in one of her Hotmail tomes:

> One reason that I "don't care for" Al Maxey is this FACT. Terry had until his time of death to pick up his appeals. Gail Evans [his attorney] made SURE that he had her cell phone # with him, in case. She waited & waited but her phone never rang. We were all in the waiting room upstairs [at the prison] & I wasn't sure why she had her phone with her. I didn't know all of this until later. Upon good authority, Gail was told in the days following [the execution] that Terry wanted to call her one hour before they gave him the pain pills or whatever they gave him (not the death cocktail, Joshua!). His "spiritual advisor" successfully talked him out of the call, although it is now known, Terry REALLY wanted to make that call.

When Terry volunteered to die, he had not exhausted all appeals, including to the U.S. Supreme Court. There is no way to know if there would have been enough time, on the day of execution, to get any of those appeals restarted. His attorney, Gail Evans, will never agree to talk to me about the case or exactly what transpired in the hours just before the execution. By all accounts she tried everything to stop it, but could never overcome her client's belief that he was born-again. Terry wrote to Jean about his arguments with Evans, "I told you she don't believe, so she can't get it that there is a better life after death. She even tried to tell me I wasn't sure what to expect . . . There really is nothing to gain from her anymore . . ." Brother Maxey tells me he gets the sense Evans feels guilty, as if she failed to save a life, which is the opposite of how he feels. Other lawyers tell me it's possible, if unlikely, that a last-minute change of mind might have prompted a delay in the execution. I tell Jean it might not have mattered if he had a last-minute change of heart. But her talk of coercion and drugging doesn't stop. She keeps saying the arc of this thing bends toward sinister. But then that's exactly where it started, and I tell her that too.

She takes to writing poems when she thinks her tomes are not getting through to me, all verses about her pain, all addressed to Jesus. She sends them to me and signs off with a prayer: *I love you Lord* ❤ *Please tell My TC, Mom & Dad I sent my heart . . . 15 minutes* ☺

Fifteen Minutes

Texas. 2:30 or 4:30 a.m. June 13, 1983. Karla Faye Tucker, Danny Garrett, and James Leibrant leave Tucker's residence after some partying. Tucker wants to go to Jerry Lynn Dean's apartment to collect some money, intimidate him a little. Two weeks prior, Tucker had talked about offing Dean. Tucker and Garrett enter the apartment bedroom. Tucker puts a pickax to Dean's head. Dean begs for his life. She strikes him with the pickax twenty-eight times. She has twenty-eight orgasms, one with each fatal blow to the head. Deborah Thornton is hiding under some sheets in the bedroom. Tucker decides to kill her too. Leibrant enters. He hears a gurgling noise in the bedroom and follows it back to where he witnesses Tucker pull the pickax out of a body, smile big, and hit the body again. Orgasms. The bodies are discovered the next morning—a pickax lodged in the chest of Deborah Thornton.

Karla Faye Tucker is sentenced to death for the murders. While on death row she finds Jesus, is converted, reborn, becomes feverishly devout. Linda Strom writes a book called *Set Free: Life and Faith on Death Row*, in which she details her role as Tucker's spiritual adviser. In the book, Karla Faye Tucker claims that from the moment the lethal injection stops her heart to the moment she arrives in heaven, exactly fifteen minutes will pass. Fifteen minutes and then she will be reunited with everyone who loves her because, in heaven, one day is equivalent to a thousand years on earth. Tucker is executed by lethal injection in 1998. *Set Free* hits shelves in 2000.

Beasts/Sunsets

October 10, 2001. Terry sits at a typewriter with his Bible. Alone. Outside of his cell for the one hour allotted each day. He types a letter, labors with a single heavy finger over the stubborn keys. He's been pondering a question about whether or not humans and animals have the same spirit. He's been researching. He's found Ecclesiastes 3:18–21. "Check it out," he writes to Brother Maxey. "We do come from or have the same Spirit, but it does not talk about the soul for animal . . . I guess we will have to wait till that time to find out for sure. Love In Christ, Terry."

Terry reads again from his Bible. *For that which befalleth the sons of men befalleth beasts.* King James Version. There is a helpful footnote. *In dealing with human beings it is God's purpose to test them.* This seems right to Terry. He marks the spot in his Bible with a small leaf he smuggled in from recreation hour last week.

November 4, 2001. Terry writes another letter. This one to Jean. Handwritten. Today he ponders a different book, one called *Set Free*.

> Heya Babe: Remember me?? I was reading parts of Karla Faye again. I got it marked out, the part about 15 . . . You just be careful when all this is over+done with. It will take awhile for people to forget. I want you safe. Your prayers should be for the Gores, so they will+can have peace . . . I always like the Fall, the colors in the trees . . . Its a time of CHANGE and soon Ill be changed too . . . Look for me in the STARS+in the SUNSETS . . . Thank you for being my friend. PROFOUND WASN'T IT??

Moral Vegetable

Brother Maxey shows me the dried gold leaf but quickly presses it back into Terry's Bible, placing the Bible on the most prominent shelf in his office. *You can't have that.* He laughs. *It's just an old leaf, but . . . I guess it's pretty neat.* He has a file cabinet full of memories connected to Terry. He opens it with a smile, shows me letters, news clippings, Terry's drawing of a dove.

When I ask Brother Maxey about Jean Ortiz, he says he doesn't remember all that much about her. She was an older woman. He sensed she genuinely cared for Terry. She fell apart at the execution. But he's not interested in talking about Jean's resentment of him or her accusations. He says it all sounds like nonsense. He remembers that Terry needed to be sedated in the hours before the execution, was given some kind of drug to calm him down. *But his heart was already made up. The drugs didn't matter,* Brother Maxey says.

I've come back to the warehouse chapel to ask Brother Maxey if he feels like he helped kill a friend. He recasts the question several times. Terry was ready to atone, accept the punishment Christianity requires. I'm asking all the wrong questions, Brother Maxey says. And I am starting to feel that way. My desk is covered in articles and photocopies and letters and many pictures of those unsettlingly deep eyes. Terry looks familiar—none of his features prominent. He's got the ambiguous characteristics of Odo, the shape-shifting humanoid from *Star Trek*. Terry could be anybody.

At his original sentencing Terry said, *I knew what I was doing. I have a five-year-old boy and four-year-old girl. The crimes that I've committed or have done, that's what they depict me as. But I don't see myself as a child killer or rapist. I just can't come to terms with myself being that, knowing how I was before.*

The district attorney responded by calling Terry *a moral vegetable who should be executed.*

After the execution Brother Maxey is penned as the spiritual adviser to whom Terry confessed all the gruesome specifics of his sins. The state's most prominent papers printed his picture on the front page, hugging Terry's Bible, saying Terry confessed all the awful things he'd never shared with anyone else, saying he was sure Terry had got right with his god. I wonder how Brother Maxey can sit so still with all those images in his head. His mustache is the same as Terry's. I've seen pictures of my father with a mustache like that. I could grow a mustache like that. I don't ask Brother Maxey about Terry's detailed confessions. I know these few facts and they are already too much:

Three shots to the head killed Dena Lynn Gore on July 17, 1986. She was nine, riding her bicycle five blocks to the convenience store for a Coke, pedaling with determination when she caught Terry Clark's eye. He didn't plan to kill her. He hadn't killed the last girl. Donita Welch was six years old when Terry coaxed her into his sports car as she walked home from school. Donita hadn't cried. She lived— and eventually long enough to witness Terry's execution. But Dena Lynn cried as Terry raped her. She cried and cried and told Terry she would tell on him. She said, *You're going to pay for this.* He panicked. Tied her up. Shot her three times in the back of the head. Dropped her little naked body in a ditch on the ranch where he worked and kicked at the embankment until she was covered with dirt.

I leave Brother Maxey's office. The sun has set and a thunderstorm is rolling in. From the parking lot of our warehouse chapel I see smoke rising off the Sacramento Mountains. I walk to a nearby park where the view of them is unobstructed. There's the Sleeping Lady. This evening the forest on her chest is burning. She's been struck by lightning. The fire spreads down to her stomach, jumps up onto her shoulders, really rages in the valley of her clavicle. I guess any forest fire so close to town is frightening but this one turns my gut. I feel sick.

I go home. My niece always wants me to read to her when I'm home. She can't wait to be in Girl Scouts. We're halfway through the first chapter of an American Girl dolls book about Girl Scout camp when I stop.

What? She turns in to me and rests her face on her hand—squishing her whole cheek up into her eye. *What, Josh?* She's laughing. *Why did you stop?*

The book closes in my hand and the room shrinks to the space between our faces. I say it before I know why I say it. *How old are you?*

I'm six, Josh. You know I'm six. I've been six since my birthday.

How do you warn a kid about evil? *Don't talk to strangers* seems woefully inadequate when the things the world can throw at them are so gruesome. It's not just that children can't understand how evil arises anywhere, anytime. We grown-ups don't have the capacity to explain it. So we say, *Don't talk to strangers.* So we say, *Don't go anywhere alone.* So we say, *Always be brave,* but that's the thing Dena Lynn remembered and that's why Terry killed her.

This night I don't sleep. I sit up in the living room, watch out the window as the Sleeping Lady burns.

Microfilm

The microfilm machine at the library looks like an archaic notion of the future—a hulking box with dials and blinking lights. And it is as imprecise as it looks. Despite many buttons and flashing lights and knobs and levers for adjustments, each newspaper page I copy from the film is static ridden and unreadable for inches around the edges. There is *auto skew correction* and *center/fit* and *masking* and *print mode* and *film type* (*text*, *fine*, or *photo*). But for all my twisting and pushing, rubbing and cursing, nothing prints anywhere near accurate. Each page of every newspaper has, imposed at the top, the words BEST COPY AVAILABLE—the antique future-machine knows, at least, how to taunt. And it lies. I make sure to utilize the framing feature before I send the film to print but the print is never framed the way I want. And it tricks. When one feature is set to automatic, all the others default to automatic and some of my prints come out as negatives. And it attacks. Three drops of blood are on a mistakenly printed article from my zoom-lens-smashed pinkie. No, the librarian says as if she's encountered this before, *I do not have Band-Aids. All blood must be immediately cleaned from the machine.* The information is lost or undecipherable or over-shadowed by annoyance because of all the problems.

The *forward/reverse* knob on the viewer has four speed settings for scanning through the newspaper in each direction. On the slowest setting there is no immediately percep-tible movement but I develop a headache as the subliminal crawl pushes left against my eyes. On the fastest setting I'm only able to decipher a few words of each headline. My eyes burn as I try to focus on the long blur of old news flashing by. I switch back and forth between the middle settings but I never get to a speed where I feel I'm both progressing effi-ciently and comprehending the information.

The mistakenly printed and mistakenly bloody article is the obituary page for Thursday, July 17, 1986—the day that

Dena Lynn was murdered. Her death is not listed—would not be announced until after her body was found five days later. On this day Colleen Gore is beside herself with guilt, calling the police to report her daughter missing, wishing she had gone to the store with Dena Lynn when she asked to get a Coke. Jean Ortiz is volunteering to join the search parties. Terry Clark is kicking at an embankment. I don't know why I stopped and printed this page. The only article that is not an obituary is an AP story that seems dropped in to fill space: "Researchers Trace Human Genes Back to Common Ancestor." The headline uses the biggest font on the page and the article sweeps across the entire breadth, overshadowing the obituaries on the bottom half. Discussed is a study suggesting that women carry a gene in their mitochondrial DNA that dates back one hundred thousand years, possibly to a common ancestor not unlike the biblical Eve or some other early member of the human race. The scientists postulate that this gene might be the key to curing hereditary disease. Maybe the article is a life-affirming attempt by the newspaper's editor to balance the list of over twenty deaths announced on this day. I don't know why I stopped and printed this page. But I've read this article many times. I've read it more than any of the articles about the crime or the execution. I keep reading it over and over.

Flatliners

My correspondence with Jean lasts nearly a year, much of it trying to parse the exact nature of her correspondence with Terry. But she remains fixated on Brother Maxey, sending me annotated articles about him, critiquing articles he'd written: *This article is not even about the Lord, it's about Al Maxey who wasn't there for MANY years, between the Baptism & the execution.* She writes that she knows why Brother Maxey advised Terry not to call his lawyer in the days before the execution, implying that the preacher wanted Terry to die, that the execution would be a good notch in his salvation belt.

She sends me a box full of material about her relationship with Terry, many of his letters, lots of newspaper clippings, a VHS full of her interviews with the local news about Child-Fund International and segments about Terry's resentencing and Dan Rather's interview with Colleen Gore about fighting to change the bond laws. Jean sends me two full front pages of the *Roswell Daily Record*. They're from November 6 and 7 in 2001, with the headlines "Dead Man Walking" and "Terry Clark Executed." On the front page of each is a subscription sticker addressed to the prison: *#34930, Terry Clark, Santa Fe.* He never saw them.

I ask Jean why she didn't fight Terry about his decision to die, and it trudges up a lot of guilt: *I feel like I signed his death warrant. I did. I did it but I knew his heart better than any other. If I did this, picking up his appeals for him, he would have been so angry with me and would have faith in no one. I wanted him to know at least one person on this Earth loved him unconditionally when he was murdered by the state. He had to die with some sort of dignity in his mind.*

After nine months, her e-mails become more sporadic. They are now mostly about financial trouble. She worries she will lose her house, have to sell her classic car. She mentions she has found a producer to make a film of her life if only I will write the book. She throws out lots of numbers such as $10,000 and $5 million and promising 50 percent to charity. *We could make some $$$,* she writes, *and I am offering this chance to you 1st. He has produced Flatliners, Radio Flyer & more . . . My whole life, my home depends on this chance.* Eventually I stop writing her back.

In the film *Flatliners* a group of medical students attempt, as an extracurricular activity, to discover what lies beyond death. They give each other lethal injections and, while medically dead, experience mostly ghosts, people and events from their lives about which they feel guilt. When they're resuscitated, the ghosts follow them back into life. I haven't seen the movie in years but I watched it a lot when I was young. A guy in my youth group at the warehouse chapel had it on VHS and we passed the tape around like unholy contraband. The film was rated R and had some sex in it, but I don't guess that's why it felt so illicit. The scandalous thing about *Flatliners*, for a bunch of Christian teens, was the depiction of the afterlife: no hellfire or pearly gates, just regret.

There's a Lot of Room for You People Up in Heaven

They call him Doorman, Greeter, Prophet, and Priest, but that's overly romantic—not incorrect, just overly romantic. The crass way of putting it: he's mentally ill and spends his days trying to sweep all the sand off a desert road. His name is Sonny and he walks up and down the streets around El Patio, waving at all the cars with a kind of peace sign/salute combo and holding doors for folks. The local businesses keep him busy with the occasional supply run or, more often, a broom. He sweeps at sand that will eventually be caught up in the wind, cause the sting and burn, and fall back onto the road.

He always says this thing to me, says it to most everyone, says, *There's a lot of room for you people up in heaven.*

I've spent the day at El Patio Cantina, wallowing and shooting the shit with Old Man Sam. Jean's schemes to profit from her relationship with Terry unsettle me. I keep thinking there's something about faith I can't quite grasp and that's why this story needs telling, that this crime and the conversion and the execution is a chance to understand more concretely, beyond all abstract theology, what it means or doesn't mean to believe in a benevolent god and grace and any afterlife at all. But then I think of Dena Lynn Gore and Donita Welch and how unfair it is to them to spend even one moment trying to understand anything at all about the man who raped them before they had even one full decade on this wobbling rock. Maybe I'm not so different from Jean. If you're reading this story, that means someone published it, that they paid me and I put a line on my résumé. *Writing is betrayal,* said a lot of us navel-gazing writers a lot of the time. The money will vanish. One line on a résumé might get scanned by a suit somewhere. The sense of betrayal will linger. I feel powerless and complicit in something. I feel my feelings make it worse.

Last week I met up with my old girlfriend Elle. We went for a run, a kind of neutral but vigorous rendezvous in hopes of tiring us out to prevent falling into all our old bad habits. She's a lawyer, works for a district attorney in another state now, works mostly sex crimes. They've been on a case, she tells me as we run, trying to solve a rape. One suspect seems like their guy, but when the cops bring him in for questioning, he pulls down his pants and shows them his dick is gone, just a mess of scar tissue—his alibi. More questions. He cut it off a while back. More questions. He sliced it up and stored it in the freezer. More questions. He slipped it in his mother's meals over a few months. We run a long way without saying anything. We were still living together when I started this story, started putting it aside. Back then she asked me why I wanted to write about something so awful when it was already all over with. I didn't have an answer. I asked her why law school. She said she thought most crimes were just a result of people being lowlowlow, that they needed help getting back up. Now we've run farther than we planned and it's going to be a long trudge back to the car. Now she says the hardest part is seeing evil everywhere she looks, trying not to become completely numb to the feeling of it.

I leave El Patio, into the sun to walk off the beer, do a few laps around the plaza with Sonny. He always wears a bandanna and has two big waves of hair slithering out from under the bandanna like a couple of water snakes. When he smiles, he tends to face down and look up at you from that low angle so his eyes roll heavenward. "Lift up thine eyes to the high places." He's got a bit of gray stubble scattered around his brown face and three deep canyons with a half dozen tributaries of smile lines on either side of his leathery lips. He's skinny as hell from all the walking and sweeping. I ask him again which prophet he is. *There are the prophets Elijah and Ezekiel,* he says. *And there is me, Jeremiah.*

Before I formed thee in the underbelly I knew thee, God said to Jeremiah when calling him to a life of prophecy. Jeremiah is known as the weeping prophet because he got beat up a lot. People didn't like the doom he was forecasting. The thing about prophets in our world is they don't get much chance to say anything optimistic. That's why Jonah takes to the belly of a whale, why Jesus disappears for all those years. But Jeremiah never minded bringing the bad news. Sonny will sometimes quote Jeremiah or channel him or, if you believe he is Jeremiah, repeat himself. He says, *But his word was in my heart as a burning fire shut up in my bones.*

But the thing Sonny says most—*There's a lot of room for you people up in heaven*—doesn't jibe with the doom Jeremiah preached. When I first heard Sonny say it to some rich tourists loading up on lattes and cinnamon buns in the coffee shop, I thought it was a joke, like leave us poor locals alone, get on up to that fancy heaven you keep talking about. But I've come to believe it's all part of Sonny's revision of the weeping prophet. Sonny never talks doom. If he ever talks about fire, it is only from those parts of Jeremiah where the prophet receives the divine word. That kind of burning is not exactly hellfire because it's the word of God, but I'm not sure if it's much better. Jeremiah's God was angry. He threatened to send lions to slay his people, wolves to spoil them, and leopards to tear them apart, serpents to bite them, dragons to roost in their homes, threatened famine and captivity and pestilence, destruction upon destruction. He talked of a mountain his people had brought to life with idolatry, said, *Behold I am against thee, O destroying mountain, which destroyest all the earth: and I will stretch out mine hand upon thee, and roll thee down from the rocks, and will make thee a burnt mountain.*

I tell Sonny how I watched the Sleeping Lady burn. I tell him the confusing part of Jeremiah is that, in his book, fire represents both total destruction on account of the sins of a few and the voice of God. I tell him Jeremiah was the first prophet to give us a glimpse of hell. *There's a lot of room for you people up in heaven*, Sonny says. Then he salutes me away, like he always does, and keeps on sweeping at the infinite sand.

A Brief History of Hellfire

Technically the place Jeremiah talks about, in chapters 7 and 19 of his book, is not yet hell. But it will become hell:

> Behold, I will bring evil upon this place, that which whoso-ever heareth, his ears shall tingle. Because they have for-saken me, and have estranged this place, and have burned incense in it unto other gods . . . and have filled this place with the blood of innocents and have built also the high places of Baal, to burn their sons with fire for burnt offering unto Baal, which I commanded not, nor spake it, neither come it into my mind: Therefore, behold, saith the Lord, that this place shall no more be called Tophet, nor the val-ley of the son of Hinnom, but the valley of slaughter.

As early as the seventh century B.C.E. the Jews had a no-tion of afterlife. The prophet Ezekiel is told by God to have a chat with a valley of bones, a mass grave of Israelites: "So I prophesied as I was commanded: and as I prophesied, there was a noise, and behold a wobbling, and the bones came to-gether, bone to his bone. And when I beheld, lo, the sinews and the flesh came upon them." This afterlife was corporeal, and since criminals would need no afterlife, or perhaps to prevent afterlife, their bodies should be burned to keep their bones from reanimating.

The Valley of Hinnom that Jeremiah talks about, at the east gate of Jerusalem, became the place to do that burning. It was already tainted by all the child sacrifices the heathens had supposedly done there, and in the centuries after Jere-miah, people began to dump all their garbage there. By the time of Jesus, it was called Gehenna, a Latin word that would

eventually be translated as "hell," a place where people used
sulfur to burn trash and criminals.

"A human limb burns a little like a tree branch," says one
forensics investigator. "The thin outer layers of skin fry and
begin to peel off as the flames dance across their surface . . .
The thicker dermal layer of skin shrinks and begins to split,
allowing the underlying fat to leak out . . . The body can sustain
its own fire for around 7 hours . . . The heat causes muscles to
dry out and contract, making the limbs move . . . Bone takes
longer to burn . . . By the end the skeleton is usually laid bare
like a charred anatomical model, coated in the greasy resi-
due of burned flesh."

Hellfire grew eternal as Christianity began to take hold,
though the fire remained literal. The New Testament includes
eight references to literal hellfire, sometimes meaning the
flames of the dump at Gehenna but also beginning to mean
fires in some otherworldly afterlife. But those fires were still
about consuming or destroying the bodies of the unrepen-
tant, the forever flame just insurance that the bones always
became ash.

The Apocalypse of Peter, composed maybe a generation
after the gospels of the New Testament, is an apocryphal text
but one so popular even in the fourth century C.E. that it was
among the last to be excluded from the Bible, though it remained part of several Christian traditions through the thirteenth century. In the Apocalypse of Peter, hell evolves into a
zoo of torment, no longer just a place where bodies are destroyed but where all kinds of sin-specific torture are performed eternally by angels for a crowd of spectators. Stroll
through this hell and see blasphemers hang by the tongue,
perverters of righteousness drown in a lake of fire, adulterous
women hang by their hair, the men who mingled with them

in the defilement of adultery hang by their feet, murderers cast into a pit of snakes and worms and the souls of their victims watching as the damned squirm among the squirming. See a gulley down below where all the gore from all the torture above washes down, washes over women and the children they aborted. See persecutors of the righteous with their guts burning and being eaten by worms, slanderers forced to gnaw their own lips while poked in the eye with a hot iron, liars gnawing their own tongues, wealthy assholes rolled atop swordlike and red-hot pebbles, homosexuals thrown from a cliff, forced to climb the cliff, then thrown down again, forced to climb again, etc. See idolaters and atheists turning their own spits, burning and turning themselves and roasting on the rivers of hellfire that course throughout the zoo of hell.

By the fourteenth century there is a greater cultural sense that hellfire as eternal torture might be overkill. In 1320, Dante writes *Inferno* and represents hell as part of a journey toward acceptance of God. The horrors of the Apocalypse of Peter are all still there but a bit more organized and not merely an exercise in chaotic sadism but also now part of an overall instruction in faith. The burning sinners are meant to help show us the way. From Canto XXII:

> And of the people who therein were burned
> Even as the dolphins, when they make a sign
> To mariners by arching of the back,
> That they should counsel take to save their vessel,
> Thus sometimes, to alleviate his pain,
> One of the sinners would display his back

In 1667 John Milton adds his two cents to the wishing well of hellfire, writes *Paradise Lost*, in which hell is not just

a garbage dump or a maze but a whole kingdom ruled by
Satan, complete with palaces and all manner of aesthetic
achievements that outstrip anything on Earth and rival even
those in heaven. Human attempts at art are rather sad in
comparison:

> Learn how their greatest monuments of fame
> And strength, and art, are easily outdone
> By Spirits reprobate, and in an hour
> What in an age they, with incessant toil
> And hands innumerable, scarce perform.

Then the Americans come onto the scene and Jonathan
Edwards, in 1773, takes us back briefly to hellfire as specta-
cle, adding applause from spectators, in his sermon "The
End of the Wicked, Contemplated by the Righteous. Or,
The Torments of the Wicked in Hell, No Occasion of Grief
to the Saints in Heaven." Edwards writes:

> When the saints in glory shall see how miserable others of
> their fellow-creatures are, who were naturally in the same
> circumstances with themselves; when they shall see the
> smoke of their torment, and the raging of the flames of
> their burning, and hear their dolorous shrieks and cries,
> and consider that they in the mean time are in the most
> blissful state and shall surely be in it to all eternity; how
> will they rejoice!

"By the 1870s," writes the historian Gary Scott Smith about
hellfire, "many Christians viewed the traditional concept's
emphasis on endless physical torments as antiquated,

malicious, offensive, inconsistent with God's character, and unjust because finite sins did not deserve an infinite penalty."

In 1881 Robert Green Ingersoll wrote, *If lunatics and idiots are in no danger of hell, God should have created only lunatics and idiots.* This was meant to be an admonishment of those who believed in literal hellfire, a mockery of the complicated justifications they concocted about exactly who would and would not be subjected to hell. Ingersoll was among the many now of the belief that hellfire was only a metaphor. Or maybe he meant to prove that there was a benevolent god by pointing out that we are, all of us, lunatics and idiots.

In 1956 Isaac Asimov writes a short story about the invention of slow-motion film, about a bunch of New Mexico scientists using that invention to watch the explosion of an atomic bomb, seeing for the first time a face that has always been hidden in the blast: "That moment of stasis—the fireball had shown dark spots for eyes, with dark lines for thin, flaring eyebrows, a hairline coming down v-shaped, a mouth twisted upward, laughing wildly in the hell-fire and horns." There was no need to worry about otherworldly hellfire anymore. Satan had come to earth.

These days hellfire is in the news all the time, in the form of a missile, named Hellfire, that we Americans keep raining down on the Middle East from drones.

In 2007 the Pew Research Center, in their U.S. Religious Landscape Survey, found that 74 percent of all Americans believed in heaven while only 59 percent believed in hell. They surveyed many religious groups and even atheists. While the percentages of belief varied greatly between the groups, there was one constant: all believed in heaven at a higher rate than hell. For some reason those conclusions feel wrong to me, perhaps a result of people needing to feign optimism in the face of a pesky pollster. The precision with which so many peoples and cultures have been able to nail down a description of hell should tell us something. Ask ten people to describe heaven in one nonabstract word and you will get lots of hesitation and ten different answers. Ask anyone to describe hell. They'll say fire. They'll say it burns.

The most recent edition of the *Stanford Encyclopedia of Philosophy* begins its entry "Heaven and Hell in Christian Thought" with this chilling thought experiment, the scenario they deem most apt for launching an investigation into afterlife:

> Indeed, despite their profound differences, many Christians (though perhaps not all) and many atheists can presumably agree concerning this: if a young girl is brutally raped and murdered and this should be the end of the story for the child, then a supremely powerful, benevolent, and just God would not exist. An atheist may seriously doubt that any future compensation would suffice to justify a supreme being's decision to permit such an evil in the first place. But the point is that even many Christians would concede that, apart from an afterlife, such an evil would constitute overwhelming evidence against the existence of God; some might even concede that such an evil would be logically (or metaphysically) inconsistent with his existence as well. It is hardly surprising, then, that a belief in an afterlife should be an important part of the Christian tradition.

Orwellian Ironies

". . . I am Terry Clark's biological son," begins the message by Justin Clark that has been relegated to the Letters to the Editor section of the *Albuquerque Journal* on the eve of Terry's execution. This special edition of the section, entitled "Hung Jury," is devoted to debating capital punishment and includes letters with titles such as "A Better Alternative: Life Without Parole" and "Clark Responsible for Own Death Sentence" and "Orwellian Ironies Will Corrode N.M. Society." The Orwellian ironies, according to the letter, are that the Department of Corrections is correcting Terry by killing him, that the Department of Health is providing the chemicals to do it.

Buried in the tiny, crammed columns of these letters is Justin's letter—"Innocent Bystanders Smeared by Association." I'm surprised to find this letter here because it has nothing to do with the death-penalty debate and because I expect words from the killer's son to be more prominent news, especially when that killer's execution is less than twenty-four hours away. But here it is, in the smallest font the newspaper prints, almost invisible on D13.

Justin writes that he is upset because the *Journal* published information about his mother, Terry's ex-wife, in a recent article; they printed her name, occupation, location, and even her hobbies. Justin argues that making such information public creates problems for an otherwise wonderful family struggling to distance themselves from an evil man. "People tend to look at you different when you suddenly become a murderer's kid. Sure, I am part of the same gene pool as Terry, but I am nothing like that man, nothing like him at all . . ."

I file that article next to the one I mistakenly printed many months ago: "Researchers Trace Human Genes Back to Common Ancestor."

Blameless

Bryan Stevenson, a death-penalty opponent who has succeeded in stopping many executions, says that for the death penalty "the threshold is not whether they deserve to die, but whether we deserve to kill." This is Jesus's old who-will-cast-the-first-stone conundrum. How easy it is to see that no one is blameless. But Terry was asking for it.

In his 2004 study, "Killing the Willing," the director of the Cornell Death Penalty Project, John H. Blume, uses Terry Clark's case as the basis of a hypothetical situation for determining whether inmates should be allowed to waive appeals and volunteer for execution. Though Blume suggests most condemned men who want to die are suicidal and therefore should not be allowed to waive their appeals—assisted suicide is illegal everywhere but Oregon—he suggests that in a case such as Terry's, the prisoner's request should be granted. Terry wanted closure for the victim's family. He believed his punishment was just. According to the court, he had a rational and factual understanding of the consequences of his decision. These three things make him the ideal volunteer for execution. Blume mostly skips over the issue of religion, mentioning only that our country has a long history of volunteer executions coerced by religious authorities. Anyway, it's an impossible topic to resolve. Terry believed he was going to heaven, believed he would be there fifteen minutes after his heart stopped. That's not a rational and factual understanding of the consequences. But in this country it is our right to maintain irrational and nonfactual understandings. It's called freedom of religion.

For Dena Lynn's parents, it only mattered that Terry died. They gave this interview to the AP two days before the execution:

> "I won't get excited until I see him strapped to that gurney and his lights go out," Jeff Gore said. "To this day, I don't care who does it, I just want the man dead." Gore, who lives in Chaparral, said he has spent many a night plotting how he might kill Clark. "Very vindictive ways that would not be quick," he said. Colleen Gore said she also has suffered from guilt. Dena Lynn asked her mother, her brother and her mother's boyfriend to go with her to the store that afternoon, but ended up riding off alone on her brother's bicycle. "We've all gone through a major guilt thing," her mother said. "She just wanted to go spend her money. It was burning a hole in her pocket."

In their story on Brother Maxey, the *Albuquerque Journal* described his take on Terry's last hours:

> Clark slept on and off that night and listened to country and western songs on his radio. He had his final visit with his girlfriend, Jean Ortiz, on Tuesday afternoon and became more agitated, Maxey said. "She said he was starting to come unglued," Maxey said. "He really had a fear of being alone. He didn't want to be alone to think. He started to get sweaty palms. He was shaking." Corrections officers gave Clark a sedative about 4pm, and Clark became less agitated but reported that he felt the room was

spinning. "I think it calmed him down so he could get through those last hours," Maxey said. Clark repeatedly said he was scared.

Brother Maxey was given a cell phone as he sat with Terry in the hours before the execution. The warden told Brother Maxey that Terry had until 6:00 p.m. to call his attorney and halt the execution. But Terry had already been sedated, and the phone was never used.

Sedatives such as Valium and other anxiety-numbing drugs are relatively common in executions, with half of all death-penalty states allowing the condemned access to such drugs in the days and hours leading up to an execution. No state has any protocol for sedating death-penalty volunteers who have not exhausted their appeals, who technically still have the right to change their minds. And Brother Maxey says there's no religious doctrine about showing up to heaven numb.

Ends

Terry is only the ninth man to be put to death by New Mexico since 1933, the first in nearly forty-two years. He remains the only man killed by the state in the modern era of capital punishment.

In 1933 Thomas Johnson got the electric chair and didn't speak but waved at the sheriff when asked for his last words. That same year Santiago Garduño got the electric chair after mixing strychnine with whiskey for his fourteen-year-old son to drink. Santiago said he had found peace with his god. Pedro Talamante's last words to a priest in 1946 included descriptions of hallucinations about movies he'd been seeing on the concrete walls of the penitentiary and the claim that a witch lived in the corner of his cell. In 1947 Louis Young sang *Use me, Lord, in thy service.* Arthur Fay Johnson loudly maintained his innocence even as the electric chair whirred into action in 1954. Later that year and in the same chair, Frederick Heisler screamed, *Don't let them do it!* In 1956 James Larry Upton asked that his face be covered because a rowdy crowd of drunks had somehow managed to gather around the electric chair and they were making him nervous. The normal execution hood did not fit Upton's big head but someone in the crowd had a parka, and before they draped it over Upton's face he said that he had no last words. *No,* he said. The parka was made of fur and when the switch was flipped and the voltage flowed, Upton's head caught fire. And in 1960, David Cooper Nelson, the only New Mexico man to die in a gas chamber, said, *Okay, Warden. God be with you.*

Terry Clark plans his last words for four months, inspired by reading about a pickax murderer born-again on death row in Texas. For months Terry repeats the chosen words like a mantra, trying them on, writing them, becoming comfortable with their sound. His last words will be *Fifteen minutes.* Then he will die. Then he will be in heaven before they even unstrap his body from the injection table.

Brother Maxey is in the execution chamber with the warden and Terry. Two experts on execution from Texas are nearby, overseeing the injection. On the way in, Terry asks one executioner if it will hurt. The Texan scoffs, *Well yeah. You're gonna die.* Terry looks to Brother Maxey, who, unable to refute the obvious, just smiles. The warden asks for a final statement. Terry gives his final statement. The state's official record of his last words will be *Fifteen minutes.* But, as the drugs course into his veins and paralyze his muscles, an addendum of sorts will pass through Terry's lips. Brother Maxey will be the only one to lean down and hear the involuntary whisper that slips out of Terry just before he dies.

Several hundred death-penalty protesters hold candles outside the death house. Many of them have been here for forty-one days, protesting one day for each year since New Mexico's last execution. Several dozen supporters of capital punishment, many friends of the victim's family, linger among the protesters, inching toward the door to be the first to quietly congratulate the state's witnesses when they exit.

Somewhere I have a firsthand account of Terry's final minutes. Something a reporter wrote—clichés such as "Time seemed to stand still for a few moments." Brother Maxey didn't notice time stand still. Or he doesn't mention it. I don't think it ever does. Time sputters and wobbles but keeps moving. Like the microfilm machine I keep going back to. Like the fan in the prisoner's witness room where Jean Ortiz sits with Gail Evans, whose phone will never ring. Like the tape recorder of the reporter in the state's witness room where Dena Lynn Gore's mother and father sit with Donita Welch, all grown up, watching through the glass as Terry gets strapped in. Twelve straps. Strapped. Tight. A sheet pulled taut and tucked neat. IV lines shoved into both arms, extended out at angles well below ninety degrees. A pillow. They provide a pillow. Brother Maxey is opposite the windows where the witnesses watch, wearing flannel again. Terry only looks at Brother Maxey. Holds still. He's promised himself he will hold still. The warden reads, never raises his eyes from the paper . . . *Hereby directed and commanded to execute the judgment and sentence of lethal injection . . . the murder of Dena Lynn Gore* . . . just hold still . . . *give a final statement.* Say it loud. Say it clear. Say it. *Fifteen minutes.* That's it, then. Well, alright. Sodium Pentothal. Pavulon. Sodium chloride. Brother Maxey leans in. Terry exhales. Whispers, *It burns a little.*

THE GLITCH IN THE VIDEOGAME
GRAVEYARD

In the Year of Our Lord 2014

I think of a world where each memory could create its own legend.

—CHRIS MARKER, *Sans Soleil*

But is it a perfect world? When everything we can recall is legend, is that a utopia or a dystopia? I guess a world like that has no choice but to play out like a hall of mirrors. When all is said and done and rubble, the ruins will only reflect themselves. But then a security guard power walks up to me and breaks my trance and wonders aloud if I should be so close to the car.

It's a time machine, I say.

Yeah, I guess it is. He watches as I try to take a picture of my reflection on the tinted window of the DeLorean, but because it is night and because I keep the flash off in an attempt to retain the perfect reflection of my face in the moonlit window of the DeLorean, the photo keeps coming out dark and empty. The guard says, *It is pretty cool.* Then he gets out his phone and points it at the time machine. He's not after his reflection but also snaps without the flash because he's trying to capture who's inside. Or what's inside—a life-size E.T. doll, belted in shotgun, all brown and wrinkled plastic with that block head and those babywide eyes gazing through the time machine's front windshield. I figure the guard's pictures are coming out dark and empty just like mine because he keeps holding his phone close to his face to inspect the pictures, and in that electronic glow I see he is missing an ear and he scratches where the ear should be and curses under his breath and snaps the exact same image again and again because it is impossible to satisfyingly capture reality when it's composed of the unreal. Then the Hollywood floodlights pop on and scare the darkness away and I see how near we are to a bank of Porta Potties and how fragile the little DeLorean is and how like a turd E.T. looks and how we are right in the middle of a landfill. I see, just over a few rolling hills of garbage, the real reason we are all gathered here tonight: the Pit.

And so I walk toward the glowing mounds of trash.

This is Alamogordo, New Mexico, on Friday night of Easter Week in the year of our Lord 2014.* It's on this day of observance about resurrection anxiety that a documentary

* Easter Friday is not Good Friday (the Friday before Easter Sunday). That's a common misunderstanding. Easter Friday is the Friday after Jesus has risen and spooked Mary and Peter and the giant rabbit has come and gone and had coffee with Pops and all the little kids have gathered up all the many-colored eggs in their little baskets and are finishing the last of the chocolates birthed by the eggs and there are so many shiny wrappers left all around everywhere because in the end this is what is left: trash. The tomb of Jesus was discovered, the story goes, empty of everything but trash, one soiled and bloodstained

crew has descended on my hometown to conduct an excavation at the dump. They hope to retrieve hundreds of thousands of copies of Atari's *E.T. the Extra-Terrestrial* videogame cartridges that, in September of 1983, were reportedly hauled ninety miles from a warehouse in El Paso, Texas, and left for dead thirty feet under our town. I want to tell the filmmakers that the time for resurrection has passed, that Easter Friday is just for shaking in your boots about running into a reanimated corpse, but that is not my place. I'm here only as a scribe, writing up the dig for what one of the film's producers keeps referring to as a *pointy-headed liberal rag.* He says, *What does a pointy-headed liberal rag care about our little dig for videogames?* And he says, *Why would a pointy-headed liberal rag send some kid?* I don't bother to point out that his second question answers his first. *I'm a hometown boy,* I say, and get out my notebook and go to work writing down adjectives for the nouns I'm seeing.

The rusty steel arm and sharp-toothed bucket of an excavator preside menacingly over the Pit, which is a hundred feet wide and dug twenty feet down into the landfill. The filmmakers hustle around, a boom mic operator in a gas mask/respirator sort of thing and production assistants in goggles and everyone else with their faces wrapped in fully

---

shroud left behind while somewhere the reanimated corpse of a carpenter roams. Easter Friday observances aren't as widespread as those on Good Friday, where the reason for the observance is clear—our Lord hangs from the cross. Easter Friday is a lot more amorphous; it's just one more day in that strange period of forty days after you've heard rumor of a resurrection but before you've heard rumor of an ascension and you are waiting around to see if the Son of God will stop by to collect on what you owe him.

grunged bandannas, all looking quite a bit worse for the wear after a day in trash and heat. They'd used the daylight to remove the overburden of garbage above the spot where their amateur science suggests the tomb of videogames lies, but they've stopped short for the night. They're saving the dramatic moment of discovery for tomorrow when a big crowd is expected to show up and gawk at the untombing. But tonight we're staging part of the epiphany anyway. I stand with about twenty townies and VIPs along the edge of the Pit, getting arranged by height for an upcoming scene.

There's the town mayor and some locals who claim to have raided the landfill and absconded with game cartridges when they were first dumped here back in 1983.

There's Joe Lewandowski, our local garbage contractor and the ostensible protagonist of the documentary, a man who's been hunting the exact location of the buried *E.T.* games for over a decade now.

There's the director of the local civic center, who put me to trash duty when I was sentenced to so much community service in my youth. I make a point of shaking his hand and giving him a look that says something vengeful about us both ending up VIPs at the dump.

There's Howard Scott Warshaw, who designed the *E.T.* videogame for Atari back in 1982.

There's a writer named Ernest Cline, who wrote a book called *Ready Player One*, which revolves around the high-stakes world of a near-future virtual reality game, an immersive simulation in which many players totally lose themselves. The book glorifies all kinds of eighties pop culture and sold to Hollywood for big bucks. In their review of *Ready Player One*, *The New York Times* printed the word *nerdgasm*. The DeLorean belongs to Cline, whose role at the dig is unclear

and unofficial but seems to be as some kind of Superinten-
dent of the Nerdgasm.

Behind me some guys in hard hats are complaining
about not getting to gather more data and do more analysis
of the Pit before the public arrives tomorrow. They're a group
of self-proclaimed *punk archaeologists* who bullied their way
into the dig by insisting that it has sufficient value as cultural
heritage to deserve some measure of methodology. They work
in the real world of stodgy academic archaeology, at universi-
ties and in private firms, but have, for whatever reason, taken
a keen interest in this seemingly minor endeavor to make a
spectacle of pop culture legend. But the filmmakers only
brought the punk archaeologists along as an afterthought.
Having actual archaeologists here makes sense like having a
DeLorean here makes sense. The archaeologists will never
get any control of the excavation but are the bookends of what
drives this dig, an obsessive nostalgia for the Spielbergian
eighties that begins with the nutball archaeology in *Raiders of
the Lost Ark* (1981), runs through the soft sci-fi of *E.T.* (1982)
and *Back to the Future* (1985), and ends with more nutball
archaeology in *Indiana Jones and the Last Crusade* (1989).*

* Just to complicate the Spielbergian cloud hanging over this event:
next year Spielberg will be announced as the director of the film adaptation of Ernest Cline's *Ready Player One*. Zak Penn, the director of
the documentary here at the Pit, will be the screenwriter, presumably
because he'll become friends with Cline during their time here at the
landfill. Alamogordo's dump is not just a tomb or graveyard for popular culture but also some kind of node perpetuating it. *Ready Player
One* is expected to be the first major feature film to extensively utilize
virtual reality technology. In the story, a media mogul creates a virtual
reality so compelling that people never want to be in regular old reality again. Then the media mogul dies and pits everyone against one

So here we are arranged by height and told to avoid looking directly into the cameras. We're told to glare into the bright lights, to gaze in collective wonder as Joe Lewandowski walks cautiously toward the source of that wonder-inducing light emanating from the Pit. We're re-creating the obligatory Spielberg shot: a group of slack-jawed humans transfixed by the strange light of E.T. going home or a spaceship landing at Devils Tower or a horde of face-melting specters roaring out from the Lost Ark. For a moment I'm transported by it, totally in awe and a little bit frightened by the possibility of what might emerge, just the way I was back in the fifth grade when I first heard about the buried *E.T.*s.

It was years after the alleged burial and years before my parents let me have videogames in the house when I first heard older guys around the local comic-book store (shout-out to Evolution Comix over on Adams Avenue) talking about an E.T. game buried under our town. I didn't immediately

---

another inside the virtual reality, sends them on a violent *Willy Wonka*–esque treasure hunt for his vast fortune, a race to find so-called Easter eggs hidden in the virtual reality game. The clues for the treasure hunt are all based on 1980s pop culture, the decade in which the media mogul was raised, for which he feels great nostalgia. But the virtual spills into the actual and high jinks and tragedy and triumph ensue. As part of his adaptation, Spielberg reportedly plans to have Penn remove from the script any references to films Spielberg directed or produced, either out of great humility or fear of being perceived as overly masturbatory. So in the virtual reality film about a future virtual reality obsessed with eighties pop culture, there may be no E.T. or Indiana Jones. All reasons we are gathered here tonight at the Pit will be erased. The node of the Pit in Alamogordo is so strong that it is writing itself out of the future.

think of the Atari 2600's toast-size plastic cartridges or the blocky eight-bit rendering of E.T. in what is commonly called the worst videogame of all time. I didn't have videogames. I figured they were talking about a board game. I thought about Spielberg's film, the story of young Elliott coaxing something alien and magical into his life with little more than curiosity and a trail of candy and then all of his buddies with him, tearing ass on their BMX bikes to save that magical creature from all the government poking and prodding and corporate exploitation. I was convinced that buried somewhere beneath our town was a game like Jumanji, meaning it was not a game at all but a portal that could transport me and my friends into the world of E.T., where we would ride our flying bikes across the face of the moon and wrest real magic from the vapid, corrupt grip of the adult world. In hindsight this was naïve, but it makes about as much sense as the real story behind the frenzy for digging up our landfill—how the rise of the gamer community, fueled by the furnace of internet rumor, made legend of the dump.

Here's a rundown of that legend for those among us not already deep into the nerdgasm. Reports in the fall of 1983 from both the *Alamogordo Daily News* and *The New York Times* suggested Atari used Alamogordo as an industrial waste dump after deciding to retool its El Paso manufacturing plant amid a downturn in business. Everyone knew Atari needed to rid themselves of *E.T.* The game was widely considered totally craptastic. Its fatal flaw was a pit into which E.T. would repeatedly fall almost as soon as the game began—the pit from which few players could help poor E.T. escape, effectively nullifying any chance for them to enact the innocence-saves-magic narrative that had made the film so successful. So gamers were left pissed at the implication that they were too iniquitous to participate in the wonder or just pissed that they'd squandered $49.95, the equivalent of a whopping $122.17 today. They returned the cartridges in droves. Atari lost $100 million on the game. Even slashing prices to $1 didn't help them sell, and *E.T.* became the first and biggest tremor in a quake that would crash the $3 billion videogame industry, bringing total industry sales to a mere $100 million by 1985 and totally bankrupting Atari. But the company refused to ever respond to reports of a massive, clandestine, and likely illegal precrash dump of their unwanted games or that the dump had been in Alamogordo, a town not far from the Trinity Site and Roswell. Atari's silence over the years led some in the online gamer community to concoct conspiracies about a desert graveyard built specifically for millions of unsold copies of *E.T.*—an act of shame when the game proved a flop or an act of desperation to clear inventory as the company neared bankruptcy or the fated final point in a kind of Devil's Triangle of the atom bomb and the UFO crash, an area in which all things paranormal congregate, where paranoia is the only useful state of mind, where all conspiracy culminates, a triangle of coordinates like the head of an arrow pointing directly from the underbelly of America toward the nation's capital, where a lizard king inside a human-skin suit now sits in the Oval Office and orders drone strikes on other lizards not happy with their king's slow play of targeted killings to wipe out the human race. Others in the gamer community found this kind of tale altogether implausible and denied any dump of any kind ever occurred, and so from the nerd squabbles of internet discussion threads rose an urban legend that has culminated in

Microsoft's Xbox Entertainment Studios funding a documentary that hinges on a bunch of us standing around on Easter Friday, knee-deep in all my town's old trash in the middle of the night and staring slack-jawed into floodlights hanging over the Pit.

Most of us in the cast complain that the floodlights hurt when stared at for so long but we try to hold our eyeballs wide and endure the pain because the filmmakers tell us to. Tears stream down my face. I did not expect to cry at the dump. The tears are involuntary but I wonder if there is any good reason to sob. I'm reminded of Gehenna, the valley outside Jerusalem that in the time of Jesus was a garbage dump, that was often lit up at night with sanitation fires fueled by sulfur. And the fires became a convenient place to unceremoniously dispose of the bodies of criminals. In this manner the fiery disposal of miscreants became a convenient metaphor for God's punishment of sinners. In this way the flames grew eternal and the name of the dump, Gehenna, eventually got translated by King James's scribes as "hell." In the beginning there was a garbage dump. That dump grew into humanity's most sustained imagining of eternal horror. This seems a good thing to explain if people ask about my tears. *Just meditating on a whole history of eternal suffering,* I'll say. But nobody asks. The documentary crew's floodlights heat unearthed garbage until a sour, sulfurous smell taints the evening breeze.

The punk archaeologists behind me grumble about the smell but mostly complain that they'd rather be doing some kind of actual fieldwork than standing around staging scenes. I'm unclear about the exact nature of punk archaeology and what this crack team of scholars hopes to accomplish here but their subtle dissent earns my respect. They're all business. Fuck the show. I dub them the Arch Punks in hopes that they will turn out to be a kind of motley superhero squad able to pull back the veil of this Hollywood spectacle. I abandon my original plan to doggedly tail the film's director and instead resolve to fall in with the Arch Punks tomorrow morning. Beyond the oddness of replicating Spielberg's paranormal sentimentality, the ethical quandary of staging scenes for a documentary, the whole history of hell, and the general weirdness of a small-town dump at night, the vibe here is uncanny and I suspect only the Arch Punks are divining it with me.

We do a half dozen takes of the epiphany scene, and when all our eyes are pretty well dripping out of our faces, we wrap for the night.

Eight a.m. on untombing Saturday and I drive through streetlights that mostly stay green and past signs that hype a man named Saint running for sheriff, past my old high school with teens hanging streamers for the night's prom dance and past the Walmart where the streamers were no doubt bought in obscene bulk. On this morning turning right onto White Sands Boulevard will take you to the Earth Day celebration in Alameda Park, where streamers are a cardinal sin. Drive on in that direction and you'll hit our town's shopping mall, which is mostly abandoned these days except for Kmart, a military recruitment office, and a little museum that is—no joke—entirely dedicated to the Shroud of Turin, the leftovers of resurrection, the burial cloth of our Lord, who can absolve all sin. But I drive straight across the boulevard, over the railroad tracks, again to the landfill, where all the streamers from all the parties in Alamogordo got dumped along with everything else from the sixties on through 1989, when this bit of desert was finally full of our trash.

Maybe a hundred people are already standing single file at the gate, waiting to stare into the Pit. Civilization is about never running out of reasons to stand in lines. And make no mistake, we are in the midst of civilization. Though this legendary burial site is often described as "out in the middle of the desert," the golden arches of the town McDonald's practically loom over the landfill's dirt road, and the line stretches back toward the boulevard and ends a hundred paces from the Hi-D-Ho Drive In. Most people in town couldn't care less about the dig, but it has dominated the front page of the *Alamogordo Daily News* for the past three days:

Atari Graveyard: In Search of 'E.T.'

'E.T.': Atari-Dig Contract Is Modified

'E.T.': Officials Discuss Dig Concerns

The *concerns* relate to the environmental hazards of digging up what was a largely unregulated landfill. A vocal faction in town is convinced the crew will accidentally unearth hundreds of corpses of mercury-laced hogs. In 1969 Alamogordo made national headlines when the family of Ernest and Lois Huckleby ate one of the many hogs they'd unknowingly fattened with grain doused in pesticides containing methylmercury. The U.S. Department of Agriculture quickly banned the use of mercury in pesticides when the Huckleby story broke, but it was too late for the family: the incident caused severe lifelong illnesses in the couple's three children and prompted decades of ultimately unsuccessful civil litigation. A photo of eight-year-old Ernestine Huckleby filled a whole page of *National Geographic* in 1970, her eyes big as she grips a teddy bear, the caption informing us that she's blind, mute, and paralyzed on account of the poisoned pork. "Clinging to life," says the caption. Last year Ernestine's brother, Amos, almost sixty and also blind and severely disabled from the mercury, was paraded before the city council in an attempt to stop the excavation of E.T.s. *Be careful,* he said. *This stuff is dangerous. Is it worth it?* Although hundreds of poisoned hogs and many thousands of pounds of mercury-tainted grain undoubtedly ended up in our landfill after the Huckleby incident, our garbage contractor, Joe Lewandowski, has promised that the hogs of '69 aren't buried near the E.T.s. of '83. *No cloud of poison will rise from the Pit,* he finds himself saying more than he'd like. But no one seems too worried this morning—the line outside the dump is growing.

Simon Chinn, a two-time Academy Award–winning producer of the documentaries *Searching for Sugar Man* and *Man on Wire,* is producing this film through the media company Lightbox with the financial backing of Microsoft, which also plans to distribute the film through its Xbox consoles.* Because of Chinn's pedigree, there's hope this will be a decent

---

* Lightbox actually came to the project late. Fuel Entertainment first secured the exclusive rights to dig in Alamogordo's landfill in 2011 after Joe Lewandowski had already been approached by numerous media outlets, including the Discovery Channel, about locating the E.T.s. In 2013 Xbox Entertainment decided to finance Fuel's beleaguered efforts as part of a series of documentaries about the digital gaming revolution, which Lightbox would produce. Souder, Miller & Associates

flick about Atari and the rocky origins of the videogame industry, an industry that has in recent years all but eclipsed
Hollywood in revenue and maybe cultural sway. Many die-
hard gamers have driven cross-country to witness this first
great excavation of the gaming age, convinced that one day
all culture will stem from videogame culture, as if soon we'll
all be living inside a simulation or a giant *Ready Player One*
virtual reality and we'll only venture back into the real world
to dig up Atari cartridges as part of a lame tour through the
artifacts that jump-started our evolution away from flesh.
They've brought their Atari games and wear their Atari shirts
and their earnest fandom electrifies the morning. Others in
line are curious locals, bewildered more than anything else,
and seeing all of them lined up to stand around in their old
trash seems an awful joke. The director of this film, Zak
Penn, is known for his writing on the scripts of comic-book
blockbusters such as *X-Men: The Last Stand* and *The Avengers* and maybe most infamously for writing the Schwar-
zenegger flop *Last Action Hero*. But Penn also once teamed
with Werner Herzog to film a mockumentary about the
Loch Ness monster and didn't bother to let the Scottish
locals in on the ruse. Few people saw *Incident at Loch Ness*,
but I exerted the not-inconsiderable effort needed to find
and watch it. My review: it is at worst a rude mockery of the

---

was brought on as the environmental firm to work with Lewandowski
on the Waste Excavation Plan. Mesa Verde construction is doing the
actual digging. People from all of these companies comprise *the crew*
and keeping them separate is difficult because of ubiquitous bandanna
usage, but the confusion of it all lends itself to that classic American
joke: How many corporations does it take to make a profitable show of
digging up one bankrupt corporation's illegally dumped e-waste?

local culture and at best totally inconsequential. But my method, as Sherlock Holmes would say, is founded on the observation of trifles.* And so here at the Pit I'm on the alert to sniff out a farce.

By 10:00 a.m. a gaggle of reporters has skipped the line. They're hovering at the orange fence erected around the Pit, many of them wearing shiny new hard hats and safety vests still creased from their packaging. Some of that packaging is discarded on the ground and blowing around. I suppose, technically, that counts as proper disposal. A few TV reporters wear blouses and fancy jewelry, and one guy is in a full business suit. They've got big ideas about a glamorous time at the landfill. John Williams's *E.T.* score plays through loudspeakers, and just for good measure, the DJ mixes in a few bars from Williams's score for *Raiders of the Lost Ark*.

---

* The excavation of this legendary videogame graveyard will eventually inspire an episode of *Elementary*, the latest TV revival of Sherlock Holmes. So that's why I coyly quoted the great detective. And also as an excuse to give one more tally of the depth of the nerdgasm we're dealing with here, the power of the pop culture node of the Pit, in case you haven't kept track. (1) We're digging for a videogame that defined the rocky beginnings of that industry, (2) a videogame based on the sci-fi blockbuster *E.T.*, (3) digging in an overtly *Raiders of the Lost Ark* style, (4) to make a documentary film for Xbox under the direction of a guy who wrote *X-Men* and *The Avengers*, (5) with a DeLorean along for moral support, a car paid for by (6) the sci-fi bestseller *Ready Player One*, soon to be (7) the first virtual-reality Spielberg film, and (8) all of it with enough intrigue to actually weasel itself into the canon of Sherlock Holmes cases. That's an eighth-level nerdgasm. And eight, as I'm sure you know, is the number of chakras some practitioners say need to be activated to achieve tantric sex. Well, alright. Also maybe relevant: in Dante's *Inferno*, the eighth circle of hell is Fraud.

Gamers fire up Atari 2600s on CRT televisions installed in the backs of their minivans. The wind gusts to match the growing pageantry of the scene. The DeLorean rolls up alongside the Pit.

When the game's designer, Howard Scott Warshaw, arrives at the dump, his failure is all the media want to ask him about. He's got a decent excuse: by the time Atari secured the rights to make an *E.T.* game in the fall of 1982, he had only six weeks to design it before a much-publicized Christmas release. He was rushed and doing a lot of drugs to try to keep up. The game suffered. But I hear him tell reporters over and over that he doesn't mind people calling *E.T.* the worst videogame ever made because, look, it's in the spotlight again after all these years and that must count for something. He says this while gazing out over the Pit, whose name is a running joke about the fatal glitch in his game. I wonder if he'd refuse a chance to saddle up the DeLorean and travel back in time to fix the code. Aren't we all supposed to be on the lookout for ways to fix what we've fucked up? But Warshaw also designed *Yars' Revenge* and *Raiders of the Lost Ark*, both Atari blockbusters compared to *E.T.* Plus, he's now a psychotherapist, primarily counseling techies in Silicon Valley. He's in the business of helping digital gurus alleviate problems with their organic networks, not through more technology but just through talking. He's pretty much at peace, settled into his new role of fixing brains glitching from future shock.

The Arch Punks, on the other hand, are all nervous energy ready to blow. They've been here since sunrise, eager to start surveying and excavating and cataloging, but have been told to wait for the public to stream in, to wait for the cameras to start rolling. As best I can tell, punk archaeology is a DIY methodology meant to be nonelite and seat-of-the-pants. In some ways it's a rebellion against academia, an attempt to keep archaeology relevant and sexy in the twenty-first century as the nature of our ruins is increasingly complicated by capitalism and globalism and technology's acceleration of the cycle from commodity to waste. But I don't fully understand the point.* E.T. and the other reportedly buried Atari games aren't rare or valuable and it's hard to fathom what the Arch Punks will learn through their excavation. But they take the work seriously and they're constantly agitated by the film crew's constrictive agenda, which makes the Punks a hoot to tail.

---

* This is equally true of other archaeologists, as evidenced by founding punk Bill Caraher's hour-long interview with a baffled and frankly stubborn Dr. Joseph Schuldenrein on the radio show *Indiana Jones: Myth, Reality and 21st Century Archaeology.* Schuldenrein seems confused by Caraher's references to Lou Reed and MC5 and the Replacements, seems confused by the idea that the chaos of punk can be translated to methodology or field practice. The point, Caraher suggests, is to never establish an overarching methodology. In Schuldenrein's defense, this is a particularly confusing concept in the context of the Pit, where the Arch Punks keep begging the film crew for a bit more semblance of methodology. Caraher's broader point is that punk archaeology fights the trend to commodify artifacts, particularly when those artifacts are coming from late capitalism where they have been discarded exactly because of the urge to commodify more and more objects. If we only value the things that will make us money, we will end up with so much trash, will end up with culture that is synonymous with capitalism. That's shitty culture. So, in an academic context, the Punks might use less field methodology in order to upset the status quo that leads to commodification. But at this commercial dig, they need to use more field methodology in order to upset the status quo that leads to commodification. Either way, their goal, stated in the simplest punk terms, is basically to fuck shit up.

Andrew Reinhard is the Arch Punks' organizer and mouth-piece. By day he's the director of publications for the American School of Classical Studies at Athens. By night he writes lo-fi anthems about punk archaeology that sound decidedly more alt-rock than punk and have names such as "Untenured" and "Miskatonic University Excavations at Innsmouth." Though Reinhard himself is not punk in any sense that I've ever used the word, he has single-handedly bullied the filmmakers into letting his team participate in the dig, the result of a months-long social-media campaign that raucously questioned the crew's ability to establish a useful methodology for the excavation and ensuing data collection. Until Reinhard chimed in, the plan seems to have been just to have a treasure hunt and not think too much about it. *These guys*, Zak Penn later tells me, *are the only thing lending legitimacy to the whole fiasco.*

Richard Rothaus is the funny bone of the Arch Punks, a reformed academic archaeologist now in the private sector who says things like *To expand on what you losers are saying* . . . in such a jolly manner that no one would ever mistake his words for an insult. Bret Weber is a historian at the University of North Dakota who acts as a gofer for the Arch Punks. He's a social worker and his temperament tends to level out the group when things get contentious.

Raiford Guins is the motor of the Punks. He's a video-game historian at Stony Brook University. He's been researching and writing about this Atari dump for years, has videogame history tattooed all over his body and never sits still. He came to Alamogordo a few years back and tracked down a local named Ricky Jones, who claims to have busted into the dump as a teen and loaded a U-Haul full with Atari games—not just *E.T.* but also *Asteroids* and *Centipede* and

Missile Command and a dozen others. Then young Ricky Jones drove west and sold his treasure in California flea markets for a handsome profit.

The soul of the Arch Punks is Bill Caraher, a University of North Dakota archaeologist who first championed the application of a punk ethos to his field. His expertise is in Mediterranean archaeology but he laces his monologues about that and pretty much everything else with so many references to 1970s punk rock that it's easy to tell where his heart lies. In Caraher I recognize a real distrust of The Man—in his eyes and shaggy beard and in the way he uses that phrase *The Man* when he gets worked up about the dire consequences of late capitalism.

I loiter with the Arch Punks as the line drains and several hundred people snake toward the Pit. Zak Penn is fitted with a microphone and climbs onto the ramp of an equipment truck, where he announces the primary rule for the day: don't go past the orange fence. This rule is in the official 106-page Waste Excavation Plan submitted to the State of New Mexico, but by the end of the day it will be broken, the fence will be ripped down by fans and tossed aside along with any sense that there had been any plan at all.

Penn says, *Let's go, start it up!* The crowd cheers as he jumps down from the equipment truck and points his hands in a bunch of different directions. A gaggle of media surround Penn and his crew, filming them as they film the excavator. Then a large portion of the crowd whips out their phones and records the media as the media record the documentary crew filming the guy in the excavator, who finally gets the monster roaring. As the teeth of the excavator's bucket dig in, the Arch Punks snug their hard hats and velcro their safety vests and assume their positions inside the fence along the edge of the Pit, holding shovels or cameras or the Microsoft Surface tablets they've been asked to carry as a kind of native advertisement in the documentary. They look undeniably cinematic. I give in and snap a picture. The Arch Punks feel to me like a kind of proxy. They're doing what I've always wanted to do, what any kid dreams of doing. They get to play around in the dirt and the trash. They even foster legitimacy by doing it.

In the one dig of any consequence that I conducted in my youth—age nine—I attempted to build a swimming hole in my backyard. About three feet down I began finding things and the project transformed into an excavation. I grew up in an adobe house built by my granddaddy in the 1950s on the outskirts of Alamogordo. I'd heard him mention that, while digging the foundation and planting the pecan trees that circle the house, he'd discovered arrowheads and pottery and also that he wished he'd kept those artifacts because they might have been important. So I brought one of my discoveries from the swimming hole into the house and examined it thoroughly for days. The thing was oblong, five or six inches in length, and obviously deteriorated—the handle of a war hatchet maybe, or a whittled icon of an Apache god. I rehearsed how I would present my findings when the talk-show hosts came knocking, probably with an anecdote about my silly pool project and lots of historical facts and plenty of flourishes with my professorial wand stabbing in the direction of the artifact, which would be housed in glass: a bulletproof, climate-controlled case with the artifact glowing under soft museum-grade lights, the kind that perfectly illuminate every angle and cast no shadows. When I finally showed the artifact to Granddaddy, he asked to see exactly where in the yard I'd dug it up. I took him out to my shallow swimming hole, which I had by then filled with water. The excavation was complete and I'd been doing a fair amount of celebratory splashing around. He paced a bit, got his bearings, and then with not too big a grin said, *This is the exact spot where I used to bury all the dog shit.*

I kept that fossilized turd around for quite a while, out of sheer stubbornness and a lingering sense of greed, like maybe one day it would turn into something of value and I'd have more than just an absurd story to tell. But that was the beginning of the end of my archaeological aspirations, a lesson that value is not a preordained consequence of things unearthed.

Eleven a.m. and the Arch Punks are elbow deep in trash. The excavator lifts out a bucketful and sets it aside and they go at it, Caraher and Reinhard with shovels, jolly old Rothaus with a tiny trowel, and Guins snapping pictures. Despite the best efforts of a water truck, 40 mph winds gust facefuls of landfill into the crowd. A layer of it cakes a family sitting in lawn chairs, chairs pulled right up to the orange fence like a sofa to a ginormous flatscreen, chairs that don't support their obesity so their asses are actually resting on the ground. But they don't move, don't flinch in the windstorm, a monklike American stasis. A food truck rolls in to serve E.T.-themed sliders, and people try to eat the little burgers without parting their lips in order to keep the refuse from rushing in. Penn climbs up on the equipment truck to announce that nothing has been found. A guy in a hockey jersey says, *Fuck this*, and throws a tumbleweed into the Pit. The crowd thins. For a time the only entertainment is a little drone in the air, fighting madly against the wind to get an aerial shot of our eternal suffering. From up there it can no doubt pan from the Pit to the Earth Day celebration down the road and zoom even farther to our beleaguered shopping mall and its main attraction these days, the Shroud of Turin Exhibit & Museum.

Among the lengthier entries in the *Encyclopedia of Dubious Archaeology* is one for the Shroud of Turin, the fourteen feet of bloodied cloth that holds the image of a crucified man, purportedly our Lord and Christ, Jesus of Nazareth. The shroud has been called the most studied artifact in the world, or the greatest hoax ever perpetrated. Hundreds of thousands of people pilgrimage to the Turin Cathedral in Italy each year to see the shroud in its bulletproof, climate-controlled case, glowing under soft museum-grade lights, the kind that perfectly illuminate every angle and cast no shadows. The roadside-attraction museum dedicated to the shroud is in our mall because back in the seventies a group of New Mexico scientists spearheaded the first and only Vatican-sanctioned scientific investigation into the shroud's authenticity, the largest expedition ever formed to study a single artifact. Most of the investigators were physicists and thermodynamicists from the nuclear laboratory up at Los Alamos. They had a notion for a hobby that might balance their perpetuation of the Bomb with a little verification of the divine. They called this the Shroud of Turin Research Project. Or STURP, which is clearly not as cool a nickname as Arch Punks. But STURP had a similarly motley team of scientists pursuing a passion project—the Passion project. After five straight days of round-the-clock analysis of the shroud in 1978 and several years of interpreting data, STURP concluded in 1981 that the shroud was the actual burial cloth of a man crucified in the manner of Jesus, that the image was not painted, and that they had no scientific explanation for how the image ended up on the cloth. Their

lack of conclusions in the last matter conveniently left open
the possibility for the miraculous, that resurrection light em-
anated from the corpse of our Lord and created the world's
first selfie. But subsequent radiocarbon testing has deter-
mined the shroud dates only to about the thirteenth century.
Although, right now another team of scientists, this one from
Italy, are researching the possibility that an earthquake in
the year of our Lord 33 could have opened up a pit in Jerusalem and caused waves of neutron particles from deep in the
earth to both imprint the image on the shroud and confuse
our radiocarbon dating of it. But it's unclear whether that
finding would verify or debunk resurrection.

The museum in our shopping mall contains a full-scale
photographic model of the shroud, created by STURP, as
well as all kinds of late-seventies gadgets used by the team—a
3-D spectrograph and interactive VP-8 Image Analyzer and
all manner of rudimentary holograms—all vintage tech that
would fit right in with our nerdgasm here at the Pit. And, of
course, we're conducting our *E.T.* excavation on the last day
of Easter Week, a week for celebrating the shroud's emptiness.
As the Arch Punks get deeper into the dump, I think more
about the shroud not because I worry our tomb will be empty
but because I'm still looking for some way to understand the
dig as more than a pop culture orgy, more than unearthing
turds. When you encounter something seemingly meaning-
less, you can accept the numbness of it or ache for profundity. Whenever possible, I tend toward the ache. *Wouldn't it
be something,* I say to Naomi Kyle, a news anchor for Imagine Games Network, *if* E.T. *and the Shroud of Turin are artifacts in the same vein?* She frowns and declines to interview
me about my shroud theories. She's worn all black today and
is busy brushing landfill off her pants to get camera ready

and doesn't buy my suggestion that filth is the original sepia filter and will make her Instagrams pop.

Perhaps the most convincing scientific theory of the Shroud of Turin's origin is that it is the world's first photograph. This theory posits that some tinkerer in the Middle Ages figured out he could record the projections of a camera obscura. A camera obscura is created by passing light through a small opening in a dark room in order to project the image of an object from outside the room onto a wall inside the room. The rudiments of the camera obscura can be traced all the way back to Plato in the fourth century B.C.E. All this tinkerer in the Middle Ages would need to have done, the theory goes, is replace the inner wall of his camera obscura with a cloth soaked in a known and readily available light-sensitive mineral such as silver nitrate, then set up his crucified corpse or statue in the light and wait for the image to develop on the fourteen-foot stretch of cloth in his dark room. There would be no record of this breakthrough in photography because the tinkerer would have wanted everyone to believe the shroud was a thousand years old, was evidence of the Lord's death and resurrection. I like this theory because it proves the hoax and adds a deeper level of intrigue, namely that we missed out on half a millennium of photography because it was a secret keeping people throwing alms at the shroud. There's not much consensus around this theory but I like it because it means *E.T.* (the videogame) is maybe a descendent of the shroud, an artifact of our technological evolution, another warp in the transformation of our visual mediums that falls somewhere between the ancient camera obscura and the near-future virtual reality of *Ready Player One*.

Well, alright.

But even if they are in the same line of our technological

evolution, these two artifacts have sort of oppositional existential value. The creation of the shroud is—perhaps—an early example of using cutting-edge technology (photography) to buttress Christian faith, to help us joyfully give existential concerns over to a deity we can never fully understand. Our excavation of *E.T.* is an example of using rudimentary technology (shovels) to revel in another relatively rudimentary technology (eight bits of Atari code) as a kind of solace in this potentially frightening age when our cutting-edge technology seems on the verge of being totally out of our control, seems on the verge of wresting from us, against our will, all existential concerns.

I don't mean to suggest that everyone around the Pit is worked up into a nervous fervor about the coming robot overlords. Most of the gamers probably welcome them, and the rest of us are just having fun. But these days our culture in general is undoubtedly more aware than ever of the possibility that our tech could turn on us or at least leave us in the dust. *Ready Player One* is a story along these lines, like *The Matrix* before it. But then also there are *The Age of Spiritual Machines: When Computers Exceed Human Intelligence* and *Superintelligence: Paths, Dangers, Strategies* and *Our Final Invention: Artificial Intelligence and the End of the Human Era*—these are not sci-fi epics but nonfiction bestsellers by some of our most respected futurists. These books evidence a primary concern of our time, that in pursuing smarter and smarter technology, we are writing ourselves out of the future.

Take, for instance, the much-ballyhooed experiments of the artificial intelligence company DeepMind, which last year created AI specifically to play Atari 2600 games such as *Pong, Breakout*, and *Space Invaders*. DeepMind says their AI "is able to master a diverse range of Atari 2600 games to superhuman level with only the raw pixels and score as inputs." The DeepMind AI has no recourse to the games' codes. DeepMind plays them just the way you or I would, by watching, but plays better than we could ever manage or even imagine. More than a few people, including the folks at Google who recently acquired DeepMind for over $500 million, are betting that this AI is laying the groundwork for a coming superintelligence—one that will not just play games but create them, create whole worlds for us, an AI with the ability to program and sustain *Ready Player One*-esque virtual realities indistinguishable from the real world so that, once we plug in, we'll have a hard time wanting, or even knowing how, to leave—a deity-like technological power totally beyond our control. So the nostalgia that gathers us all here at the Pit is not only about a fuzzy feeling for pop culture from our youth but also about a real sense that in a recent time our technology was still quaint, unthreatening, and under control—plus the accompanying sense that that time is now almost over.

Imagine if the Jews in the book of Exodus went digging for the molten calf destroyed by Moses at Mount Sinai right after he came down with the Ten Commandments. They know he's soon going to come down that mountain a second time with a fresh set of ten commandments ready to proclaim that they can no longer make their own quaint little idols because now there is only one true and all-powerful god, but they're digging up that molten calf anyway, not to learn anything but to remind themselves one last time of when they still had some control over creating their own gods, and choosing which ones to worship. Or, for a more secular analogy, we can go back to Plato in the fourth century B.C.E. and his allegory of the cave, where some of the rudiments of the camera obscura first showed up. Plato told a story of slaves chained from birth behind a wall, forced their whole lives to look only at shadows cast on the ceiling by the puppets of some sadists performing a show in the light of the cave's fire. The slaves, chained at the neck and forced to look only at the shadows of the puppet show, would never know any reality other than the shadows and, even if removed from the cave, might reject all they found there in sunlit Technicolor base reality. Plato meant for this to be a lesson about how what we know, what we learn from birth, affects what we believe. These days the allegory of the cave seems a dead ringer for a warning about virtual reality, but like any good allegory, we can apply it to most things at hand. So the creation of the Shroud of Turin, assuming it is a photograph, was a way of convincing ourselves that the reality we've experienced from birth is not the only one, that through Jesus we can wake up from the shadows and cast off our chains. The excavation of *E.T.*, on the other hand, is a way of reminding ourselves that, so far as we know, we humans have always been the ones in charge of casting the shadows, and if we were ever slaves before them, it was only because we chose to lose ourselves in the entertainment, like that family in their monklike stasis with their asses resting on the ground just as close to the Pit as they can get. Here is our tomb of the Atari, the first of our technological entertainments that we enjoyed being quite literally tethered to (via the hand-held game controller). But maybe also our party around the Pit is a prayer that we will forever continue to control casting the shadows, that our machines will never take over the puppet show without our knowledge, that we can bury and spurn and then dig up and worship our nonthreatening, nonsuperintelligent technology whenever the hell we please.

We are forever, the sadists and *the slaves, in this shadow puppet show!* is a chant I don't try too hard to get anyone around
the Pit chanting with me, even though I think that assertion
unlocks much of the anxiety that underlies all the frantic
nostalgia of our nerdgasm.

Sometime around noon, when the wind and heat and general dumpiness have run off almost all of the morning's crowd,
a flurry of activity in the Pit culminates with Penn holding up
a dirty but intact *E.T.* videogame cartridge. The moment is
altogether anticlimactic, maybe because the crowd is now
over half media, maybe because nobody makes a big speech
about the Shroud of Turin and fending off robot overlords,
and maybe because, just after the discovery, I'm standing a
hundred yards away with Joe Lewandowski. No cameras are
around us. We do not high-five. Lewandowski has been working on this project longer than anyone else. He was there as
a garbage contractor just after the games were dumped and
has put in more hours than anyone else working to locate
the games and sort out the Waste Excavation Plan. Everyone agrees that he's the only reason any of this was possible.
Lewandowski's son, Will, has driven here in his animal-
control truck, which, parked by the Pit as it is, makes it seem
we're expecting to capture a few live aliens. Will stands by
me, just across the fence from his dad, as we watch Penn
model the excavated game cartridge for Naomi Kyle in her
now spotless black outfit.

You can see where the publicity is, Joe says.

It will go viral, Will replies.

*I don't care. I just wanted to see if I could do it. It was a
guess, really.*

You knew you would find it.

Yeah. I knew I would.

Will reaches over the fence and hugs his father. No cameras record this embrace. I feel like a jerk staring at them, but it's the first sincere moment of an otherwise bogus day.

In a few months, after the documentary premieres, Joe Lewandowski will not be so laconic. He will say, *Now, that's what made me so angry about the movie*, then spend three hours laying out his critiques for me. The documentary will make little mention of the curse of the videogame graveyard that Joe battled, how he discovered that city ordinance #666 made it illegal for Atari to dump in Alamogordo, how all the garbage workers and cops and reporters who were at the initial dump in 1983 kept ending up dead, how Joe blew a tire going 80 mph in his Camaro while on the phone to seal the film deal with Xbox, how he had that strange heart attack his doctors still cannot explain. He'll go so far as to tie the curse to the 9/11 terrorist attacks, noting that one of the local cops who chased scavenger kids such as Ricky Jones away from the dumped *E.T.*s ended up a flight attendant on American Airlines Flight 175 and died when that second plane hit the World Trade Center. *The shit goes to shit*, Joe will say over and over to me, sometimes as a critique of the documentary, sometimes as remorse about the reach of the curse, sometimes as a too-perfect garbage-contractor catchphrase. Mostly he'll say it between laughs as the only way to sum up the whole strange experience: *Man, the shit goes to shit.* But for now, he's just hugging his son.

The Arch Punks fill a succession of five-gallon buckets with all the games they're uncovering. *E.T.*, *Asteroids*, *Centipede*, and *Missile Command*, everything Ricky Jones reported scavenging three decades ago. Guins hops by and says, *Very high, my man. Very high right now.* Reinhard says they're finding thousands of games, remarkably well-preserved. *Lots of returned E.T.s. with the buyer's name and address still taped to them,* he says. *Enough data for decades of Ph.D. dissertations!*

Some friends of the crew's are escorted past the fence and into the Pit. They fine-tune backgrounds for selfies by placing dirty *E.T.* cartridges carefully in different spots on the trash. The heap of unearthed garbage is now almost entirely junked Atari games and equipment. Many hundreds of cameras, professional and amateur, have focused on that pile of trash today. Here in Alamogordo lies perhaps the most photographed dump in human history but you will learn little about our town or its people by looking at those pictures. Maybe I should have been telling you more about Lewandowski's decades-long rise to garbage kingpin of town, about the bankruptcies and perseverance and how his pursuit of the *E.T.s* has now launched him into a second career as de facto town historian. I should have been telling you more about Ricky Jones, how his sandblasting business, Desert Sands Stripping over on Lonesome Dove Lane, isn't making him rich but has toughened his skin against sand, how he keeps circling the dump on his four-wheeler, appearing and disappearing in the dust devils, scouting the site to scavenge leftover *E.T.s* again, all these years later, once the cameras are gone. I should have told you more about Ernestine Huckleby, how she died a quadriplegic with mercury still in her brain at the age of thirty, over on Brookdale Drive, maybe with that same old teddy bear still in her arms. All of the sudden I fear that I've fucked up, got sucked into the node of the Pit like everything and everyone else and forgot about my own people, that I should jump in the DeLorean with Warshaw and go back and try to fix this story. When I finally get close enough to Warshaw to ask him if he wants to saddle up the DeLorean with me, he says, No thanks. He says, The mistakes make us human.

Eventually the DeepMind AI will play sixty Atari games, learning to outperform humans in more than half of them. But E.T. is not among the Atari games DeepMind's AI will attempt to play. Maybe the glitch of the Pit in Warshaw's E.T. is something DeepMind knows would send their AI into a tailspin, a mistake in the code that makes the game unplayable, too craptastic even for a superhuman superintelligence to conquer. Only a regular dumb human could figure out any use for a game like that, not even bothering to play it but just burying the cartridge and later digging it up, like a dog with a bone toy.

After 4:00 p.m. the winds hit 60 mph. The water truck has quit, and the sky is dense with dirt and refuse. The dark cloud isn't quite a plume of poison rising from hog corpses or the shadows of face-melting specters rising out of the Lost Ark, but it's more than enough to completely obscure the sun. The crew takes shelter. Ricky Jones circles ever closer to the Pit on his four-wheeler. The few die-hard nerds who have stuck around tear down the orange fence and bum-rush the piles of garbage and revel in it. The shit goes to shit. I can't bring myself to join that particular fray. Instead I wander, making a list of things I spot far from the Pit that are not videogames, the old trash of our town about which no stories will be told, stuff the Arch Punks have deemed *nonsensitive cultural material*:

> cassette tape for a Fisher-Price tape recorder
> Care Bear

    I ♥ MY KIDS bumper sticker
    checkbooks
    bottle of charcoal starter
    so many beer cans
    bottle of conditioner (extra body)
    checkered blouse
    empty package of birth-control pills
    so many unmatched socks
    bottle of foot powder
    one baby shoe, so worn

The day after the dig the Arch Punks spend hours cataloging more than 1,300 videogames recovered from the 750,000 estimated to be in the landfill.* After meticulously laying out and studying and photographing the games, they're told to sweep them all into garbage bags, still wet and now exposed to air and likely to rot, until city officials decide what to do with them. Joe Lewandowski will eventually package them individually with a homemade certificate of

---

* Everyone agrees the dig barely scratched the surface of the graveyard. Thousands upon thousands of videogames are still down there. The EPA, which I contacted about the possible absurdity of digging up just a little bit of industrial waste as a marketing gimmick, tells me the obvious: they recommend that videogame manufacturers explore reuse and recycling options before sending large deposits of game cartridges to landfills. Presumably this recommendation extends to game companies excavating large deposits of cartridges in landfills. But in Alamogordo there was never any talk of Microsoft paying to dig up (or recycle) any more cartridges than necessary to confirm Atari's improper dumping had occurred. Fixing others' mistakes is often less lucrative than exploiting them.

authenticity and sell them on eBay, netting the town just over $100,000 for the resurrected *E.T.s*.*

When we meet the next morning for breakfast at the Waffle Shoppe just east of the landfill, the Arch Punks tell me that important artifacts should not be stored in garbage bags, should not be auctioned off on eBay, should not be wrested from the custody of the archaeologists so quickly and mysteriously. Caraher compares it to the final scene of *Raiders of the Lost Ark*, when Indy expresses his concern about the fate of the Lost Ark, which he has gone through hell to recover, and a government official replies, *We have top men working on it right now.*

Indy asks, *Who?*

Top. Men, says The Man.

But the Punks are mostly cheery this morning because the dig has gone viral, with variations on "Found: E.T. Graveyard" in headlines and Twitter feeds around the world. They debate the extent to which their scholarly work was helped or hindered by the film crew. *Symbiosis*, Reinhard says. *Mutual parasitism*, Rothaus says. Caraher leans close to me and says, *I think the real deal is we were able to work around them.*

They express frustration at not getting all of the coordinates of the exploratory auger holes that were drilled in the

---

* The money Lewandowski raises from eBay sales will go to the Tularosa Basin Historical Society (TBHS). They'll use it to build a museum on White Sands Boulevard, down the road from the Pit. But the *E.T.s* will only be one exhibit in the TBHS museum. Most of the exhibits will tell the stories of this town and this land from way back, all the stuff ignored at the Pit. And in that way Lewandowski will have, in some small measure, managed to break the curse, to defeat the node of the Pit.

days leading up to the dig. They also mention that the day before the public arrived, the augers actually pulled up a load of Atari cartridges as the Arch Punks looked on. The reactions of the filmmakers suggested they wished the Punks hadn't witnessed that real moment of discovery.

It was pretty tense right up until we found the cartridges, one of the documentary's producers later tells *The New Yorker,* failing to mention they'd actually found them the day before. But Lewandowski and Ricky Jones had known the games were there. And the producers had presumably confirmed the burial with James Heller, a former Atari employee the crew paraded around the Pit after the games were unearthed. In 1983 Heller was responsible for disposing of the returned and unsold Atari merchandise. He's the one who sent the games to Alamogordo. *There is no mystery whatsoever,* Heller said. *People made it a mystery.*

As we shovel eggs into our mouths, Caraher gets worked up. At first he's just on his high horse about trailblazing a punk methodology for archaeology that accounts for how late capitalism is irrevocably shaping our landscape, and about how our precapitalist, preglobal, preindustrial contexts for archaeology cannot succeed in this new landscape—a high-minded monologue the old Waffle Shoppe doesn't get too often. *We saw in the landfill,* Caraher says, *a transition from the domestic world, your domestic world, to shit that had been injected by the industrial world. By a corporation named Atari. Traditional archaeology might suggest that Alamogordo manufactured Atari games or maybe just really loved them. Worshipped them. That's wrong. The truth is something else totally, that old archaeology alone could never explain.*

He pauses to take a phone call, then asks for help deleting a tweet. The documentary crew is pissed that he posted a photo of the Punks cataloging unearthed games. Caraher says he doesn't care about the takedown request. But censoring information of any kind for any reason clearly violates the punk ethos and fuels another rant from Caraher that is far too long to fully recount here but was forceful enough to prompt Reinhard to shush him and entertaining enough to prompt Rothaus to get out his phone and film it and profane enough to get Weber to nod apologies at the other patrons. The gist of Caraher's big Waffle Shoppe diatribe is that what has occurred in the dump is standard practice in the developing world. It's scavenging. But in Alamogordo it wasn't done for survival and was therefore unbelievably vain. The size and power of the online nerd community and the entertainment industry have enabled the film crew and the Arch Punks to be celebrated for doing this debased thing that our culture would otherwise condemn them for. The sheer speed at which this industrial waste has become celebrated as artifact, he says, as the unauthorized tweet disappears, is evidence that the world has come completely fucking unhinged.

It's a glitch, I think. Maybe we've fucked it up. But then maybe that's the only thing that will keep the robot overlords from learning to play our game better than us. Somewhere there's a sweet spot in which our civilization is ruined enough to always remain our own but not so ruined that we can't still find some joy in it. Maybe *sweet spot* is the wrong term. Maybe I'm talking about the *absurd*. Maybe I mean *the Pit*.

Soon Joe Lewandowski will announce that a few hundred of the Atari cartridges recovered from the landfill have been set aside for museums, including an *E.T.* that will be displayed among our greatest national treasures at the Smithsonian Institution. Hundreds of thousands of pilgrims will head there every year to take a gander at *E.T.*, the cartridge covered in Alamogordo grime, sitting in its bulletproof, climate-controlled case, glowing under soft museum-grade lights, the kind that perfectly illuminate every angle and cast no shadows at all.

KEEP ALAMOGORDO BEAUTIFUL

In the Year of Our Lord 2013

My great novel about the sad future is not going so well. I am stuck at the apocalypse. I don't know what happens next.

———

Grandmommy hobbles around using a broken shovel for a walking stick, wearing one pink house slipper and one floral-patterned house slipper, both dull and tattered and fastened to her feet with a bunch of rubber bands. The skin of her hands and arms and legs is translucent or her blood is darker than ever before, all visible in her veins and capillaries, not rushing anywhere anymore but just sort of tepid, dark and sluggish like the puddles of our Rio Grande. The rubber bands have stopped what little circulation gravity was forcing into her feet. Blood pools above the bands, above the mismatched slippers, dark rings like she's ankle-deep in our dying river. Grandmommy is ninety or more and pretty well blind and forgets whether she's wearing slippers. A few weeks back she got lucid and banded them on for good, to outsmart the forgetting, to keep from cutting her feet to hell on all the cockleburs when she's out preaching to the turtles. She's got fifty or a hundred of them, nobody knows for sure anymore, mostly box turtles and ornates and a few red-eared sliders, collected over half a century of walking with Granddaddy through the desert of Alamogordo. But Granddaddy's dead now so she just hobbles around the yard with a broken shovel, orchestrating her fellowship of turtles.

Grandmommy says science fiction is hogwash, says it to me and the turtles, says I shouldn't waste time on a great novel about the sad future. *Write the complete history of our Christian family,* she says. She doesn't laugh when I ask if I should start all the way back at the dusk of our apehood. She says start with Alamogordo. Start with how her granddaddy convinced her grandmommy to move to Alamogordo by saying there was not so much whiskey, not so many whores, not so much killing as the newspapers made it seem. How even before that her granddaddy's daddy was at the very birth of the town skinning jackrabbits with his bare hands. How her own daddy built the White Sands Ranch and lost the White Sands Ranch to a nuclear bomb and its progeny of Cold War missiles. How she pulled the strings for every election in the county for the last four decades. How our blood has been the blood of Alamogordo for as long as Alamogordo has existed. I keep telling her I'll get around to it someday. When we circle back to the same story about her daddy and the drunk undertaker for the third time, I get up to leave. She tries to give me money. *A little something,* she says, *so you'll write me a decent eulogy. Just like what you did for your granddaddy.* I don't want her money. I'd only waste it at the bar, trying to drink myself into the future. *But I think you might live forever*, I say, because I love her and because she's resilient as hell and because her friends the box turtles routinely live beyond a century and because I do not want to do another eulogy. I didn't get the last one right at all. She touches my face and swears she's ready to die. She tells me again how much she misses Granddaddy. She can't see it anymore but leaning against the far wall of the yard is a thirty-foot-tall VHF antenna that she's accused me, in less lucid moments, of using to kill Granddaddy. To keep from stirring her up, I take the money. I kiss her head. I bend down and readjust one of her rubber bands before heading out. She rattles a spoon in a can of dog food and the turtles hustle at a breakneck crawl. They claw over one another and stretch their snappers out of their shells, scaly necks all straining just as skyward as they can go, clamoring around and gaping as she slings the Alpo. The moist protein stuff slops onto the ground by her slippers and slops onto nearby cacti and slops onto the horde of dusty shells. Sloppy slop slop goes the whole goddamn world.

———

The three steps for embalming a corpse: sanitation, preservation, presentation. These steps are the same for a eulogy: scrub the life of its sinful parts, write down the decent stuff that's left, say it without falling apart. But it all feels a bit unnatural, doesn't it? The corpse in the casket is clearly dead but looking worse than that, all waxy with formaldehyde and like it never lived at all. Then somebody stands over the corpse giving a speech that's all waxy too. In my great novel about the sad future the bodies will not be embalmed. They will lie in the desert, bubbling and rotting, and each corpse will blossom with a whole new kind of life, the slow waltz of decay—a kind of hope that's lost with sanitation and preservation and presentation. If there's ever a eulogy in my great novel about the sad future, it must live in this way: with more than a few swear words and some of it made up right there on the spot and most of it, especially toward the end, barely comprehensible in the way a body is totally unrecognizable after a few days in the sun. I guess it's not that you shouldn't say nice things when somebody dies, just that pumping a body so full of formaldehyde inhibits the circle of life. Such meticulous preservation is at odds with carrying on. Granddaddy used to tell me that *carrying on with booze will pickle you from the inside.* That's not exactly science but I always laughed because *pickle* is a funny word and because just think of a tiny green man floating inside a jar of vinegar and surely it makes sense that preservation would have some sour side effects. In my great novel about the sad future all attempts to overcome time will be slapstick. The bodies will not be embalmed and they will all end up sour with beautiful decay.

———

Joe is up against the wall and grinning and getting choked by D Rock. Then Joe goes limp and D Rock lets go of his neck and Joe slides down the wall but then he ricochets back up but then he slumps and seizes and finally wilts to fetal. We laugh and laugh and laugh. After half a minute Joe comes back to life with resurrection stupor in his eyes but that cloud scatters after a few hard blinks and he laughs too. Then B Rizzle gets choked by Joe and D Rock gets choked by me and I get choked by B Rizzle. Ten deep breaths and my back against the wall and my eyes bulging as B Rizzle's hands push hard on either side of my throat until my blood-parched brain shorts out and I go limp and travel through time to do all the different stupid things I'll do in my life and then I'm gasping to consciousness on the floor of my bedroom and all the boys are laughing. Momma is at the hospital, getting her broken blood fixed again. We're twelve, maybe, unsupervised and learning to get fucked-up. Choking each other out. The high of going to and coming back from nothingness. Resurrection stupor. Also the whir of the VHS camcorder, hulking and purring on B Rizzle's shoulder. We stole the camera but this is the only thing we can think to record. There's no internet in our lives yet, no knee-jerk social media, so these recordings are more like prayers than boasts and that's why we'll never watch them. We'll never know what happened to them. They're gone. But I don't need to watch them because these days I can just drink and get fucked-up and time travel to any point in my life when I'm doing something stupid and that pretty much covers all of it up until now.

———

Granddaddy will be dead in one week and I swear to god on that day a thousand dead blackbirds will fall from the sky. But today he's got me on the roof, cranking at rusty bolts that have secured guy-wires to the house for thirty years. The guy-wires hold steady an antenna that towers over the house, rises into the sky forty or fifty feet, stretching to pick up signals from the mountain, the broadcast towers rising out of the Sleeping Lady. He installed the antenna when his knees still worked, became the first person in town who could watch both the Albuquerque and the El Paso news. But now his knees don't always work so good and now Obama is president and now Obama has made Granddaddy's prized antenna obsolete by making all of television digital. *It's a tiny box*, Granddaddy says. *I don't know how Obama gets all that television into it.* Each time I loosen one of the bolts, a cable slacks and the antenna teeters this way or that way in the wind, threatening to crash down like a bunch of rusty knives. There's also lightning, which Granddaddy keeps yelling about from the ground, telling me, *Heed the angry skies, sonny boy!* And I yell back, *Fine! I'll leave it for now.* And he says, *I'm just joshing ya, sonny boy. My knees are good today. Let's get that sucker down.* But I'm the only one on the roof. Grandmommy sticks her head out the door, says, *Granddaddy, you come inside. You'll catch cold.* But he wants to watch. *Joshua, you make your Granddaddy come inside*, she says. But he wants to watch out for me and he wants to witness the times changing. He hollers from the ground as the thunderstorm crescendos, hollers about what a hassle it was to get that antenna up back in the day and how ahead of the times he used to be and how isn't that just the way things go, the future looks so silly when it's in the past.

———

Before they strap Momma into the recliner she parades me around, beaming as she introduces her only son to nurses and other patients and maintenance men I've never met who ask me specifically about intimate aspects of my life. Over the years she's managed to tell them pretty much everything. They all ask about my novel. I am stuck at the apocalypse. We're in the outpatient ward, which shows just how far they've come in fixing people with broken blood. She's in here once a month but this is the first time I've visited in many years. When I was a kid, she had to get admitted, had to lie in a bed for days hooked up to lots of tubes and the nurses paid attention. Now she sits in a fancy recliner for just three hours with just one tube in her arm. The nurse sets her up with a magazine and a Dr Pepper and leaves me alone with Momma. I don't fully understand what's wrong with her. I don't understand the illness. I can write the word *agammaglobulinemia* but to me it just means bad blood. Her blood doesn't make some important thing that fights disease and so they pump her full of that important thing and it makes her sick until it makes her well and then she does it again every month, in bed for a week and then she's Magic Momma again for a week or two and then back to the hoses again. When they test my blood, they say I'm lucky because everything is there and this illness tends to be hereditary. My sisters will not be so lucky and for that I'll always feel guilty. But at least they didn't get the drinking gene. A bag of plasma hangs above the recliner and feeds into Momma's arm, which is perpetually bruised from the needle poking around for good veins, from the tourniquet trying to make them show up. The plasma doesn't drip through the IV like I thought it would. It feeds and even the nurse says *feeds* and the plasma is not coming in drops but in gushes as if her body were slurping it up and this is what I feel too. Maybe my blood has all the things that fight disease but it has this thirst—in our blood I feel from many generations back an unquenchable thirst rising up and coming in waves to slurp at whatever is near. Momma's blood slurps what it needs. She asks how the writing is coming along and I say, *I'm working through a eulogy.*

———

Grandmommy just turned nineteen. She's not Grandmommy yet. She's Maude. Maude has left Alamogordo for Los Angeles this June 1942, the first woman in her family to attend college. She walks into a bar near the USC campus and orders a whiskey. She looks around but doesn't see me because I'm dim still, because I won't be born for forty-two years and won't follow in her footsteps from Alamogordo to Los Angeles for sixty years and won't sit at this bar for another two years after that. She sips her whiskey. *Just that one sip*, she'll tell me later. Her first-ever taste of booze and it makes her feel so good, so warm and damn near euphoric, that she panics. She feels how time can get wobbly and it makes her shake so she drops the glass and runs out of the bar. Maude will finish college but then she'll return to Alamogordo straightaway and she will never leave again. She will teach music and get five decades of Alamogordo kids singing and playing the state song at every one of the town's celebrations, but she will never take another drink of whiskey again for as long as she lives.

———

Out in the middle of the cold lake I'm totally naked and sinking from the summer midnight above to the muffled moon murk below and bobbing up again and sinking and trying to find a balance between the two kinds of darkness because I'm full of panic from being fucked-up, from walking naked into the lake at midnight because I got the notion it could slow down all this staggering through time. On the shore are

KK Holiday and D Rock and B Rizzle and a dozen others, all of us a few years out of high school, a bonfire of pallets from the marina dump, a bunch of hotboxed tents, Camel-Baks full of vodka feeding straight down our throats, mushrooms and blotters and all the dope we can burn, psychonauts on a weeklong mission at the only hole passing for a lake in SNM, sacrificing all decorum in hopes of appeasing or scaring off the gods of growing up, the gods of getting old, the gods of passing time. New Mexico built this dam and dug this reservoir to harness the power of the Rio Grande—to make the future better. But the Rio Grande is dying. The water keeps dropping and you can see, one by one, year by year, the graves appear of the men who died building something they thought was the future. In five months our governor will close out 2005 by shaking hands with a British billionaire, by coming to an agreement that the future has changed, that they need to build a spaceport right over there on the other side of our lake, not a place for NASA astronauts to embark on missions but a place for average joes and janes to take a little trip, a cosmic vacation to put our redneck lake parties to shame. The moon goes grainy, the sky ridden with the static of Mexican free-tailed bats swarming by the thousands. Out in the water the stars get reflected off the surface and they ripple and twinkle and I see that everywhere in the universe is just as wobbly as here.

———

My god, those rubber bands: how Grandmommy has landed on rubber bands as an integral part of not just her footwear but also her lifestyle, like she's spent all this time collecting rubber bands and in these late years needs to employ the whole collection. All manner of documents are rubber-banded together and books are rubber-banded together and notes are rubber-banded to her telephone and bottles of pills rubber-banded together and a cushion is rubber-banded to a chair. If things can just have other things to cling to, if they can belong together: that solace: magic, even: a strategy to outsmart the forgetting: a kind of time machine—a way to remember to wear her slippers and a way to always go back to that moment when she remembered to wear her slippers so that she never forgets to wear her slippers. In the hands of a bully or serpentine around the pulleys of a motor the rubber band is all about propulsion—will conquer distance. But the simplest use conquers time: remember in the future that *this* goes with *this.* Around her little feet they constrict like a tourniquet, tight, and if you don't know any better, you might think it's just that one little line on top of her foot, might never realize it goes all the way around and is cutting things off (blood!) because it looks so innocent: just holding one thing to another like this, just tying one on like this, just the little line of a simple time machine across the top of her foot like this—

———

Before I even pull the pages of the eulogy from my pocket I hit the congregation with a little bit of nervous banter—a joke. We've just concluded a hymn and I step to the pulpit of our warehouse chapel, adjust the microphone, hear the amplified smack of my dry mouth and people shifting in the pews. *I don't know about you,* I say, *but I was singing that hymn just the way Granddaddy has always taught me—real loud and totally out of tune.*

Four out of four How to Write a Eulogy websites recommend not beginning the eulogy with a joke: "Starting a speech with a joke is usually a good way to draw the audience in. When delivering a eulogy, however, this is not appropriate." Well, alright. But the congregation is laughing pretty good and it calms me. Everybody knows Granddaddy was always a top-five loudest singer in the Church of Christ over on Cuba Avenue, him and a couple of bigger ladies with opera dreams. But he was always number one in being out of tune, like he wasn't even trying, and sometimes it was so terrible that I'd stare at him—quit singing myself and inspect him— convinced he was engaged in sabotage. But nothing untoward was ever in his big goofy grin even when it was unhinged and letting loose the hymn of a thousand dying dogs. I didn't write the joke into the eulogy—it came to me as I stepped up to the pulpit, not as a simple memory but as an accumulation of truths that did not feel like they were in the past—so that instead of saying something like *He* was *always a terrible singer,* I wanted to say something like *He has always been a terrible singer*—a full-on time trip back to the pew near the front of the church where Granddaddy sat, sits not once but always and every time he is howling "Oh, Why Not Tonight?" when I am still damp from the baptismal and howling "As the Deer" while my sister is in the hospital and howling "Heaven Came Down" as they pray for grace about my first arrest and howling "Blue Skies and Rainbows" when my niece is born shortly after my second arrest and on and on. The ongoing flow of the past hits me as I stand at the pulpit, a barrage so disorienting that I knew I'd taken too many of the pills and needed to make a joke about the howling to calm myself before starting in on the eulogy, a speech I'd finished writing only a few hours ago, finished only after starting to take the pills because the question of which verb tense to use in the eulogy was making me shake and weep. What I said to begin the eulogy was *I was singing that hymn just the way Granddaddy has always taught me*. And all the rest of it is a linguistic lie like that, situating particular moments in the past but never suggesting that he now only exists in the past, leaving open the possibility that he may soon push through the doors of our warehouse chapel belting out the hymn of a thousand dying dogs even though everyone can see he is lying right there at the foot of the pulpit, all waxy and stiff.

———

In my great novel about the sad future our hero has always been finding shovels and digging at the foot of the biggest piles of crumbled headstone. The big headstone has always been on top of the rich people. The rich people have always been with their fancy watches. Our hero has always been stabbing into the gravelly sand and tossing it every which way. Then he has always been suddenly hitting something hard and feeling the clink in his teeth, always bending down and finding another headstone that has always been small and unbroken. In my great novel about the sad future it has always been bodies on top of bodies. Our hero has always been wiping his face all over with his sweaty shirt as he has always been digging. The smaller headstone has always been inscribed with only BABY and that has always been both lazy and touching. He has always been hitting the baby's coffin first and has always been throwing it aside because babies have always never had time to amass riches. Chest deep is always how deep he has always been when he has always been finding the bigger coffin. The bigger coffin has always been a riot of bone dust when our hero has always been opening it. Our hero has always been reaching elbow deep into the dust and has always been yanking out a silver watch with a silver band studded with turquoise. Look at that beautiful watch. His spit has always been landing on the watch to polish off the bone dust. He has always been slipping the watch on his wrist and clasping the band. It has always been a perfect fit. He has always been listening for it to tick. The dial has always been stuck and he has always been fiddling with the dial and knocking his wrist on the shovel. Finally, it has always been ticking, just like you knew it would.

———

My uncle staggers out into the yard and says, *I swear to God, one time a ghost walked right through me. Through skin and blood and bones and then just kept walking. Or floating or whatever the fuck. A ghost, I swear to God.* My uncle covers his mouth when he says *fuck* because even though he's nearly fifty, he thinks Grandmommy doesn't know he cusses, thinks she doesn't know he moved home to care for her because he had no other housing options, thinks she doesn't know his forty-four-ounce Big Gulp is full of vodka at nine in the morning. My uncle is a time traveler too. But it's making him sick. He gets the shakes. If anybody knows the complete history of our Christian family, nobody's saying it out loud. But there's Grandmommy with her turtles and the eulogy bribe waiting for me. She's got a new obsession. When she's dead, she wants me to finally set the record straight about "O Fair New Mexico," our state's official song.

Over the last year she's become more adamant that her grandmommy wrote our state song, that the composer was not, as the history books say, the blind daughter of Pat Garrett, the sheriff who famously killed Billy the Kid. But Grandmommy's assertion is likely wrong. The timelines don't jibe. Elizabeth Garrett was a world-class musician who needed no help from a small-town music teacher. My uncle drinks his Big Gulp and tells Grandmommy this exact thing but he's real belligerent about it because she doesn't remember ever hearing this from him before but he's told her every day for the last year that her grandmommy did not have our state song stolen from her by a little blind girl. They go back and forth. The scene is odd and stings: an old woman with dementia and her pickled-brained son arguing about the history of the composition of our goddamn state song. They go in circles, repeating themselves in the same stubborn way but on account of different diseases. "Under a sky of azure," sings the song, "where balmy breezes blow, kissed by the golden sunshine, is Nuevo México!" Grandmommy knows she's close to the end and she's scared her family's legacy will be lost because she can smell it souring on her son's breath and hear it in his slurred voice and in the slam of the door when his Big Gulp is finally empty. She gives me the twenty bucks, this time rubber-banded to the sheet music of our state song. "Home of the Montezuma, with fiery hearts aglow, state of the deeds historic, is Nuevo México!" Grandmommy says, *At least write it in your book. Write the real truth.* I open a can of Alpo for her. The turtles crane and flick their sharp tongues and break into an ancient chorus of hisses.

Summer in Alamogordo and we're shoveling boiling asphalt out of the dump truck, smoothing and tamping it into a road. The stuff is viscous and splatters so we've got our jeans rubber-banded down around our boots and our long sleeves rubber-banded inside our gloves to keep our skin from accidently getting tarred. The big boss of the construction company pushes us to get all the asphalt down in the morning cool, but our timing was off today and it's 120 degrees from the sun and another 200 degrees rising from the boiling asphalt. We're replacing the town's water mains and we get to talking about how the water is haunted. A lot of the guys on the crew don't know the story but they call me college boy and they say, *Tell the ghost story, college boy.*

Way back at the turn of the century, when the town was first founded, the driver of the water wagon would fill up his barrels at the ditches they used before water mains. He'd drive his team of sorrel mules through the streets, wetting the dust of the streets and providing for the barefoot children running along behind him the magic of a moving water park, them laughing and jumping and wrestling in the sprinkle that shot from his punctured barrels. Jim Green was his name and people said he had a nagging wife or a drinking problem or both, and one day after sprinkling the dust of the town's streets and the dust of the town's children, he stabled his mules and wagon and unloaded his barrels and walked to the edge of the town's water ditch and pulled out his straight razor and held his straight razor for a long moment in his hands, watching the water run through town. Then he cut his throat from ear to ear and the blood ran down his neck and soaked his shirt and pooled around his waist until it found a path down his leg and then it trickled farther, off the back of his boots as he slumped there on the ditch's bank, drop by drop of blood into the town's water, except for the blood that no doubt shot from his neck, but there were no children to play in that spray. For a hundred years now you have to drink the water slow or you will go insane and slit your throat over the drain because ever since Mr. Green, the town's water is thirsty for blood. So here we are digging up the roads because the water mains went to shit, the clay pipes all corroded and falling apart, putting in new pipes and new roads trying to keep the ghosts contained. The crew lean on their shovels and adjust their rubber bands and say they've never known nagging so hard you want to slit your own throat; therefore it must have been a hangover.

In a lot of places we've dug, hardly any pipe at all was left, just roots that pushed in through joints, roots holding the shape of the pipe, a tunnel of mud running to our faucets. The new pipes are bright green, hundred-foot sections of PVC plastic that will last a thousand years. The plastic won't ever disintegrate. This pipe is strong but has weak spots where it connects. The weak spot is always the connection. Me and Johnny Gwenn leave the asphalt crew in the afternoon and push ahead to seal up joints. But first we stop off at his truck and smoke a spliff. *Tradition*, he says, *when you're joining the joint crew.* We get high and I spend the afternoon gripping my shovel trying not to float away or die. After a backhoe attacks me I'm out cold in the ditch until Johnny Gwenn holds a little of that strong glue under my nose. This is good old-fashioned government work. As I come to, I think about the miles and miles of pipe we laid, the arteries and veins of this town, thirsty for blood. I think about Mr. Green. I think about the joint crew. I'll walk the new asphalt streets of Alamogordo and I'll think about all the roots in this town, all the leaks our veins must have sprung already, all the roots finding cracks in the places where the joint crew was too faded to make things fit together the way they should, all the ghosts seeping out.

———

On the day he dies, the newspaper reports, "A Thousand Dead Birds Fall from the Sky." The ornithologist suspects lightning. If only we'd left that antenna alone, Granddaddy could have stayed out of the cold and that giant metal mess could have stayed way up there attracting public television and all the sky's nastiest bolts. And a thousand blackbirds would still be alive. But we brought it down because it was useless and an eyesore and now I agree to read a scripture at the funeral and now I agree to say a few words for the family and now I agree to do the whole eulogy because Momma says there is no one else. The cousins are all in town so we do some drinking the night before the funeral. I wake up early to write the eulogy, hungover like Granddaddy when he crashed that F4U Corsair on the deck of an aircraft carrier in the Pacific and didn't even scorch the sheepskin collar of his flight jacket. I take the hangover out of his story as I write it into the eulogy and leave only the part about how he prayed in the moment before the crash. Sanitize. Preserve. I take the first of the Vicodin prescribed to Granddaddy because he won't need it anymore and because I need to steady myself. I am worried about the verb tense. When, at the end of the eulogy, I tell the story of our last moments together in the garage, I feel alright about having taken more of the pills because I tell the part about Granddaddy mistakenly calling the garage a hangar because the numbness of the pills keeps the tears from falling out of my eyes because even though the congregation doesn't know it, I'm outing Granddaddy as a time traveler too. At the end of the funeral my uncle roots around in the coffin to make sure they don't bury Granddaddy wearing the wristwatch, and my uncle gets the watch and calls it his inheritance, the silver one with the silver band studded with turquoise, the one that never stops ticking.

———

Easter, and all the kids are hunting for eggs. We're having a good Christian time except some of the uncles have snuck in their flasks. They get excited about the hunt. They keep hiding the eggs again after we find them, or not hiding them but just putting them in dangerous places and laughing as we climb. Everybody's having a good time. One uncle does a magic trick where he pulls an egg out of somebody's ear. Another uncle pulls a whole bunch of napkins out of his sleeves. They tell a bunch of stories. They tell the one about their granddaddy and the drunk undertaker ten different times. The drunk undertaker is a centerpiece of family lore but nobody knows why. I listen close to all their stories trying to figure out what life is all about, and the gist of it seems to be that Great-Great-Granddaddy's whiskey begat Great-Granddaddy's whiskey begat Grandmommy's aversion to whiskey begat all these drunk uncles and me.

———

In one week Granddaddy will die from pneumonia. Grand-mommy will tell everyone he got pneumonia because I kept him out in the yard, in the cold, all day, playing around with his antenna. Everyone will tell me she doesn't mean anything by it—she's just grieving. I work fast and get the antenna down as a December mist gathers into a thunderstorm. Granddaddy and I drag the antenna to the far side of the yard and lean it on the wall where it will stay for years, a futile jungle gym for turtles. We take shelter in the garage. We were out dismantling the antenna for maybe thirty minutes but we stay in the drafty garage with the door open, watching the rain come and go, for hours. He wants to give me cash for helping him with the antenna. He wants to give away his money before he dies. I say, *Keep the money. Live forever.* He says, *Take the money, I'm on my way out, sonny boy. But you better know I won't die before my wife.* He has always been faithful to her, all sixty years, but he believes she will die before him. *I pray to live longer than her,* he says, and it sounds callous but this is the way love goes. The old man needs to make sure his wife makes it out before he follows after.

I hope you can find a little wife like that, a woman to love like that, he says. My hair is long and dirty and my face is never shaven and he suspects that I might not always do the right thing, the Christian thing. He starts up with war stories, tales of flying F4U Corsairs in our Second World War. One day he comes in for a landing on the aircraft carrier and the old boy on deck is telling him, *Too slow! Too slow!* At the last minute the old boy waves him off—*Abort! Abort!*—but Granddaddy wants to land, wants out of the air and the sky and needs the ground so bad that he goes for it anyway and hits the deck and the plane busts in two and bursts into flames—breaks in half right behind the cockpit. Just six inches from his seat. He climbs out and the sheepskin on the collar of his flight jacket isn't even scorched. He says, *I was a bit hungover and that was my fault. But the Lord was looking out for me. I let go of the flight stick and prayed and the Lord was looking out for me. And I have to ask myself why. And I guess it's to live longer than your grandmommy.*

He is always on the verge of tears when telling war stories. He is always choked up and pulling at his neck, trying to keep the tears from spewing—pinching the loose skin of his neck near his Adam's apple like he's a wizard using his long beard for deep contemplation but he has no beard— he's just pinching his neck and pulling. He does this right now, the pulling, to stave off the spewing, and now he is telling another story about another plane exploding. This one is sitting on the deck of the carrier and a Japanese fighter plane comes round and lights it up and lights up all the boxes of .50-caliber ammo waiting to be loaded onto the Corsairs and the bullets all rise up in a fiery rush to everywhere. He doesn't know what to do, doesn't know the protocol for when your air is nothing but buzzing cones of your own damn American steel. Somewhere there's a foam gun the firemen use and he has a notion to soften things with it but the pilots haven't been trained on the foam. He pulls the damn trigger and kicks the thing and .50-caliber rounds are whizzing by and only this sorry little drip of foam comes out of the cannon. He grins. A little tear squeezes out of the corner of his big blue eye because he's pulling at his neck so hard that he's squinting too, but the tear gets stuck in the bag of wrinkles under his eye and a tear is only a tear when it has the dropping shape. So he's not crying yet and anyway the cold draft in the garage whisks the thing away. He gives up on the foam and wanders around as the whole ship catches fire. A lieutenant comes walking at him from the hangar belowdecks, saying something, flinching. His mouth keeps moving and he keeps walking and Granddaddy is trying so hard to hear the orders that it's a whole lifetime before he notices the lieutenant has a .50-caliber hole right between the eyes. Takes the hit. Keeps walking and jawing. But with a bullet in his brain. Granddaddy laughs, chuckles as if the man walking around with a bullet between the eyes is the punch line to a cosmic joke. Finally they call for all hands on deck and the lieutenant sits down, leans on the bulkhead, and closes his eyes. Granddaddy snaps out of his daze and joins a group of pilots heaving five-hundred-pound bombs off the ship. Everything is fire and they don't want to be blowing up more than they already are so all the pilots unload their bombs and heave them into the Pacific Ocean.

A little wife, he says. *You need a little wife you can love all your life.* He says he saw Grandmommy walking down by the old Hotel Alamogordo on New York Avenue when he was just back from our Second World War and knew right then that he would marry her. He says her daddy, GB, my great-granddaddy, never liked him at first. He says, *Old GB was a rounder and GB thought I was a rounder and he didn't want anyone anything like himself around his daughter at all.* Granddaddy pulls at his neck. They're throwing the bombs overboard, live bombs, and then they start pushing whole airplanes off the deck because the fire is growing and the whole carrier is close to capsizing and this is desperation. Granddaddy's lost his sheepskin flight jacket somewhere. He ripped it off on account of the hotness of the fire and the hotness of the heaving and when one of the bombs slips and rolls toward the bulkhead where the lieutenant is resting his eyes including the hole between them, where the hangar is licked over with the flames, all Granddaddy knows is that his sheepskin jacket will be scorched this time for sure. He pulls at his neck. He keeps using the word *rounder*. Says I need to exercise every day, go for a long jog and stop being a rounder. Says I don't have to say anything because he can tell, he used to be a rounder too. Says *rounder* a whole bunch of times. He pushes himself off the garage wall he's been leaning on and stands hunched waiting to see if his knees will work. He shoves the cash into my chest, says, *You go. I'll close the hangar door behind you.* And I walk out through the garage that is no longer a garage and will never be a garage again because now it is licked over with flames.

———

Grandmommy holds the money for a long time. Keeps it in her lap as she shells pecans. She grinds her teeth and touches the money in her lap once in a while to make sure it's there and says, *When I die, I need you to do my eulogy.* I wait for her to start up about the state song but she doesn't. She's got a new habit of shelling pecans that keeps her mind from getting stuck too much, an entirely tactile task that suits her new blindness. She stays busy with it for many hours at a time. I munch the pecans slowly, careful to pick out the shells she misses. *I've already written my obituary,* she says. *You can copy some of it if you want.* She wipes the nut dust from her hands and passes me the twenty bucks rubber-banded inside her obituary. *You remind people how much I loved your granddaddy. Remind people how hard I worked to keep Alamogordo beautiful.* She'll hold on to life for years and will still be living and shelling pecans even as you read this and every few months she'll give me another eulogy bribe. Maybe you think her mind has gonegonegone and that she has no idea she's already paid the bribe so much, but I think she's just sweetening the pot year after decaying year because the one thing she knows for sure is that she wants the decay edited out.

———

I run along the Rio Grande. I run down by Mesilla, where the river is mostly forgotten even by water though there is a sense of oasis still, enchantment lingering, the last gasps, spatterings of creosote and wolfberry and yuccas with their haunches of bayonets and still the spirit of Billy the Kid killing and fleeing through mesquite, still Coronado lost in the dust and broke on dreams of gold, still Apaches brandishing scalps like the Spanish taught them but with the ears still attached and hollering at the heavens, still the long-faced dinosaur lumbering and my Nikes landing in the fossils of its awkward tracks as the roadrunners dart across my path into the seepwillow to ponder the absurdity of their wings as I sweat out twenty bucks of whiskey, cough tar, grit my teeth, and churn out six miles, seven miles, in the summer burn beside the big mud snake, through onion fields gone to seed and the stink of their blossom orbs rising like a universe from the dust, blindly through acres of chili tweaked in its genes to stay green but burn harder, acres of capsaicin heat rising, colliding with sun rays at the height of my eyes, nose, lips, the singe in my face, and still I run for miles along the Rio Grande because something primal is in me, this movement, shoulders rocking independently of the head, ligaments in the feet like springs, left foot, right foot, the emergence of skin from fur and the evolution of sweat glands like an infinite cool breeze so I can move across the world eating and growing my beast-fed brain big enough to be conscious of teetering at evolution's apex, and then my left Nike lands askew in one of the awkward tracks and a small stone catches in the deep flex groove along the outsole of my ergonomic running shoe and my ankle twists inside the sock liner and were it not for asymmetrical lacing reducing pressure over my foot's top ridge, I might stumble all the way, crash, knock my head silly and have my eyes pecked to caves by flight-shy birds, but these shoes are made of science, made to re-create the feel of barefoot running as it was in the dusk of our ape-hood with the bonus of neoprene cushion and impact absorption so I can heel strike when my ancestors would only lean forward, striking always on the balls of their bare feet, the natural cushion, more on their toes and leaning into the hunger that kept them chasing prey six miles, seven miles along the big mud snake, but these featherlight foot-conforming canvas-mesh shoes have set us back on our heels, the unnatural posture of the modern runner: I am not hungry. I am enacting hunger poorly or I am terrified of the hunger. I run past the horse apple tree and the acrid smell of dropped fruit rotting in the heat and a snake with its guts exploded out of both ends and the middle of him flattened in an awkward track but there are no long-faced dinosaurs anymore. Whose tracks are these? In the distance, spanning the dying river, is an overpass and semitrucks roaring across. On the banks of the dying river, in the flickering shadows of the passing semis, is an army of tractors, their mounds of dirt and the bright yellow and slick oil of heavy construction. Here come the bulldozers and all the ground in their wake is pressed into awkward tracks from the symmetrical grooves of their steel traction belts. Here comes the future. They're building a road to the spaceport.

—

The 1922 Model T carved-panel hearse rattles along the un-paved roads of Alamogordo. The drunk undertaker is at the wheel and my great-granddaddy sits shotgun, and I'm not anywhere near alive but I'm along for the ride. Somebody has died. There's been a big funeral and we're easing toward the burial. Out the back of the hearse, over the coffin, I see the whole funeral procession snaking along. There's D Rock and B Rizzle wearing CamelBaks and Johnny Gwenn with a spliff. There's Momma in her hospital recliner and all the uncles doing their magic tricks. There's Granddaddy drag-ging his antenna and Grandmommy with her whole fellowship of turtles in tow. Somewhere, way in the back, maybe there's a little wife for me. The procession circles the young town's sparse cemetery once and stops. The drunk undertaker leans out the window of the hearse and shields his eyes from the sun and looks around. The procession circles the cemetery again, then weaves in and out of the rows of headstones and circles more. Round and round and round. By now the mourn-ers are breaking rank, scratching their heads. The drunk undertaker takes a drink and passes the bottle to Great-Granddaddy. And me. *Well, shit,* says the undertaker. *Nobody remembered to dig a damn grave.*

A MILLION TINY DAGGERS

SCENES FROM THE AFTERMATH IN A CITY FORMERLY
KNOWN AS MURDER

•

In the Years of Our Lord 2014–15

June 16, in the Year of Our Lord 2014

The other day a stray mutt trotted through the gate with a severed hand in his teeth. Nobody went looking for the body. *We burned the hand with the trash,* says El Pastor. *No problem.* We're eating breakfast in the big kitchen of his asylum, Visión en Acción, a ragtag cluster of cinder-block buildings just far enough from Juárez to make it feel like the middle of nowhere, fifteen miles west of the city and fifteen miles south of the border, along the lonely road to Ascensión, a stretch of desert where so many of the bodies ended up. *Anywhere is a grave,* he says. *Ah, but not here.*

Some of the residents wander in and out of the kitchen, doing their morning chores. El Pastor points and tells me their origin stories. He loves origin stories. They're the first thing he says anytime he introduces me to a resident of the asylum, a way of communicating the successes of his ministry by relating the sad or horrific past of an individual who now stands on his or her own two feet, cleaning the griddle of eggs or emptying a fifty-pound bag of beans into a cauldron on the stove. This person came in totally mute. This one came in with maniacal cries and a headful of huffed paint. This one came in with his mother's blood on his hands and this one came in with lice and this one came in with his fingers falling off from gangrene. Then he says their names. Shouts them really, not by way of introduction but as an exclamation, announcement of rebirth. *Josué! Memo! Gaspar!*

They're not really patients because there's not a whole lot of treatment because there's not a whole lot of money. El Pastor says, *The only treatment is us crazies.* One hundred twenty of them living in the desert, feeding one another and clothing one another and sometimes bathing one another. A whole wall of toothbrushes hangs above names written on little tags of duct tape. The names sometimes get changed out more than the toothbrushes. Juárez proper has only one public mental health facility, with only thirty beds, and those are mostly for patients totally incapacitated by their illness or its medicines, patients more or less docile. But out in the desert, here at the asylum, residents get the run of the place. *We are addicts helping addicts. Mexicans helping Mexicans,* El Pastor says. *That's all we need.*

I don't even get halfway through a thought about the possibility of love conquering all things when El Pastor says that just yesterday a guy on the street in Juárez gave him the finger. And El Pastor said, *Fuck you, guy*—yelled, *Fuck you, guy!*—because the guy didn't know, didn't have any idea what El Pastor could do to him. He looks at me and says he knows how to handle guys like this. He knows what to do with guys that tell him, *Fuck you.* He puffs up in his chair so I can see how big he is, over six feet and barrel-chested at sixty-three, both priestly and menacing in his customary all-black getup complemented by slick waves of silver hair. He laughs and bares a few missing teeth and takes a bite of eggs. He motions for me to hurry up and finish my food. There is so much he wants me to see. The asylum is a complicated place.

He became El Pastor by trying to kill one. He was back in Mexico after a decade in California prisons, loitering and gulping a bottle of booze, watching a street preacher shout his Jesus shouts. But El Pastor didn't particularly like the Jesus shouts and was lost in a bender so he emptied the bottle down his throat and took it to the preacher's head, beat unmercifully at the preacher's skull to keep him from shouting any more sermons. When the street preacher was on his way out of consciousness and maybe the world, he reached up and wiped his own damn blood from the face of his assailant, took ahold of his assailant's whiskey-soaked head, and prayed for the poor man's soul. In that moment the drunk ex-con known as José Antonio Galván decided not to stab the preacher with the broken bottle and dropped the bottle altogether and felt, for the first time, the presence of his soul, not in his body but sort of rising out of his chest. And around the plaza were all the souls risen out of all the Mexicans' chests and the souls were dragging their bodies around. Galván knew he could find a better way. He gave up all drugs and booze and rage. He became El Pastor and within a few years he'd started building himself an asylum in the desert where others could learn to give up their rage too, help their souls settle down until that time when they will rise up finally for good. He doesn't tell me what became of the street preacher he beat to shit. The point is, Galván was converted. El Pastor was born. He makes sure I know that the point is not that he can mercilessly beat a man but that any man can change. *Old dog,* he says. *But learns tricks. Ah, you see? I learn the needles.* El Pastor points to the man I've come down here with, Ryan Bemis, a young acupuncturist from New Mexico who's been visiting the asylum for the last few months, training El Pastor and some of his residents to treat one another with needles. Needles are cheaper than prescription drugs. In the ears are acupuncture points that anyone can learn. *Brilliant,* Bemis says, *for reducing stress, which makes all illness worse. In that way, it is kind of a cure-all.* El Pastor smiles and laughs and says, *Pew pew, pew pew,* making baby-gun noises as he mimes how he pushes needles into ear after ear. He throws the imaginary needles all over the room like so many tiny spears. *I nail them all. Ah, you see? A million tiny daggers in the heads.*

El Pastor has run the asylum since the late nineties. I first heard about the place in Charles Bowden's book *Murder City.* The cartel wars were at their bloody apex—before 2007 Juárez had not had more than 300 murders in a single year but then had 2,754 murders in 2009 and 3,622 in 2010, and the trend seemed likely to rise until it swallowed the city whole. *Murder City* is Bowden's scramble through the worst of Juárez in 2008. He writes of the asylum as the home of a woman he becomes obsessed with, a beauty queen from Sinaloa who is driven insane after gang rapes by the municipal police, a woman brought to—discarded at—the asylum by those same police when they were done with her. Bowden characterizes El Pastor's place as a kind of beautiful collection of lunatics in the desert, the only truly sane people on the border, an oasis where Mexicans are all but killed by a perfect storm of evil—of cartels and government corruption and U.S. immigration policy and poverty and NAFTA exploitation and general fucking human darkness—could finally take care of one another. *Murder City* gave the impression all of Juárez would drown in blood and rape and drugs and even probably the asylum too but at least El Pastor was making a real go at building an ark to weather the wrath. Then, in 2011, for the first time in years, the Juárez murder rate dropped. By 2012 there were just 803. Even though the rest of Mexico seemed to pick up the slack—nearly 30,000 murders nationwide in 2012 with only 523 of those resulting in a conviction—the American media was impatient to write a feel-good story. "Ciudad Juárez Weighs a Neglected Notion: Hope," said a July 2013 *New York Times* headline. By December the paper was less ambiguous: under the headline "Ciudad Juárez, a Border City Known for Killing, Gets Back to Living," it highlighted the return of bars and restaurants and young people dancing in a club with "fake blood on the walls, as if mocking the violent past, hoping to render it harmless."

A city does not just dance away from 12,000 murders in six years, does not just bounce back from an exodus of nearly half a million citizens fleeing the violence. But like most of us I want to believe that humans, alone or altogether, can just decide to be better humans and then, almost miraculously, it happens without hardly any work at all. Our souls find a better fit. We stop getting dragged along. *Old dog. But learns tricks.* When I heard an acupuncturist had begun visiting the asylum outside Juárez to teach residents to treat themselves, it seemed a good measure for how things were healing. Visión en Acción is a microcosm of all the suffering along the border—families torn apart and brains melted by drugs and bodies cut and shot and raped by cartels and spirits and bones ground down by twelve-hour days at the maquiladoras making all manner of American bullshit—and acupuncture, just a handful of little needles, therapy on the borderlands of science and mysticism, seems a Hail Mary, a miracle or a wholly futile endeavor, one small indicator of whether anything at all can ever heal along the ceaseless wound we call la Frontera.

From the kitchen we head out into the plaza, the pulsating center of the asylum, me and Bemis and El Pastor out into a crowd of residents, half lounging and the other half pacing, moaning, screaming, slapping at the air. The plaza isn't large and everyone is bunched up at the outer edges against cinder-block walls, lingering in tiny cells of shade as the sun climbs to its burning place on high. An old basketball hoop in the middle of the plaza gives the sense of a school playground. There's a big green gate and stone benches and pink walls, vibrant like an actual village plaza. Two stories of cinder-block rooms are built into the outer wall like a roadside motel or a ramshackle fortress. The bottom floor of rooms are real cells with real bars and people on the other side of the bars holding on, residents deemed too dangerous to roam. Everywhere clothes hang drying, like the yard of a big family, secondhand clothes from the empire to the north, all the brand names and logos faded or torn. There are exercise bikes, in disrepair. The one bike with a seat gets use but only for sitting. A guy named Yogi jumps off that seat, runs up to hug each of us. Yogi has been here since he was unceremoniously dropped off as a boy, is still exuberantly boyish on account of his Down syndrome, can't speak much but never stops smiling and squealing approval. He touches things, pets them really, inanimate objects: the bike, a tree, a cup. He runs around and touches everything like this and then comes and touches me, pets my hand and arm. Then pets the bike. Then the tree and the concrete. Nothing is dead. For Yogi everything is full of life.

Ah, my army of insane, says El Pastor. He often calls the residents *insane* or *lunatics* or *human garbage,* which is not so much passing judgment on them as it is passing judgment on the society that has treated them this way. *My recycling center,* he says. *For the human garbage.* Even through his big grin of what seems to be genuine love, it's hard to hear El Pastor say this kind of thing without wincing, at least at first. But everyone gets used to it. I think of the writer Harry Crews and how he always said his books were about *freaks* but also said that when he said *freaks,* he was just using a kind of shorthand and what he meant was *people with special considerations under God.* Crews was crass and a freak himself but there was no mistaking how he meant *freak* as a term of endearment for the only people he considered worthy of endearment. And El Pastor reminds me there is no point to political correctness out here in the Mexican desert. The asylum is a complicated place.

You see? My family, he says as Yogi grabs ahold for another hug.

Gaspar, who dresses like a soldier in unmarked second-hand fatigues, fighting for a nation unknown, shakes my hand. *Gaspar!* says El Pastor as he points at another resident, bellows another origin story: *He was burning down houses and eating dead dogs.* Elisabeth carries an empty purse, has a mischievous smile and a freshly shaved head. She speaks English, and when she hears me speaking English, she comes up to ask for a cookie. El Pastor doesn't have an origin story for her. Nobody shouts her name. She says she's lived in Los Angeles for years and has only been here at the asylum for three days. She says she is looking for her lost children. She rubs her shaved head to show me how new she is. She touches my hair, tells me I'm too old to be wearing it so long. *It is good hair,* she says, *but we will shave it or you will get the bugs.* Elisabeth is a flirt, crossing and uncrossing her legs to show off her black platform shoes as she plays with my hair and asks for a cookie over and over. I don't know it yet but much of what she's said is a lie. She's been in one of those cells for at least two years on account of her propensity to attack other residents. They've just set her free and that's why they've shaved her head, trying to keep whatever infects the cinder-block cells out of the general population.

Most of the residents do not speak English, and I don't speak great Spanish. El Pastor and his right-hand man, Josué, speak English. Bemis translates whenever I get lost. An old woman, Favela, rolls up in her wheelchair. Favela says that I am beautiful, that I look like her son. She talks about how proud she is of her son and how hard she worked when she cleaned the seats of city buses and how proud that made her feel. She scrubbed seats. She scrubbed walls and wings. She scrubbed the sky. She will scrub the sky and let me sit there. I am her son. The sky is big and has no seats. Her hands go up in the air and she double-times her rate of speech. Bemis has difficulty translating, says it has all become nonsensical. His attention drifts to another resident pulling at his shirt. Favela keeps reaching up high from her wheelchair, does not take her blue eyes off me as she rants, eyes sitting so deep in her face that their brightness is sort of tunneled or channeled and comes out like beams. I try to listen to every word but comprehend almost none of them other than *cielo, cielo* or *mi hijo.* I pay attention to her inflection, her eye beams. I'm twice removed from rational comprehension—without her language or her singular rationale—trying to feel what she has to say, trying to listen in a way we rarely do in our lives, without our ears. I don't expect to understand every word so I am not thrown off by non sequiturs. Everything seems of the utmost importance. How necessary is language? I can never find the right words, which is why I use so goddamn many of them. In a perfect world, this story would be exactly one word long, just the right word, maybe not even a word but just a sound, and you'd understand it all. Ah, you see? I'm also searching to excuse not knowing a language I should have tried harder to learn all the years I was growing up just fifty miles north of here. I've studied French and Spanish in language classes, but like most of us Americans I can't have a real conversation in any language other than the language of our empire. And even then I say *eye beams*, struggling to convey what it is to have Favela looking up at me from her wheelchair, in this place and smiling still—all the way alive still even though I can't quite tell you her story.

El Pastor gets annoyed as I linger in the plaza. He's ready to move along, show me everything else, keeps listing off all the things I'm about to see. I realize he's guiding me through a pretty standardized tour, something he's done many times since Bowden first wrote about his asylum five years ago. Every few weeks or months another media outlet shows up to get their five hundred words about a glimmer of hope in Juárez, to snap their pictures of El Pastor and his maimed flock. Or another church group shows up to do the tour and a few hours of group prayer and post blogs about their dangerous forays to minister to the criminally insane south of the border. El Pastor has become as much a public relations man as anything else. He knows I will want to start my story with the tale of his violent conversion and that's why he tells it to me within twenty minutes of my arrival. He knows my readers will want all the horrific details of the residents' origin stories and so he shouts them even before their names. Whatever pristine isolation the asylum once enjoyed is gone and I'm just one more brick in the road toward a bona fide media sideshow. El Pastor makes no bones about it: my job as the gringo writer is to tell all the other gringos about his saved Mexicans so they will send him money so he can save more Mexicans. In this way there is nothing disingenuous about El Pastor's tour—it is some of that new sincerity that feels like the oxymoron of a heartfelt wink.

We make our way to the chicken house, where sixty chickens lay the breakfast eggs. El Pastor keeps smacking my back like he does and says, *Ah, my army of insane,* about the chickens. He winks but it's an unsettling joke because of its heartfelt part. The chickens mill around in the same arbitrary manner as the residents in the plaza. There is the same kind of constant, dull chatter. But I don't feel drawn to connect in any emotional way with the chickens and that is a kind of relief compared to the plaza, at least until an intense wave of guilt for feeling relief about not having to empathize with the residents sets in. Then I want to run back to the plaza and talk to everyone and help however I can. El Pastor has mapped out a perfectly evocative media tour.

We visit the goats and the pigs and the stained block upon which the pigs are slaughtered. El Pastor is particularly proud of an area where he has run electricity for a cinderblock-making machine. With this machine they will build more walls, grow the asylum to make room for more residents. *Three hundred,* he says. *I want three hundred crazies. Three hundred just like the movie.* He enacts some version of Spartan violence from the film *300,* a big kick to the chest of his invisible enemy. He throws his arms wide and slaps the concrete of the slaughter slab. *I will really have my army!* I guess it's the kind of dark humor that inevitably develops after decades of living in the desert with addicts and orphans, schizophrenics and murderers, and now all the cartel corpses. But an actual suit of armor is in El Pastor's chamber and swords are on the walls, with many paintings of Roman centurions throughout the asylum, and a big Roman-style crest he has adopted for Visión en Acción is painted on the entrance gate. When I ask about all the ancient military stuff, he says of course they are at war. But then also he just loves the whole aesthetic of ancient Rome. He relates the plots of his favorite movies, *Gladiator* and *300*, and he cannot remember all the names of the ones he watched when he was young, but he's talking about *Spartacus* and maybe *Julius Caesar* and definitely *Ben-Hur*. We're in the laundry room now and one big rat is in the corner by the wash bin eating one little rat as El Pastor recounts at length the scene from *Ben-Hur* in which Jesus has a cameo. *The first time you see Jesus*, he says. *And he gives water to the warrior!* El Pastor kicks the big rat off the little rat but only kicks the gnawed corpse an inch behind the washer. The big rat immediately jumps back on. *And the warrior gets his revenge. Do you know this movie?*

El Pastor's latest project is a new plaza being built to look vaguely Roman. Five residents work filling molds with plaster for its columns. A mural will show Daniel in the lion's den. Already cast in concrete is a lion's head that will be placed atop a giant fountain. El Pastor's spent ten grand and will probably need seven more. *It will be my Rome*, he says. To cut down on violent incidents, he wants to separate some of the women residents from the men, give the women their own high-class plaza. But also he wants a place to showcase the grandeur of his vision. So, a new plaza, the first thing any visitor will see, the volunteers and the media and the stray dogs, gazing upon El Pastor's white columns and the busts of lions and the fountain and the women residents milling around.

I wonder if El Pastor knows how the Romans treated his Lord and Savior Jesus Christ. I wonder if he knows the cartels have this obsession with all things ancient Roman too, if he knows about cartel leaders, such as Sinaloa's El Ondeado, building themselves half-million-dollar Greco-Roman-style mausoleums. Or the Zetas reportedly organizing gladiatorial combat with hundreds of kidnapped Mexicans, a game to see who will be the last man standing, who will be pressed into service as their next assassin, their next *sicario*. And *sicario* itself, a word from the Latin *sicarius*, a member of a group of Jews, the Sicarii, who rebelled against Roman rule in the first century C.E., a name meaning dagger wielders. "These Jews," says the historian Josephus, "who slew men in the daytime, and in the midst of the city; this they did chiefly at the festivals, when they mingled themselves among the multitude, and concealed daggers under their garments, with which they stabbed those that were their enemies." But the Sicarii were not killing Roman soldiers, just other Jews who sympathized with Roman rule or got in the way of their rebellion. Like the cartels kill each other some and Americans rarely, but mostly they kill innocent Mexicans who get in the way. But down here the cartels are the empire, not the rebels. So, etymologically, *sicario* isn't the right word for cartel assassins because the cartels are not the disenfranchised. Who is the real *sicario*, wielder of little daggers, rebel with eyes toward the empire's demise? The point is, a lot of what you might call ancient Roman memorabilia is at the asylum.

Well, alright. It's an absurdity of the kind one can't question in any satisfying way. Like the asylum's brief business of manufacturing apple-themed décor, a kind of art therapy turned moneymaking venture, kitschy décor one might find in the pages of a Pottery Barn catalog but here is a room full of it at the asylum. Like the wooden apple El Pastor gives me or the apple-shaped clock with crooked hands he gives me that will hang in my momma's kitchen for years, telling a lie a second or still just stuck on asylum time.

El Pastor's next project is a garden for what he calls *the hopelessly insane*. These are the residents kept locked up in the cells of the old plaza's outer walls. *They are always naked*, he says. *They are always eating their own shit. I want to build for them a garden. A big garden where they can walk around naked and eat their shit and be just as they are, in my garden. Ah, just like the garden of the Bible.*

Have you noticed how El Pastor likes to punctuate his sentences with *ah*, not a word so much as an epiphanic sound that communicates succinctly the grandeur of his vision?

Ah, here is that wooden apple in my hand, red and shiny and about the right size of an apple but not at all the right shape of an apple, the bottom totally flat and the top far too narrow, a warped apple plucked from the asylum before it ever has a garden. What knowledge is stored in this apple's tree, which is not a tree but the hands of El Pastor's army of insane? What will be the consequence for learning such knowledge? I will carry this wooden apple for years and never take a bite.

Lunchtime and we head to the plaza for beans and bread. The beans are distributed in multiliter soda bottles with the tops sawed off. Everyone gets something like a liter of beans, the makeshift bowls filled up just past halfway, bread balanced on top. Some dip. Some scoop. Some slurp from the bottle and wipe their faces with the bread. In late afternoon the sun relents a bit, clouds drift in, and many of the residents disperse from the edges of the old plaza. But just as quickly Josué rounds them up, lines them up.

Time for the needles, everyone.

The metal door to the multipurpose room slams. The residents sit in plastic Office Star folding chairs, circled up, totally solemn or making silly faces. A guy wearing a hat with the logo of a billion-dollar energy-drink corporation makes farting noises. An old man in a bathrobe stands and sits and stands and sits. Gaspar is at attention. Yogi is the king of silly faces and takes down all challengers with a puff of his cheeks, a tug of both ears. Elisabeth holds her purse, crosses her legs, and flaunts her platform shoes. Smiles.

At the back of the room are three showers. A dusty plastic Christmas tree. And a pulpit in the corner, surrounded by homemade TV lights, fluorescent bulbs and lots of aluminum foil. El Pastor is sometimes a TV evangelist. And sometimes a painter. The multiple purposes of this room are meeting hall, treatment center, shower, storage, TV studio, art studio, and gallery. Many of El Pastor's paintings hang on the walls of the asylum, including the one over Elisabeth's right shoulder: a skeleton scratching his chin at Jesus, who sits on a heavenly throne, and at the left edge of the painting, Satan overlooks the scene, his face covered in American Stars and Stripes. The only picture on the wall that isn't amateur art done by El Pastor or a resident is the painting above Elisabeth's left shoulder: a Roman centurion with his sword raised for battle.

The circle is composed of thirteen men and seven women.

Favela has been wheeled in over by the pulpit, out of the circle. I think we are waiting for El Pastor to administer the treatments, but he will not come. Josué and another of the healthier residents, Jesús, will do the needling. El Pastor is out directing the construction of his columns.

Josué tears open the needle packets with his teeth and his good hand. The other hand is missing three fingers from gangrene that ate at his body as he lay in the gutters of Juárez in the months before arriving at the asylum. He holds the needles in the good hand and starts with Elisabeth, tilts her head, his mangled hand on her buzzed scalp as she breathes. He breathes. He's stocky but right now all his bulk is channeled into an unlikely delicacy as he slips the needles into the cartilage of her ear. Then the next ear. The next resident. Ear after ear. *Pew pew, pew pew.* I think of the Sicarii and their little daggers. I think of an alternate universe where the word *sicario* has its roots in the little daggers of acupuncture rather than the little daggers of assassins and the possibility that in that parallel universe there are no cartel hit men in Mexico, no twelve thousand dead, no Josué or Elisabeth at the asylum, no need for the asylum at all.

Nearly every time Josué gets the needles into another ear he looks back at me and grins. He looks to Bemis for approval, and when Josué gets the nod of assent, he flexes his biceps. He and Jesús have only been learning the needles for a month, still under the watchful eye of their teacher, Bemis. He's training them in a protocol called NADA, just five insertion points in the outer ear, a technique used by the National Acupuncture Detoxification Association as "a no-nonsense, non-verbal, no-drug pharmaceutical free, and barrier-free approach to behavioral health." All the negative constructions in their slogan play on the idea that *nada* is

Spanish for "nothing." Just ten needles in the ears. *De nada.* The soul will fall into place.

Jesús doesn't quite have his needle legs under him yet. He's clearly guessing a bit about the location of any single insertion. There is much poking and jabbing. When Jesús first arrived at the asylum, he could not stop shaking; he'd done nothing but booze for decades. The shakes have mostly passed but there's nothing elegant in his work with the needles and he knows it. He avoids looking at Bemis and soldiers through the wincing of the face between whatever ears he's stabbing.

From under the energy-drink hat, the farting noises start up again. But then Josué gets to the farter and sticks him with the NADA protocol. The last resident needled is Gaspar, soldier of a nation unknown. Gaspar is also the name of one of the three wise men in the novel *Ben-Hur* and I wonder if El Pastor is choosing residents' names. In the novel, each wise man tells his own origin story. Gaspar is the Greek bringing frankincense to baby Jesus. The reason Gaspar gives for blindly following a twinkling star out into the Judaean Desert seems to pretty well summarize why El Pastor is out here in the Chihuahuan Desert, why I'm out here, maybe why anyone at all ends up in the asylum.

It happens that two of our philosophers, the very greatest of the many, teach, one the doctrine of a Soul in every man, and its Immortality; the other the doctrine of One God, infinitely just. From the multitude of subjects about which the schools were disputing, I separated them, as alone worth the labor of solution; for I thought there was a relation between God and the soul as yet unknown. On this theme the mind can reason to a point, a dead, impassable wall;

arrived there, all that remains is to stand and cry aloud for
help. So I did; but no voice came to me over the wall. In
despair, I tore myself from the cities.

With Gaspar the circle is complete. Forty ears. Two hundred
needles. Nearly everyone is silent. Calm. Some with their
eyes closed and others with the kind of distant stare that
suggests contentment rather than absence. They will sit like
this, quietly in a circle, all heads needled, for a half hour or
more. Out in the plaza the residents are always a cacophonous organism on the brink of going totally to shit, the pacing and the shouting and hand-wringing and lounging and
occasional slap or bite or corpse carried away or dragged in
piecemeal by mutts, all of it feeding the whole living, breathing whirlwind of enfeebled humanity in the plaza, and if
anyone stops pacing too soon or howls too soft or repeats repeats repeats himself one too many times, then the delicate
balance of madness and routine shatters and the organism
implodes and even the cinder-block walls all fall down. But
here, for now, it is quiet. In the multipurpose room—with El
Pastor's army of insane all now brandishing their little daggers in this strange way, five needles shooting an inch out of
each ear like a mad science experiment or some *Hellraiser*
congregation or so many antennas in search of a connection—
there is silence.

   In the corner by the pulpit Bemis bends over Favela in
her wheelchair. She gets more of the full-body treatment,
needles in the ears and head and legs and feet. Bemis is a
pro, effortlessly twisting the needles so deftly it's almost like
his fingers create a kind of propulsion that launches the steel
into the flesh. Ah, you see, here is a different kind of steel
piercing the flesh. The cartels have stocked up on AR-15s

and AK-47s, some bought from the American ATF or manufactured in clandestine cartel workshops in Jalisco or Gua-
dalajara. Steel-jacketed ammo will ruin a gun barrel, but
with high-volume shooting it's cheaper to replace barrels
than it is to spend more on brass ammo—$500 cheaper per
five thousand rounds—so the cartels have been saving many
thousands of dollars a month littering Juárez with steel casings, firing steel-jacketed bullets that will fragment just cen-
timeters into the flesh, the bullet often passing all the way
through a body but the steel jacket fragmenting, stopping,
staying in the flesh, one or two grams of steel resting inside
the skin. So many of the bodies in this desert with one or
two grams of steel resting in the skin. I bet that's about the
exact weight of those steel needles sticking out of Elisabeth's
ears—one or two grams of steel resting in her skin. Her leg is
really shaking now. She's tense, gripping her empty purse
and her platform shoe hitting the ground, that click of rubber on tile the only sound as we sit waiting for this new steel
stuck in the side of her head to fix the terror of all that other
steel. And Elisabeth's buzzed head just slightly rocking, all
those needles in her ears pointing up to the Roman centurion on the one side or tilting and pointing toward Satan in
Stars and Stripes on the other side.

July 16, in the Year of Our Lord 2014

GOD IS ON YOUR SIDE says the billboard as we drive I-10
along the border toward Juárez. Today I'm headed with Bemis not to the asylum but deep into the city, to a church in
south Juárez called Santa Margarita, where pastoral workers
are learning the NADA acupuncture protocol along with

another form of traditional Chinese medicine called moxibustion. Bemis rummages through boxes of needles in a duf-
fel bag and pulls out some moxa, dense bricks of black, dried
mugwort that'll get burned on the flesh of a patient with
particularly chronic issues. He has me sniff the moxa to get
a sense of it, how it looks like pot and smells a bit like pot
when it burns but it is not pot. Then he stuffs the bricks in
the bag along with all the other boxes of needles. *You've got
to be careful taking this stuff across the border,* Bemis yells,
but the bag stays in plain view behind us. He's yelling because
we're on the freeway and his window won't roll up. He's
thinking about using duct tape to keep it closed, but the AC
doesn't always run good and this is a roasting summer. So
the window is stuck down and he's yelling about duct tape
and he's yelling a story heard from a friend of a friend about
a student of moxibustion in Guatemala or Uganda who
found a woman in labor on a jungle road and burned moxa
on her belly to get the baby turned around the right way and
delivered safely. These kinds of stories always crop up around
the talk of traditional Chinese medicine. You've probably
heard about patients in Shanghai undergoing open-heart
surgery without anesthesia, no drugs and only acupuncture
to manage the pain. They're stories that sound too good to
be true, like miracles, and you can either spend your life trying to dissect the specifics of the unbelievable account or
simply accept the human need for stories that break the terrible cycle of tragedy. There's no way to sift through the specifics of the moxa birth by yelling at Bemis over the noise of
speeding along the border in his Ford clunker, so I choose to
believe it. Also, I hope my little bit of faith will grow and
envelop us and glue the vehicle together as we clunk, windows wide-open, through the terrible unpaved roads of some

neighborhoods that only show up in the news when another corpse is found.

We cross into Juárez and I catch the yawn of a guy on the corner just as some federales speed up alongside us, the officer riding shotgun leaning out his window and getting pretty damn close to leaning right into Bemis's window, checking out the bag he's no doubt been alerted to by the inspector at the border crossing. Extortion is easier once you're a few blocks into the city. Bemis has been pulled from his clunker in alleys by local police with assault rifles and gotten the shakedown for as little as the twenty bucks he keeps in his sock. He's in his thirties, grungy with a hint of hipster, looks neither dangerous nor rich, but that doesn't stop the shake-downs. The federales swerve in front to stop us, then grill Bemis about the bag. He responds by saying *zapatos* a whole bunch. I don't know how in the world this satisfies them but it eventually does and they drive off without opening the bag, which is good because even though no money or drugs or guns were in it, there were no *zapatos* either and that would have been enough to ruin our day.

There is a moment I fear we might be smuggling drugs, both now and every time I'll cross over or back with Bemis. There's the similarity of moxa to *mota*. There's the general paranoia lingering from my stonier days that I've left a joint in my backpack or pocket. There's the fact that I don't yet know Bemis all that well, met him for the first time when we went to El Pastor's asylum. And then the big issue is that in this place—la Frontera—drugs make a whole lot more sense than traditional Chinese medicine, like it would be incredibly mundane if we were smuggling drugs, but all the little needles and mugwort, that's absurd and totally outside all reason. This is how the authorities see it. So, coming or going,

with the Mexicans or the Americans, no border official will
ever let us pass without incident. A couple of long-haired hippies in a clunker must be up to no good, particularly when
they concoct some bullshit story about one of them sticking
people with needles at a chapel while the other one watches
and takes notes. When we get pulled out of the clunker on our
way back from this trip and separated for questioning while
U.S. ICE agents tear the car apart, I'll try to explain my theory
about the congruity of steel in bullets and needles while
Bemis just lifts up his shirt and shows what looks to be a knife
sheath on his belt and the agents will hold their hands on
their guns while he slowly pulls from the leather case, bead by
bead, a rosary. This always seems to agitate them because
maybe they wanted it to be a knife and sort of lusted after the
kind of confrontation that makes sense to them in these violent times and now they feel a bit guilty with Bemis just dangling the crucifix in their faces, and maybe they are even
having a flashback to a moment of faith in their lives or a moment when their own good intentions were misconstrued,
and the combination of all those complex emotions in the
sort of people we've got manning our border is usually enough
to short-circuit their single-minded investigations and finally
get us on the road again. This is the power of the rosary, of
any object with no utility but for faith.

    We arrive at Templo Católico Santa Margarita Maria
Alacoque in the *colonia* Constituyentes—a warehouse of a
chapel that reminds me of the church I grew up in, except
this one looks quite a bit more fortified. There are iron gates.
We leave the SUV parked on the street along railroad tracks
that run across the face of the chapel to an industrial park a
few miles north. Right there on the south corner of Santa
Margarita, last May, a woman was gunned down in a hit that

mimicked one on nearly the same corner at the height of cartel wars in 2009. Though everyone I'll talk to at mass today agrees the violence is over, they only mean The Violence is over, that it is no longer every day they wake up to another massacre, that murder is no longer the only thing on their minds. This parish includes the impoverished *colonias* Constituyentes and Independencia II, and here the blood still flows too much, just not enough to be abnormal. A scan of *El Diario*, the Juárez daily news, for terms such as *la víctima* or *asesinato* or *arruinar* in these *colonias* surrounding the chapel since cartel fighting in the city supposedly began to ebb in 2012, tells of a woman's body in a Ford Explorer, bound hand and foot by duct tape, head wrapped in a plastic bag. And two convenience-store owners gunned down for refusing extortion. And a convicted murderer released early only to return home and immediately kill his neighbor. And a handful of carjacking murders. And a severed head found in the sewer. And a stabbing spree at a dance party. And the bullet-riddled corpse of a woman in the street. And a man walking with his family, executed by a truckful of armed men. And a jogger executed. And a mechanic executed. And an unidentifiable body, bound hand and foot with duct tape. As we walk into the chapel, duct tape holds a flyer of announcements to the big iron gates. There's a cliché about duct tape, how it fixes everything, and it's true that duct tape will hold a sign or keep a clunker's window up or patch a space suit, but it has also been accomplice to so much murder. If a single sound could relate to alien civilizations how much ingenuity and barbarism we humans pack into our modern civilization, it would be the dull, hollow screech of duct tape coming off the roll.

And maybe it was duct tape just barely holding together

the candy factory down the road at the industrial park when it exploded eight months ago—eight people dead and dozens more maimed and burned. They call it Blueberry, the factory that makes candy for the American company Sunrise Confections, and its explosion was not exactly murder but just indifference toward 250,000 impoverished Juarenses employed for about eight bucks a day to make American furniture and laptops and sweets. The Blueberry factory had appealed nearly twenty labor and safety infractions before it exploded, and as all that sugar and flesh burned, there was so little help because the city's already woefully inadequate fleet of twenty-four ambulances was operating suboptimally— five were broken and fifteen had no gasoline.

Yes, at least The Violence is over, they say.

So here we are in a hard pew for mass. The iron gates are rolled open like a whole wall of the warehouse chapel has evaporated and the city is spewing in, the street and its gory gutters just feet from our pew and the railroad running to the exploded candy factory. Stray dogs meander in and out of the chapel throughout the homily, runts all filthy and starved, in and out of the aisles. The youngest kids roam the aisles too, sucking on candy to keep them quiet, free sweets a perk for parents slaving away at Blueberry. The entire service is run by women and girls. Altar girls and girls reading the Scriptures and leading the hymns and a nun giving the homily. I think it's progressive but I'll learn it's just what these parishes resort to when the men stop showing up because they've been otherwise occupied with The Violence. But slowly people are coming back. The chapel holds hundreds, though only thirty are here today. That's clearly an increase because during Communion they run out of wafers. A nun crumbles the last wafer in the big chalice and the final dozen parishioners sip until they feel they've ingested a crumb of divine flesh and then everyone leaves or mills, waiting for the needles.

Today the treatments are administered by two parishioners Bemis has trained, Rudolpho and Rosario, and a nun, Sister Maria Rosario. Bemis trains them for free so long as they agree to treat people for free. Sometimes patients donate a few pesos to cover needle costs, a second tithing for the day. About ten people grab chairs or pull up some pew as the three needlers work their way around, wiping and poking ears. Bemis adds needles to the head of a boy with epilepsy. Rosario lays a woman down on a table and burns moxa on her back. I talk to two small children, Ricardo and Mariana, who say they are being treated for weighing little things. They say *la pesadilla* and I should understand it means "nightmare," but like any novice language speaker I'm translating too literally. I'm thinking of quesadilla. I'm thinking, what is this illness of weighing little things? Eventually we get around to saying *malos sueños* at each other like an epiphany. But the disease of *weighing little things* sticks with me, how it is a nightmare to pay attention to the tiniest details.

Ricardo and Mariana's mother comes along and clarifies that their problem was not bad dreams so much as sleepwalking. No one on their block could sleep well after a body was dismembered in front of their home but then it got worse: the children began to sleepwalk. For months the mother would barricade the door to keep her kids from sleepwalking out into the horrors of the night. They wouldn't wake up no matter how loud she screamed. But when her children get the needles, she doesn't have to rearrange the furniture. They don't sleepwalk anymore. *Faith moves mountains*, she says. I try to figure out exactly what it is that she has faith in, trying to parse if she thinks of the needles as medicine or as an adjunct to her Catholic faith or as another brand of spiritual undertaking altogether and after several minutes of our going around and around she smiles and pats me on the knee to let me know I have too many questions. *Faith is everything*, she says.

But I am weighing little things.

One or two grams of steel.

NADA protocol generally requires a whole group of folks to be needled simultaneously, ears poked and sitting together quietly for up to an hour, some falling asleep, others just resting their eyes. So there is a long stretch of stillness in Santa Margarita. I whisper with Rudolpho a bit, who, when I ask him about Bemis, says something like *De médico, poeta, y loco, todos tenemos un poco*. Every human has something of the doctor, the poet, and the lunatic in their disposition— but Bemis especially. Rudolpho asks why I've come here. *It's boring to watch a bunch of people sleep, no?* Bemis has asked me this before and will ask me a bunch of times over the next year as I follow him and his needles around Juárez. I say, *Sure, nothing is happening. But that's when the mind roams.* Rudolpho is a mechanic and a massage therapist and a butcher and a single father and now, after learning from Bemis, an acupuncturist. He doesn't like to sit still. Staying busy quiets the mind. Needles quiet the mind. He points out that a roaming mind is sort of the opposite of the meditative state acupuncture encourages. He says he can help quiet my mind by poking my ears but I guess he knows I'm not ready yet because he says nothing else and walks off to inspect his patients. I want to explain to Rudolpho exactly why it's interesting to stare at needled ears in a chapel, why I am not bored. But I could never get out the convoluted explanation in conversation, an explanation that begins with something like *Ah, ears are so weird.*

"Those ingenious labyrinthine inlets—those indispensable side-intelligencers," wrote the nineteenth-century essayist Charles Lamb in "A Chapter on Ears." Something like ten pounds of pressure will rip an ear from its head, about what it takes to tear through fifteen pages of paper—grab hold of the front matter of this book and tug to get a feel for it. Once the ear is off the head you can appreciate its oddness. An average adult ear weighs just over one hundred grams, or the equivalent of a small tomato. An average adult ear is two and a half inches long, with three-quarters of an inch being lobe. Turn that ear around in your hand and trace the labyrinthine inlets and think about everything that has passed through. Recent studies of Devonian fish fossils suggest our ears evolved from gills, meaning the history of our ears, beginning about 400 million years ago, is about ventilation of water or air. In the womb we still grow our outer ears on our lower neck in six gill-type perforations. The sensitive bones of the inner ear evolved from the jaws of our reptilian ancestors about 195 million years ago. So the history of our ears is also about chewing. First, ears were expelling what we didn't need, and then they began to help us chew what we did need. By the time we homo sapiens emerged as we are today, around two hundred thousand years ago, our ears were fine-tuned to sense one another's voices and pick up pretty well all the other sounds of our world—a hole for collecting so much of the invisible around us. And in this way ears become sort of magical. The Ebers Papyrus from around 1550 B.C.E. Egypt, one of the oldest known attempts at a medical text, talks about ears as forces with great existential power: "There are four vessels to his two ears together with the canal, two on his right side and two to his left side. The breath of life enters into the right ear, and the breath of death enters into the left ear." If we believe our Bibles, just one hundred years after the Ebers Papyrus was authored in Egypt the Jews made their great escape from generations of Egyptian slavery. If we don't believe our Bibles, it happened a thousand years after Ebers or never at all. The point is that the story of the Exodus—and the Ten Commandments that come out of Exodus and go on to shape all of Western religion—hinges on the problem of magical ears.

Moses is taking too long—chatting with God atop Mount Sinai—and the Israelites are itching to worship something. Aaron is down at the base of the mountain trying to keep the people behaving but he senses a riot brewing and decides to pacify the people and says to them at the beginning of Exodus 32, "Take off the rings of gold which are in the ears of your wives, your sons, and your daughters, and bring them to me." Maybe one thing evolution didn't account for was that, as our ears grew to hear more and elongated to hear best the frequencies at which human speech occurs, we'd find their folds and curves and lobes irresistible locales for personal décor. The Egyptians knew all about the spirits of death slipping in through the ear hole and this is one reason they began to use earrings, to ward off the demons. But also—and like all things—earrings could represent status. The big gold earrings of a pharaoh could ward off the demons more effectively and that for sure meant that he was better than you. So the earrings of the Israelites are no minor detail in this story; they are symbols of foreign culture, a culture that had until recently enslaved the Israelites, remnants of Egyptian polytheism that the jealous god of the Israelites could never abide.

Then, Exodus 32:3–4, where the story blossoms with

blasphemy: "So all the people took off the rings of gold which were in their ears, and brought them to Aaron. And he received the gold at their hands, and hashed it with a graving tool, and made a molten calf."

The molten calf, that most famous of idols, is made of metal from a foreign culture that the Israelites had poked in their ears. And here we are in Juárez in a chapel after the homily and all the Mexicans have this Japanese steel for practicing Chinese medicine poked in their ears.

Then the people of Israel have a dance party around their molten calf and call it Lord and that pretty well pisses off God. Moses talks him down, calms God down. But when Moses sees the molten calf for himself, he smashes the stones on which God's commandments are written. He demolishes the calf, grinds it to powder, scatters it upon the water, and makes the people of Israel drink it. We often forget this last part of the story because it is a strange punishment, like making a child smoke a whole pack of cigarettes as atonement for puffing just one. Or more like making a child eat a whole pack of cigarettes as atonement for puffing just one.

The story's focus on the earrings as the raw material for the idol, as the material on which God and Moses cast their ire, likely exists to scold the Israelites—the earrings being a visible way in which the Israelites had lost something of their identity by assimilating with their captors. But then, the practice of drinking gold was also part of Egyptian culture, something they did to treat illness and promote general spiritual purification. If the Israelites assimilated so much of their former captor's culture, then God is quite literally giving them a bit of their own medicine when he makes them drink remnants of the idol made of earrings, not to heal them, but to punish them. The healing ways of

one culture become an abomination in another. Your medicine is my blasphemy.

Finally God sends Moses down with a second set of
tablets and, lo and behold, the first commandment is don't
worship your ear piercings, or "Thou shall make thee no
molten gods." Exodus actually has two different accounts of
the commandments, so a whole lot of stuffy debate concerns
what exactly was inscribed on the first set of stones and if it
jibed with what ended up on the second set of stones, but the
first commandment is always the same. There's no questioning that God gets jealous when his people make an idol out
of their ear piercings—the immoral idea that life or death or
any old god could float into our ears at any moment, that a
bullshit piece of some foreign nation's metal could even
feign the power of truly regulating or demolishing gods and
demons. Throughout the rest of the Old Testament, pretty
much anytime anyone hears the voice of the one true God,
their naked ears tingle.

My point: the metal people had in their ears nearly threw
all of monotheism off track. God wasn't hip to the lobe décor. Sitting here at the chapel in Juárez, staring at all these
needled ears just moments after the homily, I wonder if God,
or the priests who are now his proxy, will get jealous again.

This may sound outlandish but it's not at all beyond the
realm of possibility. Take Reiki, for instance, a kind of Japanese laying on of hands in which practitioners scan a body
by hovering their nondominant hand over all its parts and
then spend a half hour just resting their hands on different
areas of the body whose energy seems to need realigning,
beaming through their hands the healing energy of Reiki.
Sometimes they call the practice a spiritual massage, which
means not that it is a physical massage with potentially spiri-

tual consequences but that it is a literal working over of the
spirit, with minimal physical interaction. In 2009 the United
States Conference of Catholic Bishops' Committee on Doctrine released a document called "Guidelines for Evaluating
Reiki as an Alternative Therapy." The misleadingly named
document was essentially a ban on Reiki for all Catholics:
"To use Reiki one would have to accept at least in an im-
plicit way central elements of the worldview that undergirds
Reiki theory, elements that belong neither to Christian faith
nor to natural science."

And: "Superstition corrupts one's worship of God by turning one's religious feeling and practice in a false direction.
While sometimes people fall into superstition through ignorance, it is the responsibility of all who teach in the name of
the Church to eliminate such ignorance as much as possible."

Finally: "Since Reiki therapy is not compatible with either
Christian teaching or scientific evidence, it would be inap-
propriate for Catholic institutions, such as Catholic health
care facilities and retreat centers, or persons representing the
Church, such as Catholic chaplains, to promote or to provide support for Reiki therapy."

Bemis says, *Woo-woo*. He calls the sort of spiritual aspects of acupuncture woo-woo and distrusts the woo-woo
even though he's got years of expensive training in Eastern
alternative medicine and he's a Western-churchgoing guy.
He gives a lot of credit to evangelical churches that saved
him during some rough times in his youth but he was raised
Catholic and now attends a nondenominational church.
When I first visited his acupuncture clinic in Las Cruces, he
escorted me to his office in an old bank safe and showed me
where he'd hung some bland artwork over a spot at the back
where a previous tenant had painted *Bow down to The Lord*.

The covering up of this command in his clinic is less about his personal beliefs and more about his constant attempt to separate acupuncture from the woo-woo—regardless of whether that woo-woo is of the Eastern or Western variety.

Bemis encounters lots of Catholics in Juárez who are interested in pressure points in the palms and in the feet, the locales of stigmata. He tries to deflect that particular interest as the expansion of NADA in Juárez requires that it not get on the wrong side of the Church. According to Bemis, deployment of NADA after mass is a matter of convenience more than a matter of spiritual ritual. That much needs to be clear to any clergy who bust in with a hankering to clarify dogma. Bemis often points to the recent history of NADA as evidence of its nonspiritual nature. But if you go all the way back to NADA's origins, they are mired in woo-woo.

Before NADA there was the auricular therapy of a guy in France, Dr. Paul Nogier. I'm tempted to go beyond Nogier, back into the origins of acupuncture itself, but those origins are just as muddled as the modern science that tries to explain acupuncture—many variations of needle therapy have existed in China for about twenty-one hundred years, all waxing and waning in popularity, and the vast majority of recent medical studies of modern acupuncture conclude its efficacy in treating most illnesses is nonexistent or equivalent to placebo. Digging much deeper than that opens up a maddening spiral into mountains of biased research and history from both practitioners and decriers of quackery. Best to stay focused on the ears. In the 1950s, Dr. Nogier was cauterizing people's ears to treat back pain and having so much success burning patients that he decided to start poking them. He studied acupuncture and made maps of the ear that were less like traditional Chinese medicine's maps of qi—life energy—in the body, and more like the popular nineteenth-century pseudoscience head maps of phrenology. Nogier figured the external part of the ear had points that corresponded to every bodily system and that any ailment could be cleared up with some deft massaging or needling of the ears in just the right places. Upper earlobe for toenail situations. Lower lobe for throat and tongue situations. The spot where your ear first curves back toward its high point for anus situations. And so on for over fifty points. His mapping of these spots eventually led him to conclude that the ear was not at all labyrinthine in shape but that it had the exact proportions of a miniature inverted fetus. He traced these inverted fetuses into his ear diagrams—the ear drawn to look exactly like an inverted fetus—as a way to exemplify how the ear might be a microcosm of the whole body, one magical and accessible spot where any ailment could be remedied. Nogier's acupuncture diagrams, if you look at them even just once, will irrevocably change the way you see ears forever after. The closest approximation I know is the way a friend of mine dressed up as Princess Leia for a party in college, but she was in a punk phase of her life and had shaved her head and so to get that famous Princess Leia hairdo she just glued some honey buns to the side of her face. Now, whenever I see or even think of Princess Leia, there are those honey buns. But with ears, after Nogier, it's fetuses, just hanging like sleeping bats from the sides of heads. Obviously we're still heavy into the woo-woo here. Though, technically, Nogier's early experiments with auricular therapy were not yet NADA. But then his ideas get transported across the Atlantic in the 1970s and his over fifty points on the ear get distilled down to just five. The five points that became popular with practitioners of auricular therapy in America are the ones for the lungs, liver, kidneys, and two points associated with the nervous system, the Sympathetic Point and the Heavenly Gate Point. That these points correspond with areas of the body most ravaged by addictions—smoking and drinking and snorting and shooting heroin—is no coincidence.

The people practicing and popularizing these five points of ear acupuncture were in the South Bronx at Lincoln Hospital's drug detox center, a place run in part in the 1970s by groups such as the Black Panthers and the Young Lords. Lincoln Detox began as a methadone clinic but those beginnings were tumultuous, complete with the alleged murder (and cover-up via staged heroin overdose) of a detox doc, killed (allegedly) to stop him from pursuing more public funding. All kinds of more legal and better-documented manipulations were made by the elite of New York City to keep methadone and other resources from the clinic, to maybe keep the troublesome elements of society addicted and in that way pacified, not stirring up issues of civil rights, etc. Here in the fires of poverty and rebellion against all kinds of institutionalized discrimination, the NADA protocol was solidified—an epidemic of addicts being treated for their problems as cheaply as possible, all rounded up in the auditorium of a hospital in the South Bronx and quietly needled in the ears to fix their lungs and livers and kidneys and nervous systems, anything to wean them off the dope. There was little woo-woo about it. Just regular people desperately trying to help other regular people who were stuck in a spiral of hurt. Communities trying to make themselves better without any need to rely on the government or any of the other institutions that had been oppressing them for so long. As the addicts at Lincoln Hospital seemed to get better, NADA spread, caught on as an addiction therapy in urban detox centers and prisons across the country. Because it was so simple to teach and practice—just five points in the ear, *de nada*—and extremely quick to deploy, it expanded into disaster relief, no longer just an adjunct to detox therapy but now becoming a kind of general stress-reducing, pain-relieving behavioral-health therapy. NADA was in New Orleans after Hurricane Katrina and in Haiti after the earthquake and in Joplin, Missouri, after the tornadoes. The U.S. Center for Substance Abuse has guidelines for the use of NADA. So do the United Nations and now the Departments of Defense and Veterans Affairs. There are variations of NADA for use on the battlefield and variations for PTSD. NADA was in Guatemala after the civil war and in Manhattan after the towers fell and thrives in places of constant conflict such as Uganda, the Gaza Strip, and Lebanon. Bemis points to all this stuff when he talks about the history of NADA being totally separate from the woo-woo. Three decades after NADA took root in the Bronx, Bemis was trained there at Lincoln Hospital and he is steeped in that history of individual healing intertwined with community organizing. Yes, maybe Nogier was a nut with his inverted fetuses hanging from the head but there are all of these examples of NADA practitioners moving in quickly after catastrophes, before even the Red Cross or any other NGO can get set up, and empowering communities by teaching them this simple kind of health care. When all those other organizations do show up, whatever structure has been put in place for NADA therapy can be used to dispense all sorts of other health care.

But this evolution of NADA may not be so easy to explain to the Mexican clergy, especially with no medical science to verify the efficacy of acupuncture therapy. Even if the priests know nothing of the ear as an inverted fetus, they may walk

through the big iron gates of Santa Margarita and see their
parishioners, still in pews after the homily, meditating toward
the sacristy, toward the giant loinclothed Jesus hanging from
the cross, with one or two blasphemous grams of molten god
sticking out of their ears. A whole cultural, religious, socio-
economic revolution of possibly pseudoscientific proportions
is tied up in these ears. That's what I want to say to Rudolpho,
but I don't know how to translate the words.

The NADA session ends and we're clunking again, through
alleys and the wrong way down one-way streets. Bemis generally drives like a maniac but that's more often than not how
traffic flows in this city and he's just going with it, over medi-
ans and through stop signs and up a hillside in the northwest-
ern part of the city to a slum barrio and Casa Tabor, home of
Father Peter and Sister Betty. They've been instrumental in
helping Bemis make the connections, build the trust necessary to start needling people in chapels. NADA is not a
church-sanctioned practice, but it is not yet banned, and
when you know the right people, you can ease it in here
and there.

   Father Peter and Sister Betty have been in Juárez since
1995, helping out wherever the archdiocese needs them.
Casa Tabor is their home and ministry, a shelter and a clinic,
a respite and a rebellion, one house in a hilltop slum with
the dual purpose of spreading the word of God and indicting
U.S. policies that destroy the hardest-working Juarenses.
Father Peter just turned ninety and Sister Betty is only a decade behind him but they haven't slowed down much in
their devotion to the Church or their railing against NAFTA.
We drink tea and they rail. God is good but the Free Trade

Agreement has wrecked small Mexican farms and the liveli-hoods of all those farmers. God is good but the Free Trade Agreement has brought to Juárez countless factories of Amer-ican companies that pay 90 percent less than they would north of the border even though the cost of living in Juárez is only about 10 percent less than it is in the big cities of Texas. God is good but the American willingness to pay for drugs . . . to pass out guns . . . God is good . . . but the human . . .

Betty has painted a whole cosmos on the cinder blocks of the wall outside their kitchen window, a mandala of sorts, great swirls of blackness and swirls of stars and even the gritty gray of the unpainted cinder block seems pulled into the domain of the metaphysical. I marvel at the wall's ability to stand despite the weight and warp of infinity. *The universe is beautiful*, Betty says. *That's why we must destroy the world.* She says it with a smile and I know she means only to destroy the world of evil and sin and all that NAFTA bullshit but that doesn't make her words sound any less apocalyptic.

She's got another wall, opposite the cinder-block cosmos, painted with murals unfurling like scrolls, murals with paint-ings of doves and so many brown faces in anguish and at the center of each scroll is a big space filled with a tiny font, thou-sands of handwritten names—all the murdered and disap-peared of Juárez.

Betty tries to write all the names, tries to record everything taken from the city by The Violence. Almost the entire wall is full, four scrolls maybe three feet wide and five feet tall, the writing so small that all the ink looks like nothing, like maybe just some splatter from one of the swirls of the cos-mos on the opposite wall got a bit out of hand, but when you get close, when your nose is almost touching the splatter, there is a name, or a word to let you know there was a name. *Yolanda Tapia. Unidentified. Jorge Chaparro. Unidentified. Unidentified.*

Betty tries to write a few names a day. She asks visitors to write a few names. And still she has stacks of pages of names that she needs to add to the scrolls. She asks if I want to add a name. She consults her many pages, riffles through them looking for where she last stopped. The next name on the list is Joshua Reyes. *How about that,* she says. *Your name is Joshua.* I take the marker and add his name to the list. Later I'll notice his name already on a scroll. It is tough to keep track of so many names. She will never catch up, will run out of wall or time, she worries, because she is getting old. I won't tell her that Joshua's name is already on the wall. She must have lost her place in the pages, doubled back and repeated. What does it matter? He might as well have died twice. Efficiency and accuracy are not the point. I don't guess she aims to finish. This is not a memorial in the way the Vietnam Wall is a memorial, the names stuck in stone because the war is over and the killing done. This is an act of meditation, a constant engagement with what has been lost, what is being lost in a world that must be destroyed.

Also in the yard, between the cosmos and the scrolls of the dead, is a serpentine path of stones, a labyrinth Betty has made for the women she counsels, for them to pace through after sixteen-hour days in the maquiladora or after beatings by their husbands or after the murder of their children. I walk the labyrinth. Being in its curl is comforting, makes me feel small but not lost, more like held or even carried. Like maybe a fetus is not so different from a labyrinth. I follow its spiraling path that makes me face the cosmos and then the scrolls of the dead and then the cosmos and then the scrolls of the dead and I spiral all the way to the center, where there is no clear way to face at all.

April 4, in the Year of Our Lord 2015

Another labyrinth, this time in the desert of Chaparral, New Mexico, with people who call themselves The Ruined. *Those countless ones,* they say, *throughout the ages who have encountered the presence of the living God to such an extent that they are ruined for the things of this world.* The Ruined is a collection of a half dozen families who've removed themselves from society, who joke often about how others see them as a cult. *We are not a cult,* say The Ruined, laughing.

Tomorrow is Easter and Bemis and I will head to the Valley of Juárez for dinner with some pastoral workers but tonight we are spiraling. These labyrinths are popping up everywhere along the border, little manifestations of confusion and the need to have a path, however circuitous, through it all. I'm supposed to be meditating on my relationship with Jesus as we spiral but I think of a murder just written up in *El Diario.* Yesterday in *colonia* Independencia II, near Santa Margarita, a young couple stabbed an old man to death after trying to steal his TV, probably to pawn for dope money. Maybe this kind of news is good, not the fact of the murder but the style: no unidentified men with automatic weapons jumping out of a Toyota, no beheading, no duct tape, just your run-of-the-mill junkies-in-love stabbing that could happen in any city, the kind of thing *El Diario* might never have reported in recent years.

Bemis currently lives with The Ruined because of some turmoil at home with his wife. He doesn't offer many details about the situation and I don't pry. I don't ask if she's grown weary of his choosing to spend so many days and nights in Juárez rather than at home with her. I don't ask if she's had some revelation about acupuncture as a sham. I don't ask anything except how long he thinks he'll be with The Ruined. *I don't know,* he says. *I like it here.* Bemis and I have a simple understanding, that he will spread the needles far and wide and I will follow them and we will not worry too much about each other as humans. The arrangement is easy but also strange because his job as a healer is to empathize with people and my job as a writer is to empathize with people and yet we share a slight distrust of each other that keeps us from being pals. I have my suspicions about whether his needles heal. He has his suspicions that I will write that I have my suspicions about whether his needles heal. So I don't ask any of the questions I should to help you empathize with Bemis but this is not a story about Bemis. He says, *I don't want to be another gringo parading around like I know what's best for everyone.*

His long hair is uncombed and his clothes wrinkled and his eyes are so tired as he makes his way through the labyrinth. Perhaps by way of letting you know Bemis a little bit better I can offer this observation: his name is one you might recognize from toilet seats. Well, it's not his name exactly but for several weeks after I met him I felt I recognized his name and then one day there it was on the bottom of a toilet seat. The Bemis company so dominates that market they own the domain name toiletseats.com. They manufacture nearly half of the toilet seats in use in America. *Your bare ass has been on a Bemis* is the slogan they don't use but could. *It's the only thing keeping you from falling in.* To be fair, the acupuncturist I've been following around is not of that particular Bemis clan. But something about the association, when it strikes me, helps me understand him so much better, like he is of the category of things that you might never notice because they do their job quietly, a seemingly unremarkable entity that you will probably never fully appreciate for keeping you, and everyone you ever have to ride in a car or elevator with, from being soaked in some serious shit.

But also out of fairness I dig a bit deeper looking for a less crass association to cement to his name, some other image to have in mind so that I'm not constantly smirking at him when I think of it. *Bemis* originates from the Old French *beau* and *mes*, meaning "beautiful mansion," a phrase that originally denoted not just a house but something like a wedding hall, a fancy place to live but also to conduct religious rites outside the church, somewhere comfortably secular that also, when necessary, has the guts to house the Holy Spirit. Well, alright. Somewhere in the collision of toilet seats and secular chapels is Ryan Bemis, an unassuming blue-collar type with a bent toward the spiritual. Somebody who just does what needs to be done. Somebody who more than a few people have told me is *an honest-to-God healer.* Somebody whose soul pretty well fits, who keeps others from falling in too much shit. I guess that holds true whether or not his needles work.

We spiral ourselves to exhaustion. At the labyrinth's center, one of the youngest among The Ruined gives a sermon, a boy no older than nine. There is no conviction like the conviction of the young. I miss it terribly. The boy shakes as he recounts an encounter with God, shakes on account of both the cold night and his fiery conviction. God hugged him. He and God are pals. At the moment I can find no good reason to doubt the boy. Then The Ruined ask me to share something. I mention I'm chasing Bemis's needles.

I mention I've just come from Trinity, spent the morning walking around the obelisk monument that marks the location of the first-ever detonation of an atomic bomb. I say it was a pilgrimage of sorts, that hundreds of us caravanned and then circled the lava obelisk like Muslims around the Kaaba but with quite a bit less intent and fervor, that I guess it wasn't all that different from walking this here labyrinth, that I don't guess there will be many days in my life bookended by such strange circumambulations, chasing the zenith of our technological bend toward savagery and then the nadir our technological bend toward vigor. Nukes and needles. Amen. We light some candles and send them skyward in paper lanterns and they float on and flicker off into the darkness of the star-pocked sky except for one that immediately catches fire and crashes into creosote. The bush burns. The Ruined rush over and extinguish the burning bush with stomps and then we all go to sleep.

April 5, in the Year of Our Lord 2015

In El Paso, Bemis and I pick up a couple of chickens for Easter dinner and cross over at Fabens, Texas. We follow Sister Maria Eugenia down into the valley. She wants to meet us at the border, escort us to Barreales. The Mexican army has moved into the Valley of Juárez in the last few weeks and they're stopping everyone, extorting everyone, *El Diario* says. Our Easter birds need safe passage and the nun will provide. We follow close behind her little white jalopy of a car with wheels so thin and wobbly it looks more likely to get somewhere slithering than rolling but she manages fifty-five and has no fear. On her back window is a decal, big and faded: the Looney Tunes bird Tweety.

At the chapel Sagrado Corazón de Jesús we sit through mass led by Padre Ramirez. Only twelve of us are in the pews. Barreales is abandoned. The whole Valley of Juárez is abandoned. The towns of Guadalupe and El Porvenir and La Esperanza, the whole fifty-mile stretch of farmland, from the eastern boundary of Juárez down along the spout of Texas, all unequivocally forsaken on the Mexican side. Somewhere around 90 percent of the nearly twenty thousand people who lived in the valley are gone, most fled but plenty missing or killed in the last seven years. While Juárez racked up all the headlines, these small farming villages amassed a higher per capita murder rate. And here The Violence hasn't yet let up. We walk from the chapel toward the home of Beatrice, a pastoral worker who's attended Bemis's NADA trainings in Juárez. Sister Maria Eugenia is needle-trained too and she and Beatrice had hoped to set up a clinic here, like the one at Santa Margarita, but they cannot heal anyone when there is no one to heal. Nearly every adobe house on every block is abandoned, many of them burned to the ground, the charred spine of their vigas sunk in ash. The village is about six square blocks around the plaza but Beatrice has a hard time counting more than ten houses that are currently occupied. We pass a dilapidated day care with Tigger and Winnie-the-Pooh painted on a crumbling wall. Next to Beatrice's house is a baseball field. Six weeks ago there was a gunfight at the ball field. A battle, really. A waging of war. Two dozen men and forty minutes of nonstop gunfire and grenades. We walk out onto the sandlot. There is no grass. There are no foul lines. There is no sense that it was ever any kind of diamond or that anyone ever played here. There is desert and steel shell casings.

For many years the Juárez Cartel ruled this valley, the premier corridor for moving drugs and people over the border of rural West Texas. In 2008 the Sinaloa Cartel made a play for control of the valley in the midst of the chaos of President Felipe Calderón's crackdown on cartels in Juárez proper and that was a war for a while but the Sinaloa pretty much won and now they are fighting among themselves. After the recent ballfield gunfight, El Negro, the head of the Sinaloa Cartel in the valley, was arrested. El Papacho, the jefe of Sinaloa's *sicarios*, was also arrested. He would show up at 2:00 a.m. at the houses of anyone who hadn't fled the valley yet, threatening people and kidnapping and killing and burying bodies under porches. Now that he and El Negro are gone there is a vacuum of power and that is why, just last month, State Attorney General Jorge González Nicolás sent five hundred soldiers from the Mexican army to live at a gymnasium down the road from Guadalupe. Nobody knows what's next. Two days ago *El Diario* reported that El Papacho ratted out the whole Sinaloa operation in the valley, gave up locations of mass graves and weapons caches and names. When the soldiers aren't shaking down the locals, they are helping to dig up their families' bodies. Maybe the Sinaloa Cartel is done here for a while but that doesn't give Beatrice much solace. She knows only that vacuums fill always with blood.

We sit down to the Easter chickens. Even through the thick mud walls of the house we hear Beatrice's dog, an epic bawl and roar that drowns out Sister Maria Eugenia's prayer. *He's hungry,* Beatrice says after *Amén.* She got the dog when her husband died in 2010, after she shut down the little bodega next to her house from fear of extortion. *The dog is my gun*, she says.

Sister Maria Eugenia has a Tweety Bird key chain and hangs it off her habit alongside her rosary. She worries Tweety more than the rosary. *I like the little bird*, she says. *He is small but makes trouble*. The thing I remember most about Tweety is that he was always on the verge of being eaten alive. We shred the chicken and drop it into corn tortillas. *Five years ago Easter was not so quiet*, Sister Maria Eugenia says. That day hundreds of flyers were dropped all over La Esperanza and El Porvenir, little posters issuing a warning for everyone to leave or die. That night the chapel at El Porvenir was burned down. Nobody fought the fire because they were hiding or packing to leave.

For many years Beatrice and Sister Maria Eugenia were absolutely resolute that they would never leave the valley, both nearly sixty and stubborn as hell, two old pals not likely to let a bunch of punks run them from home. But that last gun battle at the sandlot spooked them. They will not lie to me—for the first time ever they thought of leaving. They talked about it for hours over the phone, afraid to go outside. Then, the night after the ballfield gunfight, Padre Ramirez showed up at Beatrice's house. He'd never had any interest in her acupuncture but he showed up that night falling apart. She laid him on her bed. Cleaned his ears. Stuck them with the needles. *De nada*. She knew then that she would stay.

Sister Maria Eugenia is more reticent about the needles. She thinks they help people but she does not proselytize about them like Beatrice. *If people come to me, then people come to me*, she says. Next week she's headed to a big convention of nuns and padres to discuss the role of the Church in bringing Juárez back from the brink of the abyss but she doesn't plan to bring her needles. Even the other nuns she lives with don't know that she's trained in acupuncture. She is worried the Church may crack down on needles, like they've done with other folk remedies. Mostly she doesn't want to draw attention to herself. In the valley, anything might be interpreted as taking a stand. And people who take a stand do not last long. Of everywhere I'll go with Bemis, the valley is the only place I'll never see the needles used.

Oh, but people are painting! says Beatrice. This is a filament of hope she's lately strung through her heart to keep it afloat. After dinner we'll drive over to Guadalupe so she can prove it. She will point out a lot of abandoned cotton farms and a lot of murdered people's houses and the infamous Reyes/ Salazar Bakery, owned by a family of six who were gunned down, no police ever bothering to investigate the murders. She'll show us exactly where people are painting. Past the plaza and its benches, where the decapitated heads of the Guadalupe police were once displayed, is the town hall, with one fresh coat of peach paint on one wall. *A good sign*, she'll say, *when they paint. Even just to cover the blood.*

Lukas is the name of Beatrice's dog. Eventually he gets to making so much noise, impossibly shaking the thick adobe walls with his bark, that we interrupt dinner to look in on him in the backyard. Beatrice says he's a Doberman, but he's Doberman mixed with tyrannosaurus, a towser lumbering out of the shadows, the whole shadow of the house seemingly come to life, monstrous and looking inbred for insanity and reared for bloodlust. In my boots I'm a man of average height and this dog is on all fours looking me straight in the eye, panting real slow right into my mouth. His eyes are bloodshot cue balls drooping beside his snout. Once daggers aimed heavenward, his ears are now permanently folded into stubs where demonic horns might have been sawed off. He's emaciated the way the Valley of Juárez is now emaciated but all the more terrifying on account of it. Every last pulse is a chance to eat you alive. He's all ribs and teeth, his pendulous jowls once muscled enough to rip a human torso in half with a single bite, but now it's clear he'll have to gnaw some because the strength has waned. With her bodega closed, Beatrice can't afford to feed him as much as she should. That makes him angrier. The thick chain around his neck is the most solid thing on him but there's no question he'll rip free of it whenever he likes. He quits breathing and starts to roar. He rears back on his hind legs and towers and he's got this hard-on, this big red dog boner that seems impossible to sustain in the midst of such emaciation. Anything truly monstrous is wrought only on account of the parts that are beyond all comprehension. Bemis and I cower. Sister Maria Eugenia worries Tweety. Beatrice reaches out and pets the beast.

June 6, in the Year of Lord 2015

We drive up over the train tracks, passing four Border Patrol agents on horseback and a sign—WARNING: ENTERING BORDER PATROL FREE FIRE ZONE. More agents are in SUVs along the fence on either side of the vigil, one every fifty or so yards. Just one federale is on the other side of the fence. We're here on the fifth anniversary of the death of Sergio Adrian Hernandez Guereca, a fifteen-year-old Mexican boy killed for allegedly throwing rocks, shot twice by Border Patrol agent Jesus Mesa, Jr., the two bullets fired from American soil, tearing over the Rio Grande, hitting and settling into Sergio's back flesh and skull bone under the Paso del Norte bridge in Juárez. Our Border Patrol shoots brass rounds. Sometimes they shoot through the steel fence. Last week an American judge ruled that Sergio's family has no right to sue his killer in our courts. Our constitution, the judge said, does not apply to foreigners on foreign soil. Because the bullets crossed twenty feet over an imaginary line called the border, it is as if they came from nowhere.

In a few years the U.S. Supreme Court will hear this case on appeal, but will decide to return it to lower courts, in part over concerns about the implications for modern warfare. Justice Breyer will ask the attorneys for Sergio's family, *Are we, in deciding for you, deciding as well that anyone who suffers a drone strike can come to New York and bring a law case? . . . What words do we write so that this opinion doesn't affect a drone strike?*

Today the Border Patrol has warned us that they don't want to see anyone hanging on the fence from the American side and they definitely don't want to see us passing anything through the fence. Here by Anapra at the southeastern corner of New Mexico, away from the big cities, there is no wall. There is only a chain-link fence. But it is enough to pry wide-open the wound of la Frontera. Last year Shena Gutierrez, whose husband was also shot by Border Patrol, was manhandled and arrested at this vigil. Today she speaks to a hundred or so people gathered on both sides of the fence, shouts against complacency. Some Mexican media are up on ladders, hanging over the fence to snap her photo. Sergio's mother, Maria Guadalupe, takes the bullhorn on the Mexican side and weeps into it, says over and over that she cannot understand how her son was shot in the back. Through the fence, through a heart made of paper doves stuck into the chain links, I watch her fill the bullhorn with tears. *Shot in his back*, she says. *In his back*.

As Father Peter from Casa Tabor leads the crowd in prayer, I walk to the vigil's edge, talk to three boys on the Mexican side, hanging on the fence in front of a truck draped in a banner: WHO PROFITS FROM WAR. They are not much younger than Sergio was when he died. We do some high fives through the fence. They ask if I want to take their picture. I tell them it will be hard to get their faces through the chain links. I take a picture and show them how something imaginary made manifest with steel can make everything blurry. Through the fence the littlest boy hands me a rock, innocently maybe, or maybe to see what happens when a white man throws it. *In solidarity until the final consequences*, someone shouts into the bullhorn. Then the bullhorn is held up to a woman playing a wood flute and we disperse to the electronically amplified sound of wind through reed.

We cross over and head to Santa Margarita, me and Bemis and two volunteers he's brought to help with a NADA training tomorrow. Bemis is in high spirits, despite the lingering somberness of the vigil. *Interest from pastoral workers across a lot of parishes in south Juárez has grown*, he says. *The needles are taking root. The training's gonna be packed.* Also, Bemis has left The Ruined of Chaparral and has himself a new bachelor pad. We clunk through Juárez at an unusually relaxed pace.

Today is the weekly church clinic and about fifteen people get needled. I talk for a while with Alfonso Garcia, a doctor who visits the clinic regularly, to give people pills when the needles aren't enough. He has a goatee down past his chest and runs his hand through it and then rubs the ostrich skin of his boots and then back to the goatee. He's never been needled but he doesn't see any harm in it. He mimes popping pills to show me how he thinks people really get healed. But then he also keeps saying, *Faith before medicine.* He says, *This is why the church is good for a clinic. You go to God first.* From the air in front of him he grabs a fistful of faith and with the other hand he grabs something else. I ask him what's in that other hand. He smiles and mimes popping more pills.

We stay the night with Josefina, a Santa Margarita parishioner and one of Bemis's NADA students. She lives not far from the chapel with her husband and their children and their children's children, an overfull house stuffed more tonight. Over dinner there is much debate about what does and does not require invocation of the divine. About ten of us are eating Josefina's enchiladas, all folks connected in some way to the NADA clinic at Santa Margarita. I guess I started the commotion when I asked Sister Maria Esther what the needles have got to do with her faith. She tells a long story about a priest once destroying her cabinet of herbal remedies, storming in and ripping the flowers apart and smashing drawers and shouting different stuff about blasphemy. She thinks the priests get jealous when people come to the nuns for healing. Even though Reiki is now banned, she still practices it occasionally, along with the needles Bemis taught her and those herbal remedies she learned working for years with the indigenous Tarahumara. She'll try anything when people are sick. The problem with Reiki, she says, is that too many people were claiming it could make them levitate, and levitation scares the Church. She doesn't think anyone has such silly ideas about the needles. Carli, one of the American volunteers, says of course these old priests who have had for so many centuries the power of healing in their hands, in their hands alone, would be scared if suddenly anyone could call on the divine energy of the universe and channel it through his own hands and use it to heal. And how much more threatening is it, she suggests, when all these new healers are women. All the women laugh and agree that the problem is men. But not everyone agrees with Carli when she doubles down and says acupuncture is the same as Reiki, that the invocation of divine energy is the same, but that it is simply less threatening because it is channeled through a tool, a needle, rather than the hands of women. This gets Sister Maria Esther stirred up. *God is not in the needles*, she says. Even Bemis tries to steer Carli clear of the woo-woo but Carli is New Age through and through, says she's not even talking about God because there is no God but just the divine feminine force that breathes life into the universe, and that statement dampens the conversation to murmurs.

But everyone needs to get on the same page about the issue. Juárez has a new bishop and in the morning Bemis will meet with him to lay out his plan for introducing NADA to chapel clinics throughout Juárez. Too much talk about the outlawed Reiki and/or no-God-but-just-the-divine-feminine-force-that-breathes-life-into-the-universe might scare the bishop off the whole thing.

June 7, in the Year of Our Lord 2015

Down the stairs in early morning I creep-stomp, trying to both announce myself and keep from startling any sleepers. The staircase is a rickety spiral ladder that drops right into Josefina's bedroom. Josefina's daughter is down there alone, changing in front of a gun locker. I sort of avert my eyes and make a guttural apology noise but she says it's alright, she's almost done. Both she and her brother are in their twenties and have joined the municipal police in the last year. As The Violence ebbed in Juárez, the police force, gutted by murder and corruption, needed repopulation. They are good jobs in the sense that the money is decent, better than at the maquiladoras. But the money is only good because the chances are still high that you will be killed or pressed into service by cartels. She smiles at me. Pulls a bulletproof vest over her head and buttons up her uniform. She takes an assault rifle out of the locker, inspects the gun, wipes it down, and shoulders it. She kisses her kid on the head and leaves to do god knows what for the day. The rest of us go to mass.

Hundreds of parishioners cram into the Virgin de Luz chapel to catch a glimpse of the new bishop, José Guadalupe Torres Campos. When we arrive at 8:00 a.m., it is standing room only and even then most of the standing spots are outside. Josefina is having none of that and sneaks our group inside by herding us behind the swinging incense into the bishop's procession. I find myself walking in stride with the guy, him with his dazzled staff and vestments and towering miter, me in my Nirvana T-shirt.

Most everyone here has come for an audience with Bishop Campos. At a potluck after mass he is swamped with people crowding for kisses and blessings. Bemis ends up getting less than five minutes with the guy, just long enough to say a few words and offer up a gift: something called guerrilla prayer flags—a string of rags in the Tibetan tradition, each rag with a different symbol, a lotus petal or the Virgin Mary or the yin-yang of the I Ching or the logo of Bemis's American acupuncture clinic, Crossroads. The logo is a crucifix with a highway cutting it in half. The gift is a whole cultural/religious mishmash. The bishop is confused as he inspects the flags. They are about as woo-woo a gift as one could present a bishop. I realize, not for the first time, that Bemis is more conflicted about the woo-woo than he lets on. Sometimes he wants his needles to be nothing more than wrenches or scalpels, utilitarian objects in a rational, physical, and scientific vocation. But then he throws his acupuncture logo on some prayer flags alongside all the symbols of the world's faiths and presents it to the bishop and it's clear his aspirations are of the metaphysical variety. One might easily see this meeting with the bishop as less of an audience and more of a challenge. But Bishop Campos smiles and folds up the rags and passes them off before blessing us and dismissing us and sitting down to a bowl of steaming menudo.

As we head to Santa Margarita, Bemis tells me he's surprised the bishop seemed to have no idea about the NADA clinics. He'd supposedly been briefed about the gringo giving away acupuncture training in the chapels but clearly knew nothing about it. This is either good or bad, that the highest church official in the city is oblivious of the needles seeping into his parishes. Bemis will go back and forth on the issue all day. *Do you think I surprised him, man? Do you think he just doesn't care? Or what? Should I maybe, like, not have said anything?* Bemis tends to have that stoneresque amazement toward a lot of things others might worry about. He's gonna keep doing what he does regardless—no reason to fret. But there's no harm in being amazed. One time he drove to Juárez, drove all day around the city and on the highway back home, with a wheel falling off his Ford clunker, the car shaking ever more violently the faster it went, the lips of his passengers starting to bleed from nervous biting and also accidental biting from the quakes of the wheel, loose on its axle. But all day Bemis never worried, just went on remarking to his passengers how wild it was that his car had become the shaking kind.

At Santa Margarita, Carli gets all the nuns and pastoral workers, all women save Rudolpho, the mechanic/butcher/massage therapist, doing some mild calisthenics in the chapel courtyard, a kind of lazy yoga to prepare their spirits for needle lessons. I sit in the chapel and talk to a stream of NADA patients, lots of maquiladora workers, young and old, suffering from insomnia, headaches, kidney failure, osteoporosis, vertigo, and gobs of hypertension. Bemis says lots of people want to give me testimonials and I can hardly keep track of them all. Testimonials are a big part of alternative medicine, like they are a big part of religion, there not being any kind of definitive science to trot out. Almost all of the several dozen patients I talk to discuss the needles in terms of faith. They all say variations of *I waited to try because I didn't believe. Now I believe.*

At day's end the students are ready to experiment with new points they've learned, ready to stick each other in the forehead and hands and feet. They're moving beyond NADA now, for reasons unclear, no longer concerned only with the labyrinthine fetal voodoo dolls hanging like bats from the head's flanks. Bemis has outfitted the chapel with zero-gravity chairs, sort of reclining lawn chairs, in which to needle people. They circle up the recliners, in front of pews by the altar, in the wake of the life-size crucified Jesus, loinclothed and rippling with muscles, hanging in the sacristy and observing us rather sullenly. I'm recruited as one of a dozen test patients. After a year of chasing needles, I finally recline with the others, submit my flesh to steel—a new Commu-

nion without blood or wine or crumbs. It feels like art, somehow, us all collapsed into a painting or performance but also
outside it gazing in, staring at one another in the circle, each
without our shoes or socks, pants rolled up, needles sticking
out of foreheads and feet and ears, each meditating on his or
her own anxieties but also watching the others in the circle
meditate on their anxieties, and illness and pain and depression and despair. It is the first time in a long time that I've
been comfortable in a church. The recliners are an improvement on pews. But the steel tingles a bit, in the skin, and it is
easy to imagine it catching the frequency of angst broadcast
by all the other steel, in all the other skin. It is easy to imagine the needles as receivers and broadcasters of pain, a network that, if spread wide enough, may in some equitable
and tolerable proportion disperse the pain. For many of us,
that means we must feel more. Be less comfortable. It is easy
to imagine that Rudolpho and his children will have a peace-
ful life, that he will one day get a shop in which to butcher
hogs and the dark red stain in the dirt outside the front door
of his house will fade, easy to imagine that all the dark red
stains will fade or be obliterated by a fresh coat of peach
paint. It is easy to imagine that Josefina's daughter and son
will never have to witness the decapitations of their col-
leagues on the Juárez police force. Easy to imagine that at El
Pastor's asylum Elisabeth will get needled enough and get
well enough that she walks out of the asylum and finds her
children and moves again to California, where she will live
out her life on the beach, watching her babies swim out beyond the white breakers, swim back to shore, grown and full
of vigor. It is easy to imagine El Pastor building on the outskirts of Juárez a Rome of such splendor that no one in the
place wants for anything or suffers from anything. It is easy

to imagine that *El Diario* will go the vanishing way of so many newspapers, not because their reporters keep turning up assassinated but because they will have nothing to report beyond relative happiness and deaths of old age. It is easy to imagine that name after name on Sister Betty's wall of the disappeared will themselves disappear, the scrolls rolling up on themselves without the weight of mournful ink to make them unfurl. It is easy to imagine that the needles will spill out of this chapel and into the streets and into all the labyrinthine inlets of side-intelligencers so that everyone in the city becomes a little less anxious, easy to imagine that the needles will spill even farther, that there will be such demand that even the big steel wall prying open the wound of la Frontera will need to be torn down to make enough needles. Ah, but who will slave in that factory? It is easy to imagine the Catholic Church in a hundred years, all the priests placing a wafer on tongues followed by all the nuns slipping needles into ears, Sisters Maria Rosario and Maria Esther of Santa Margarita becoming the patron saints of the needling nuns. It is easy to imagine that, given enough time, all of the world's religions and superstitions and pseudosciences will blend into one practice, easy to imagine that this is finally and only what is really human—unreasonable faith—that as our bodies evaporate into the cloud of information that now besieges the ever-wobbling earth, one small pocket of something still like the old humanity will be left, a tribe whose practice includes sitting still and quiet in a warehouse chapel in the wake of a crucified man, with needles in their ears. It is easy to imagine every labyrinth unfurling into a straight path, easy to imagine the human ear flattening, evolving to become nothing but a platform for our new network of dispersing pain in tolerable and equitable proportions. A simple steel implement—*pew pew, pew pew*—in the hands of a desert tribe crawling to the edges of the earth and over them, moving ear by flattened ear, in search of ever more flesh to remind that it is flesh, that it must feel its portion too. It is easy to imagine.

Bemis and his volunteers cross back over the border but I stay this night at the house of an acquaintance who lives in one of the many gated communities in north-central Juárez, the relative middle-class *colonias*. These areas of the city seem a world away from the impoverished *colonias* just a mile or two south. They are no different from most neighborhoods just across the border in El Paso, apart from ubiquitous tall steel walls that encircle the blocks, with big gates and guards. We go to a store and to a bustling *mercado* for dinner and stop at a street vendor for chili-lime *raspados*. In this neighborhood are professional acupuncture clinics where an individual treatment costs five hundred pesos, the fancy kind of spas where most acupuncture happens in America too. This is a good neighborhood. Tonight the streets are run by strolling families, the children testing in all directions the outer bounds of their parents' pull and bouncing back again, disorderly orbits of *raspado*-stained satellites. This is the Juárez where it is easy to imagine that because the murders have ebbed, everything will be just fine.

June 8, in the Year of Our Lord 2015

Do not worry about hitting people with your car, says Sister Maria Esther. *People will jump out of the way. But the sad dogs, they will just let you run them over.* Some 150,000 strays run the streets of Juárez and most of them seem to be on the rutty dirt roads we're driving around Santa Margarita. Sisters Maria Esther and Maria Rosario are letting me tag along on their daily rounds. Usually they walk but today we're dodging strays in the car. They're a dynamic duo of needling nuns, Rosario with big glasses on her round face and close-cropped silver hair, Esther with long silver hair and that slight hunch from a dozen years walking everywhere with the indigenous Tarahumara on mountain paths, another dozen years on these unpaved city streets. These sisters prefer denim skirts to habits. They wear matching silver crucifixes.

Their order of nuns is charged with service of the poor. *Being in service of the sacred heart is a lot easier than being in service of the poor*, says Rosario. But they would not trade their work for any other. Alternative medicine was not something they learned in the nunnery. But some brought it with them to the city after working with the Tarahumara. Until 2008 their use of herbal remedies was mostly clandestine because of dogmatic priests. But once The Violence started, the nuns were pretty much left to do whatever they wanted. Their clinic for herb therapy grew and in 2011 Bemis showed up with needles. Since then their daily rounds have expanded, with folks from all five chapels in the parish coming to Santa Margarita for the needles, and requesting that the needling nuns come to them.

We go to the homes for very sick people, Rosario says. *If they can walk to the chapel, they should. It is easier to make people sit still in church. But not everyone can walk.*

We visit Antonieta Aguilar Alvarado, fifty-two, who cannot leave home because of vertigo. She has had many health problems over the years but *one day the whole world just started spinning*, she says. *It always spins*, Rosario reminds her. *It finally made me dizzy*, says Antonieta. Rosario pokes her ears once a week, enough for her to sit up and watch mass on TV.

We visit Bacilio Hernandez, fifty-one, who is almost dead from liver cancer. His daughter Rosa and wife, Negrete, sit beside him on a bed in their house, which is one room with dirt floors where they live along with Rosa's six children. The hospital will not treat Bacilio anymore. *They say he is dead already but he is not*, Rosa says. Bacilio rolls his eyes to communicate. When he tries to talk, blood dribbles from his mouth. *The needles make him calm*, his wife says. Rosario holds his bony hand and needles his ears and his eyes roll and the children outside scream as they chase chickens and Rosario prays. Bacilio's eyes close.

We stop and pick up Veta and her two-year-old grand-daughter, Andrea. Andrea is our key. She is small enough to slip through the bars of the fence around the house of Graciela Salomé Mesa, forty-seven, who cannot open the door herself because of brain damage from strokes. Graciela cries as I talk to her, *from the memories*, she says. For many years Graciela helped Rosario and Esther stock and distribute their cabinet of herbs but she has not left home much since the first stroke two years ago.

Graciela has albums of obituaries, funeral cards with pictures and brief eulogies pasted into the repurposed pages of her children's old math textbooks. She wants me to look through them but cannot tell me why. Flipping through the book of obituaries and all the equations swirling around them, it's clear almost all the deceased are old. Rosario looks over my shoulder, says, *These are not the murders*. Graciela, both before and after her stroke, has collected all the announcements of people who died of old age, friends, acquaintances, strangers. She tries to explain why she's done this but can't, and each time I pose the question in a different way she cries again. Rosario and Esther say she has always been a bit odd, a bit obsessive in this way. They show me a room of her house with towers of hoarded newspapers. Graciela's albums of obituaries remind me of the scrolls of names Sister Betty etches onto the walls of Casa Tabor. Sister Betty meditates on lives interrupted. Graciela meditates on lives that have run a full course. Glued as they are atop pages of elementary equations, Graciela's obituary collection seems the calculus of a mad genius; here is what it is all supposed to add up to: no one dead at the hand of another.

We drive on and from the backseat Veta narrates the toll The Violence has had on all the places we pass. *We have children*, she says, *but unfortunately children behave like they have no mothers*. Esther says, *The whole world is mothers*. This is either a pun about Mother Earth or a pun about nuns because they all laugh. But something about it is exactly a notion that's been dawning on me for a while, since I first visited Santa Margarita last year and the women were running everything. These clinics have spread to many chapels and the number of NADA practitioners has multiplied from a handful to nearly a hundred in the last year alone. And it is almost entirely women who have taken up the steel, who have done over thirty-five thousand treatments, poked over 350,000 needles into ears, well on their way to unleashing a million tiny daggers on the city's side-intelligencers. I will not say the needles empowered them, because that maybe suggests the women in this city weren't always the ones keeping it afloat.

Before The Violence there was The Femicide, the notion that from the 1990s through about 2005 Juárez saw over four hundred mysterious murders of women by, as one researcher put it, "street gangs, organized crime syndicates, powerful families, a satanic cult, an underground snuff film industry, the police—or all of the above." The story of The Femicide casts a long shadow over the women of Juárez, suggesting they've been powerless victims since long before the cartel wars. But Molly Molloy, a researcher at New Mexico State University, who has tracked violence in Juárez since talk of The Femicide began, says it is an unfortunate myth. "Female murder victims," she told *The Texas Observer* in 2014, "have never comprised more than 18 percent of the overall number of murder victims in Ciudad Juárez, and in the last two decades that figure averages at less than 10 percent. That's less than in the United States, where about 20 to 25 percent of the people who are murdered in a given year are women." She says that 75 percent of those four hundred mysterious murders of women were solved, a rate exponentially higher than the number of murder cases that were closed during the subsequent years of cartel warfare. She says The Femicide is little more than a grotesquely sexual media narrative that obfuscates the complex social pressures that victimize all the impoverished, the vast majority of people, in Juárez:

> Some of the writing about these cases I find to be pushing over into the extreme and eroticizing the victims in a way that makes them appear a lot more helpless and powerless than women in Juárez are . . . I just don't think that's a re-alistic depiction of life in a place like Juárez. Many of the women, who do the work and are the only breadwinner, are quite powerful. Many of them are mothers, and workers, and take care of other people. They're not the powerless

people that some of the literature portrays them as. And I find that, as a feminist, to be counterproductive in the extreme.

After a year of chasing the needles I still have no clear understanding of their medical value. I've collected many testimonials praising their power but just as many studies suggesting they are little more than placebo. Two years ago, *The New York Times* headline was "Ciudad Juárez Weighs a Neglected Notion—Hope," and I wondered if it was true, if the needles were proof. But I suspect you could give Rosario and Esther, all the other nuns and all the other women who now practice NADA, pretty much anything, needles or moxa or herbs or handfuls of nothing but air, and they'd find a way to use it to ease the suffering of those around them, even just a little bit, just by showing up, just by coming together and making it clear that hope was never a thing they neglected. In this desert, there is no force greater than its women. You don't need any amount of science or faith to understand that. Even our mountains are in their image. The Sleeping Lady, woke for good. Go: see the needling nuns. Be healed.

July 31, in the Year of Our Lord 2015

I meet Morgan Smith and his nephew in the parking lot of a Carl's Jr. in El Paso. A Corolla rolls up next to us and an old guy named Art gets out, opens the trunk, shows us the haul we'll smuggle down to the asylum. We all nod a bunch: it is a good haul. We load up and caravan to the Santa Teresa port of entry, across the border, and past the Border Patrol's million-dollar pond and the Foxconn plant of six thousand

Mexicans making thirteen thousand gadgets a day for Apple and Nokia and Motorola, the rear end of Art's Corolla riding low to the road, nearly dragging because his little trunk is packed to capacity with wieners and buns and chili.

Morgan is a former public official and lawyer from Colorado who's been visiting the asylum for five years, bringing treats and snapping photographs and trying to help raise awareness about El Pastor's mission. Art and his team are a group of Christian retirees who recently linked up with Morgan after hearing about the asylum on NPR and feeling called to charity. I'm tagging along with this group because Bemis has pretty much stopped visiting the asylum, decided to focus on places where he sees the most progress, the church clinics in Juárez proper. The asylum, he says, has more basic struggles. NADA is not exactly a luxury but it only seems to distract from keeping the people there clothed and fed and protected. And El Pastor can be a tough man to work with. He's scrappy. He wants to know the monetary benefits of the charity he receives, whether that charity comes in the form of art classes or acupuncture or chili dogs. He wants it to feed his vision of the asylum by getting his story in the press and by lining up grants and donations to help him build Visión en Acción into an empire. This rubs some folks the wrong way, El Pastor always putting on the pressure for more help and more money, especially when, despite all the aid, the living conditions of the residents don't seem to improve all that dramatically but fountains are being built.

The new courtyard is much more developed since my last visit. Back then there were a few columns and one or two molds for busts of lions but now it is pretty well built out with about twenty-five concrete lion busts in varying sizes and two full-bodied lions guarding a fountainhead, which is an openmouthed lion through which water, when they have any extra water, flows. Right now they do not have any extra water. The fountain spouts nothing. Nada. The new courtyard is a rough approximation of grandeur, beautiful but oh so temporary. El Pastor isn't here right now, but when he shows up in a few hours, Morgan's nephew will ask him about the lions and the columns and El Pastor will talk about *Ben-Hur*, will talk about *Gladiator*, will go on and on like he does about his beloved ancient-Roman period flicks and I'll see rising in the kid's eyes the tide of uncanny, which will eventually break to worry as he struggles to make sense of a world so close to his own where a place such as this actually exists. The kid is headed to law school next year. He's wide-eyed. The asylum is a complicated place.

I track down Josué, rearranging the toothbrush wall that seems to have a lot less brushes than it did before, lots of names with no toothbrush hanging there. I ask him how he's set for needles. *We don't have them,* Josué says. *They are good, the needles, but we don't have them. We don't use them now. You bring some next time and maybe we stick everyone again, but I don't know.*

Art unloads over three hundred wieners and buns and sodas and fifty pounds of chili and twenty pounds of candy and Morgan stuffs a couple of cartons of cigarettes into his jacket and all of this is the treatment for today. The process swings into motion pretty quick, the dogs dumped into huge industrial pots and the chili heated in huge industrial pots and before I know it I'm arranging food on a rolling cart, Art having bunned the wieners and sent them down an assembly line of slopped chili and squeezed mustard, me at the end of the line trying to fit them two at a time on a three-level rolling cart and in an arrangement that maximizes the number of dogs on each level without smearing their chili, an arrangement that allows us to get the most possible dogs out the door in a single roll of the cart, out into the old court-yard. A chili dog for Yogi, who pets it before he eats it. A chili dog for Memo and Gaspar, who eat theirs in two bites as they pace concentric circles into the dust. Favela eats hers from the wheelchair, nibbling in a sophisticated way, smiling and showing off her manners. I carry two chili dogs around look-ing for Elisabeth, but she is not here. No one seems to know where she's gone. She's gone and no one knows a thing. I sit with Yogi and eat Elisabeth's dogs.

El Pastor arrives after everyone is fed, singing "I Believe in You." He says, *This is what I feel when I see you bring the dogs!* He belts the song to the group of retirees in the kitchen as thanks for their generosity, messing up most of the words but powering through full-blast anyway:

> *I don't believe in Supermans*
> *Organic foods and foreign cars*
> *I don't believe in expensive gold*
> *I don't believe in growing old*

El Pastor says he loves the great country band Alabama, but I think he's confused; the song was recorded by Don Williams and I don't guess any band like Alabama ever covered it. Bette Midler did a cover for her '95 album, *Bette of Roses*, and that should give you some idea of the song's character, a kind of lounge-piano cabaret tune suffused with so much sappy sincerity and so outside the traditional Western ethos that it's hard to believe it was ever at the top of the country charts. But it was, in 1980, with Don Williams, the Gentle Giant, meandering through guitar licks, just barely keeping his head above the molasses flow of that laconic groove, his throat rolling down past baritone in the chorus. El Pastor sings it just exactly like a show tune, loud and with a huge grin on his face, the butchered chorus echoing off the concrete walls of the asylum, twangy professions of belief in babies, love itself, and you. El Pastor believes in you.

Morgan takes advantage of the distraction to distribute the cigarettes he's smuggled down. He knows smokes might be frowned upon by the Christian retirees but he can't help bringing them every time he visits. *They get so little here,* he says. *One smoke won't hurt.* But still he carries around a bag of candy, delivering it in handfuls around the cigarettes to be a bit less conspicuous. He's got to get them passed out and smoked up quick so El Pastor doesn't stockpile and ration them. Morgan wants everyone to get a smoke all at once, right after the chili dogs: a communal activity. I take the two packs he hands me and go back to Yogi and Favela—one each and a light. Then a swarm of residents grab from the open pack and it's empty. All around the courtyard the hundred or more residents have chili on their hands or faces and a lollipop in one hand and a cigarette at their lips. This is the antithesis of the needles. The asylum is quiet like it was the first time I saw the residents needled, only here it is not a handful of folks circled up in the multipurpose room, but everyone in the whole courtyard, mostly holding still and puffing and the smoke rising into the laundry hanging overhead. I wonder if this is giving up, the way our hospitals will pump people full of morphine at the end of their life. But here there is no morphine. In the streets of Juárez there's booze to guzzle and paint to huff and crack to smoke and that is what lands most residents here in the first place—giving up and being given up on. But even though the needles aren't around, everybody's ears still look like inverted fetuses. And that makes me happy, though I don't know why.

El Pastor is still bellowing in the kitchen. I can't hear the exact words but I know them anyway. I know the song. This isn't the kind of tune I'd ever be caught queuing up on the jukebox at a honky-tonk but it's the sappy kind that runs through my head whenever I get the sense all of life is a slow process of giving up but I'd rather not just now. El Pastor sings about heaven being everywhere, switching to Spanish at times—*cielo, dios como amor*—and it sounds alright.

Yogi smokes with a fist, a full hand wrapped around the cigarette's filter and his thumb and two fingers splaying around his face when he wants a puff. He hands it to me when there's not enough left to fist and motions for me to smoke the rest and asks for another. He pets the new smoke and I light it for him. He takes my hand and pulls me back to the northwest corner of the courtyard, to the cells like the one where Elisabeth spent two years. In this corridor are two cells, two men in each cell behind the rusted bars, men whose minds have collapsed from illness and addiction, men who have murdered, men who will attack other residents. If not for the cigarettes, the smell of feces would reign. This is the worst part of the asylum, there being no way to look around and come even close to justifying use of the word *humane*. These men are not dead on the streets, El Pastor would say, as they would be if left to the government or the cartels. But they are not exactly alive in here. These seem like conditions that would get any zoo or animal shelter in America in trouble. Just twenty miles up the road is the million-dollar pond at the border crossing and a string of multimillion-dollar factories making billions of dollars of American goods but there is not a single cent to spare here to preserve human dignity. They have none, crouching naked on their side of the bars. But I, staring in from the other side, have none either. We have none on our side.

The only man in the cells in any condition to talk, the only one wearing pants, steps up to the bars. He's known only as El Ratón—the little rat. He was in the asylum years ago, left, and last year was brought back by the police when they were cleaning house, *destroyed and sick*, El Pastor says, after years of being neglected in a Juárez prison. The police don't know his name either so it was easy for them to drop him off at the asylum. El Ratón rasps through the bars, mostly asking without real words for a smoke. Yogi kind of pets El Ratón's rasp in the air between us as if letting me know it's okay to rasp back, though Yogi's not about to do it if I don't, but there's no such thing as harmony in rasps. I pass the cigarette through the bars and El Ratón says, *Gracias*. His posture changes as he smokes, as he enjoys this base human pleasure. He stands up straight. I guess this is why Morgan always brings the smokes, five years of coming down here with volunteers and money and gifts and none of it can make things better, can never make things alright, but at least with cigarettes at their lips everyone has a kind of undeniable dignity, the primal mastery over fire that first made us human, the knowledge that we can do a thing even though it's harmful and the will or ignorance or sadness to go ahead and do it. The choice. I've got two cigarettes left and El Ratón and me and Yogi pass them around, blow smoke at one another through the bars, we three masters of the primal inferno.

El Pastor has quit on his country show tune. I miss it already. His version, specifically, with all the wrong words.

Translation is the attempt to erase borders, but the whole history of civilization is the creation of borders, so translation is a Sisyphean mess. That's why, when something manages to pass through so effortlessly—like the sentiment of bedrock faith in human goodness through the sap of Don Williams and the atonal hollering of El Pastor, like smoke through the bars between me and El Ratón—you just got to shut up, let it echo through your labyrinthine inlets, give your fetal ears a real chance to grow into a worthwhile soul.

As we pack up to head out, I ask El Pastor why they've stopped needling, if they can't easily get needles from Bemis or have Morgan bring them or pick them up when El Pastor or Josué are in El Paso. El Pastor's eyes get big and he says, *Ah, but the miracle has happened!* Out of his closet he drags a bag from Express, grinning and loosening the drawstring so I can see inside, see many little boxes covered in Japanese glyphs. El Pastor was late to the chili-dog party because he was retrieving these needles from an old lady in the city who didn't need them anymore. *I don't know why she has needles but then she gives them to me. Like that.* It does seem like a little miracle as I shake the boxes to make sure they're full. *Yes,* he says, *her son died this morning.* El Pastor had gone to visit the woman because her son had been a resident at the asylum, spent a year here after his family got overwhelmed by his violent outbursts and dropped him off. Then came the call that the boy, having returned home several months ago, just this morning hanged himself after smoking PCP. His mother had bought the needles for him because he'd received NADA treatments at the asylum. She thought they might continue to help in his recovery. Only one of the boxes is opened but in it only a single packet of needles remains. He must have tried to get better, must have believed in the needles a little bit, for a little while. I show El Pastor the lonely packet and he says, *Go ahead.* I put the needles in my shirt pocket. This boy who hanged himself was one of the few who got out of the asylum and made it home and these were the last needles he looked at and decided against. *A shame*, says El Pastor. *But this is how the miracle works. Ah, mysterious, you see?* He closes the bag and pats me on the shoulder and pulls me in for a hug.

As we leave the asylum, there's Benito, the goatherd, on his bicycle chasing some strays off the road. He had a bipolar episode every January until they put him in charge of the animals. And there's Memo, with a big staff walking among the goats. Gaspar stands at attention in front of the gates, salutes us away. Art and his crew head north, back across the border, but Morgan and his nephew and me, we go the other direction. We stop and buy Cokes at a little shop where some boys in the back are watching *RoboCop.* We head toward Palomas, another Mexican border town to the west. We stop off at a lonely highway shrine for Santa Muerte, the saint of death, whose veneration has long been condemned by the Catholic Church and more so lately because of the way the cartels have taken to her. Shrines like this one have risen up all over the war zones, little shacks painted black and purple, covered in murals of a skeleton holding Earth in its hand or a skeleton praying with rosary beads, shacks housing a statue of a black-robed skeleton sitting on a throne of skulls holding a scythe. Morgan wanders into the desert to take a leak and his nephew grabs as a souvenir one of the many candles burned at the shrine. I step up to the grim reaper and look her straight in the skull holes and drop the packet of needles at her feet bones. All hail Santa Muerte of la Frontera. I make this sacred offering, a few grams of steel. Even you must weigh little things. The sun gets big and fiery like it does when it falls and looks to bounce off the distant sandy plain. We drive into Palomas and there in the road at the edge of town is a woman with three small children, the kids running around her and screaming as she playfully herds them down the road. And of course it is not Elisabeth. Of course it is not. Nobody knows what happened to Elisabeth or where she went, and generally when residents leave the asylum and do not return, it means they are gone for good but what if this is Elisabeth, her hair down to her chin, exactly the length it might have grown after her head was shaved last year, reunited with her kids and fixed up totally with her soul fallen into place, the concrete cell and the bugs a distant memory but the ping of the needles still in her ears as she drifts along a road that disappears into the ball of fire landing on the horizon, as she heads not into the sunset, heads not even for the sunset but stops, just now, to sway around it, her dancing just like that, to the perfect pitch of one or two grams of steel, and singing all the words just exactly right:

But I believe in love, I believe in music, I believe in magic, and I believe in you.

NOTES

ix The definition of *acid western* is a mash-up of phrases from Pauline Kael's blistering review of Alejandro Jodorowsky's film *El Topo* (*The New Yorker*, November 20, 1971) and Jonathan Rosenbaum's blissful book-length review *Dead Man* (BFI Modern Classics, 2000) of Jim Jarmusch's film of the same name.

THE LIGHT OF GOD

19 *Highly skilled, highly trained people can only eat*: A Predator drone pilot said this in the article "Boredom May Be Worst Foe for Predator Drone Operators," published November 16, 2012, in the *Las Vegas Review-Journal*. The article cites an MIT study that claims remote pilots are likely to make fewer mistakes if they distract themselves with snacks or music because they won't get bored. Creech Air Force Base, forty-five minutes north of Vegas, is where the military operates most of its Afghanistan drone missions from. Most drone strikes in Pakistan are likely carried out from CIA offices in Langley, Virginia, because we (the United States) are not officially involved in military operations there—but

this, like all things covert and drone, is hard to pinpoint. Also hard to pinpoint is which locale makes for more sinister remote killing, a steel cargo container in the Nevada desert or an air-conditioned office building in Virginia.

19 *For most missions nothing happens*: Another drone pilot, quoted in "Boredom, Terror, Deadly Mistakes: Secrets of the New Drone War" by Jefferson Morley on April 3, 2012, on Salon.com.

20 *I can't sleep at night because when the drones are there*: From an interview with a man injured in a March 17, 2011, drone strike on Datta Khel in North Waziristan. This interview and others more disturbing, all conducted with Waziris on the ground in Pakistan, are from the report *Living Under Drones* published through a joint effort by the Stanford Law School and the NYU School of Law in 2012. The report is the most comprehensive evaluation of the effect of drone strikes on civilians in the FATA regions of Pakistan. The report also includes a description of Hellfired bodies, used later in this essay: "dismembered, mutilated, and burned beyond recognition."

23 *Obama has a "kill list"*: Jo Becker and Scott Shane, "The Shadow War: Secret 'Kill List' Proves a Test of Obama's Principles and Will," *The New York Times*, May 29, 2012.

23 *"Among the elements that could combine for a lethal signature"*: This is from Andrew Cockburn's *Kill Chain: The Rise of the High-Tech Assassins*, which, when published in 2015, will be the definitive history of America's drone warfare up to that point. Cockburn establishes that much of our drone warfare results not from its effectiveness as a surgical weapon but from the need to feed a trillion-dollar (too-big-to-fail) defense industry. Most drone-related technology, including the much-vaunted Gorgon Stare, he will characterize as absurdly ineffective and inaccurate, writing that the military has often known this before its deployment in combat but kept it quiet to keep the cash flowing.

26 *"data at rates of 10 to over 1,000 times projected communications"*: *Operating Next-Generation Remotely Piloted Aircraft for Irregular Warfare*, United States Air Force Scientific Advisory Board, April 2011, 10–11. The Gorgon Stare, while portrayed in this government

document as an almost omnipotent surveillance tool, will never actually work (see *Kill Chain* by Andrew Cockburn).

26 *the USAF Scientific Advisory Board recommends "automated processing"*: Ibid., 21.

26 *"The new technology should be accurate"*: Michael Endler, "Baseball Meets Internet of Things: Bye, Bad Umpires?," Information Week.com, April 5, 2013.

26 *When a reporter gets into the Reaper Ground Control Station at Holloman Air Force Base*: This exchange occurs at Holloman AFB in the 2012 Al Jazeera documentary *Attack of the Drones*. An almost identical scene occurs at Holloman in the 2012 ABC Australia documentary *Rise of the Machines*.

28 *One of the few photos I've seen*: Photos by Noor Behram, in Spencer Ackerman, "Rare Photographs Show Ground Zero of the Drone War," *Wired*, December 12, 2011.

28 *The government reported no civilian casualties for this strike*: The Pentagon remained silent about this strike, while Reuters reported only three dead, all combatants. The Bureau of Investigative Journalism used eight sources, including locals and Pakistani officials, to estimate that seventeen to twenty-one people were killed in the strike including nine to thirteen civilians, of whom six were children, including the seven-year-old brother of the children in the photograph. The most accurate public information on all American drone strikes is on the bureau's website, www .thebureauinvestigates.com/projects/drone-war.

28 *light that looks like it's coming from heaven*: From an interview with a former Predator drone pilot conducted by Omer Fast for his film *5,000 Feet Is the Best*.

CHILDREN OF THE GADGET

45 *Joseph Masco's got this idea in his book* The Nuclear Borderlands: Masco's book brilliantly explores the complexities of complacency regarding the Bomb and delves into Northern New Mexico culture in a way this book doesn't even attempt to. You should definitely read it. But as I prepare this book for publication, I can't

help but feel both Masco and I are behind the times, though this essay is just two years old and Masco's book is only nine years older than that. Right now, in the summer of 2017, Americans cannot stop talking about nuclear war because we have a president who seems willing to wage it on a whim. Fearmongering is never useful. But part of me hopes that more than a little bit of our anxiety from this political shitshow persists, to keep us from ever becoming complacent again about the monster we have created.

50 *"Exposure rates in public areas from the world's first nuclear explosion"*: From the *Los Alamos Historical Document Retrieval and Assessment (LAHDRA) Project: Prepared for the Centers for Disease Control and Prevention (CDC) National Center for Environmental Health Division of Environmental Hazards and Health Effects Radiation Studies Branch* (2009). That's the actual thirty-two-word title, which is not a title so much as a list of bureaucracies. It's an incredibly eye-opening report if you can keep your eyes open through all the bureaucratic obfuscation.

53 *"A few people were probably overexposed"*: LAHDRA.

65 *0545 Hours—July 16, 1945 (Fifteen Minutes After the Blast)*: This section is an edited version of a July 21, 1945, report to General Groves, included in *LAHDRA*.

69 *The first public tour of the Trinity Site was organized in September of 1945*: All quotes about the first public Trinity Site visit are from a September 11, 1945, article from the Associated Press, reported from Alamogordo, that ran in almost every one of the nation's newspapers, often headlined by variations on words such as *Destructive*, *Death*, *Devastations*, etc., even as the article itself promotes the idea that no danger lingers from atom bombs beyond the blast itself.

70 *"secured some good pictures of the cattle"*: This from a December 13, 1945, article in the *Alamogordo Daily News* headlined "Paramount Picture Corporation 'Shoots' Bombed Cattle." The headline is one of those puns newsrooms get off on, but really the sad joke is that the mutated cows, all of them, should have been shot (gunwise) and removed from the food supply.

71 *A 2011 study of the aftermath in Chernobyl*: Alexander M. Danzer and Natalia Danzer, *The Long-Term Effects of the Chernobyl*

Catastrophe on Subjective Well-Being and Mental Health, discussion paper series no. 5906, Forschungsinstitut zur Zukunft der Arbeit, 2011.

72 *"These people are sick"*: Dutch psychiatrist Dr. Johan Havenaar, in Michael Specter, "A Wasted Land," *The New York Times*, March 31, 1996.

72 *0530 Hours—July 16, 1945 (Fourteen Seconds After the Gadget's Detonation)*: Compilation of descriptions of the explosion from Manhattan Project members Frank Oppenheimer, Isidor Isaac Rabi, Val Fitch, and Kenneth Bainbridge.

ADDITIONAL SOURCES

Bowden, Charles. *Trinity*. University of Texas Press, 2009.
Couffer, Jack. *Bat Bomb*. University of Texas Press, 1992.
Eckles, Jim. *Trinity: The History of an Atomic Bomb National Historic Landmark*. Fiddlebike, 2015.
Hersey, John. *Hiroshima*. Modern Library, 1946.
Price, V. B. *The Orphaned Land: New Mexico's Environment Since the Manhattan Project*. UNM Press, 2011.
Rhodes, Richard. *The Making of the Atomic Bomb*. Simon & Schuster, 1987.
Wilson, Jane, and Charlotte Serber, eds. *Standing By and Making Do: Women of Wartime Los Alamos*. Los Alamos Historical Society, 1988.

SO LET ALL THE MARTIANS COME HOME TO ROOST

SNM EXTRATERRESTRIAL READING

I cannot speak to the validity of the claims in these books, but they make for great entertainment for the brain.

Berliner, Don, and Stanton Friedman. *Crash at Corona: The Definitive Study of the Roswell Incident*. New York: Marlowe & Company, 1994.

Fry, Daniel. *The White Sands Incident.* Horus House Press, 1992.

Jung, Dr. C. G. *Flying Saucers: A Modern Myth of Things Seen in the Skies.* Translated by R.F.C. Hull. Signet and Mentor Books, 1969.

Marden, Kathleen, and Stanton Friedman. *Captured! The Betty and Barney Hill UFO Experience: The True Story of the World's First Documented Alien Abduction.* New Page Books, 2007.

TRUTH OR CONSEQUENCES AT THE GATEWAY TO SPACE

After this story was first published, a Virgin Galactic *SpaceShipTwo* crashed during a test flight in Mojave, California. One of the two test pilots died that day, Halloween 2014. Much debated (mostly in the geeky New Space Race threads of the Net) was whether Galactic's public response to the crash was in poor taste. Galactic characterized the dead pilot as a hero sacrificed for a noble cause. But *Wired* wrote, "When various corporate representatives eulogize those two pilots as pioneers who were helping to cross the Final Frontier, that should make you angry. That pilot died not for space but for a luxury service provider." The situation was further complicated when, nine months after the crash, an investigation concluded that the primary cause was human error—the dead pilot pulled a lever too soon. This conclusion was obviously advantageous for Galactic, a company that already had many millions of passenger dollars invested and could not afford to have celebs such as Gaga and Brangelina asking for refunds on account of faulty/fatal technology. Some saw Galactic's eagerness to publicize the findings of human error as a kind of second sacrifice of the test pilot and used this story as evidence for Galactic's poor corporate conduct. I guess you'll reach your own conclusions about Galactic, but I want to take a moment to tell you the name of that test pilot: Michael Alsbury. He was thirty-nine, had a wife and two kids and a twin sister. In one sense, Alsbury was just doing his job. He was also doing what he loved. His death was a terrible tragedy, no matter what you think of Galactic. I hope Alsbury's kids get the chance to experience space, to taste a bit of the Overview Effect, to know that their father's dreams, at least, were never in the employ of any corporation.

BEFORE THE FALL

All of the highly specific data from this fall is available on the BDED website about their stunt. Much of the information in the essay comes from the "Key Facts Summary" and "Scientific Data Review" documents. The site also includes hours and hours of raw footage of the stunt, interviews with crew and stuntman, slick documentary recaps, and endless advertisements for the ED.

153 *A 2010 complaint in Los Angeles Superior Court*: BDED Corp briefly paused the production of their stunt in October 2010 as a result of this lawsuit by Daniel Hogan, though BDED maintained they'd done nothing wrong. The suit was settled out of court in July 2011 and BDED resumed production on their stunt soon after.

159 *"The Anglo-Saxons of Eilmer's days were beginning to show Christ almost jet-propelled"*: This quote and much of the information about Eilmer, including possible inspirations for his feat, come from "Eilmer of Malmesbury, an Eleventh Century Aviator: A Case Study of Technological Innovation, Its Context and Tradition" by Lynn White, Jr., *Technology and Culture*, vol. 2, no. 2 (Spring 1961): 97–111. White, like many writing about Eilmer, claims he "flew 'spatio stadii et plus,' or more than 600 feet." But that's likely impossible, given the height of the tower and what we now understand of physics. Eilmer fell.

160 *"bespattered the emperor with his blood"*: From the Harvard University Press edition of the Loeb Classical Library translation of *The Lives of the Caesars* by Gaius Suetonius Tranquillus.

ADDITIONAL SOURCES

Goble, Ronald, and Stephen Hall. "Archaeological Geology of the Mescalero Sands." *Plains Anthropologist* 53, no. 207 (2008).

Kittinger, Joe, and Craig Ryan. *Come Up and Get Me.* University of New Mexico Press, 2011.

RAGGEDY, RAGGEDY WABBITMAN

This essay fleshes out family lore about how we ended up rednecks in Alamogordo. It was either jackrabbits or poker, they say, depending on whom you ask and when you ask them. Many of the cited newspaper clippings were included in a boot box of family documents I was given by Aunt Yvonne, passed down from George Bradley Oliver, saved through the generations for god knows what. But I am glad to have found the scraps and expect to add this book to the box.

ADDITIONAL SOURCES

Gilbert, Beth. *Alamogordo: The Territorial Years.* Starline Printing, 1988.

Sonnichsen, C. L. *Tularosa: Last of the Frontier West.* New York: Devin-Adair Company, 1960.

Traphagen, Myles B. *Final Report on the status of the White-sided Jackrabbit (Lepus Callotis Gaillardia) in New Mexico.* New Mexico Department of Game and Fish. June 1, 2001.

LIVING ROOM

The names Kate and Johnny have been changed out of respect for their families. But sometimes, because I don't use them in this essay, I barely remember their real names at all. That bothers me. So I leave this space where their real names can be recorded in my copy of this book and never forgotten: _____ and _____.

182 *Bodies in the Rubble*: This uses information and quotes from Thomas M. Walsh and Thomas D. Zlatic, "Mark Twain and the Art of Memory," *American Literature* 53, no. 2 (May 1981): 214–31.

190 *Said Mark Twain*: Written in a letter to his wife, Olivia Clemens, while he was on a lecture tour in Bennington, Vermont, November 27, 1871. The letter begins, "Livy darling, good house, but they laughed too much . . ."

190 *Said Others*: "Take heed of a gluttonous curiosity" is from the

seventeenth-century writer Thomas Fuller's book *The Holy State and the Profane State.* Fuller's book begins, "Who is not sensible, with sorrow, of the distractions of this age? To write books, therefore, may seem unseasonable . . . Now I will turn my pen into prayer . . . I will stop the leakage of my soul."

One more time, so you know I mean it: Now I will turn my pen into prayer, I will stop the leakage of my soul.

192 *Forgotten Ear:* All quotes are from the article "The Abyss," by Oliver Sacks, published in a September 2007 issue of *The New Yorker.* Other information is from Jonathan Miller's 1986 documentary about Clive, *Prisoner of Consciousness,* also referenced in Sacks's article.

194 *Static:* Quotes from several articles written by Laura London in the *Alamogordo Daily News* from November 2007 to April 2008.

196 *Mirrors, Held Close Together:* This quotes directly (1) a *Science Daily* article from September 16, 2008, "How Memories Are Made, and Recalled," by Mark Wheeler; (2) "The Brain: A Story We Tell Ourselves," by Antonio Damasio, in the January 29, 2007, issue of *Time*; and (3) an interview with Antonio Damasio by David Hirschman on the website Big Think.

The hammering-monkey study was conducted at the University of Parma in Italy, where Giacomo Rizzolatti was studying how macaques' brains control their hands. The hammer experiment was initiated only after a graduate student was eating ice cream in the lab and noticed that when the macaques watched her eat the ice cream, their neurons fired as if they were moving their hands, as if they were the ones with a spoon eating the ice cream. But the macaques were not moving their hands, were not eating the ice cream, were just sitting completely still watching the graduate student move her hand to her own mouth to eat the ice cream, which may or may not have been peach sherbet.

203 *Said the Psychologists:* Excerpts freely from Helen Phillips's "Mind Fiction: Why Your Brain Tells Tall Tales," in the October 2006 issue of *New Scientist* (much of the excerpt is Phillips quoting University of Oxford professor Morten Kringelbach). The first paragraph of this section, however, is quoted from *The*

Truth About Confabulation, by Daniel Pendick, published in 2000 on the website Memory Loss and the Brain.

203 *Use but Little Moisture*: Gathers information about the shirt belt from a 2001 U.S. Patent and Trademark Office press release (#01–61). Other information about the scrapbook is from "Celebrity Invention: Mark Twain's Scrapbook," by Rebecca Greenfield, published in *The Atlantic*, November 12, 2010. Copies of Twain's original scrapbook design are available from the University of Virginia Library.

205 *Mine of Her*: References an article about a superachieving candy striper written by Cindy Kleiman, published in the *Toronto Star*. I've since lost this scrap, though, and can't tell you anything more about it than that.

THINGS MOST SURELY BELIEVED

Much of the information about the trial/appeals of Terry Clark are from coverage by the *Albuquerque Journal*, *The Albuquerque Tribune*, Associated Press, and *Roswell Daily Record*. Much more of the information is from letters, memos, and court transcripts I've collected, as well as interviews I conducted between 2009 and 2011. The following is a list of things quoted directly from these and other sources. Some quotes include the original document's idiosyncrasies—grammar, spelling, etc.

212 *Art*: This section is based on a drawing of Terry's given to me by Brother Maxey, as well as Brother Maxey's recollections about why Terry drew it. "Lord, I've been changed. Angels in heaven done sign my name . . ." is from the spiritual "Lord I've Been Changed," as performed by Tom Waits on the album *Orphans: Brawlers, Bawlers & Bastards*. That song is only relevant because I couldn't stop playing it while writing this essay.

216 *An Account of Jailhouse Immersion*: This baptism account is taken from a December 30, 2001, letter written to the Reverend Floyd Harris, Jr., from a young convict, Michael Jamison, who recounts the spiritual conversion of a fellow inmate in a California prison. The letter was given to me by another prison chaplain when I

tried, but failed, to find official records of Terry Clark's death-row baptism. However, Jamison's account is quite similar to the death-row baptism of Terry, as recounted to me by Brother Maxey and Jean Ortiz. Terry was immersed in a laundry cart filled by a recreation-yard garden hose. Brother Maxey pushed him under. The water overflowed. That said, Brother Maxey does not feel Jamison's letter accurately characterizes Terry's baptism, which Maxey calls "simple" and "joyous" and "very primitive." Brother Maxey, I imagine, is suspicious of the naïve tone, suspicious that I included Jamison's account in this essay ironically. But I see sincerity in Jamison's words—a respect of magic—that I could never approximate because I am too steeped in a culture that distrusts sincerity. I want to believe in a god to the point that it makes me clumsy with joy in a trash can or laundry cart, but I do not have things most surely believed. So I'll leave the specifics of Terry's baptism for Brother Maxey to tell. You can read about it on his blog, *Reflections*. Jamison's is the account that moves me.

217 *Sane and Ready for Heaven*: Some of the dialogue here is taken directly from written correspondence between Brother Maxey and Terry about the last meal. Other dialogue, as well as the rest of the details, are from Brother Maxey's recounting of the scene.

226 *Fifteen Minutes*: The first paragraph of this section is taken from court transcripts of Karla Faye Tucker's sentencing hearing. I've edited tense and punctuation.

239 *A Brief History of Hellfire*: This section is guided in part by *The Origins of Christian Hell* by Dimitris J. Kyrtatas, as well as *Changing Conceptions of Hell in Gilded Age America* by Gary Scott Smith. The forensic scientist is quoted in Linda Geddes, "Body Burners: The Forensics of Fire," *New Scientist*, May 20, 2009. The Isaac Asimov short story is called "Hell-Fire" and can be found in his collection *Earth Is Room Enough*.

248 *Ends*: Details about the history of New Mexico executions and last words are from an article by Mark Allan, "Capital Punishment or Compassion—Executions in the State of New Mexico: The Death Penalty Since Territorial Days," published on the Angelo State University library website.

THE GLITCH IN THE VIDEOGAME GRAVEYARD

The theory of the Shroud of Turin as evidence of early photography seems to have originally been posited in 1993 by Nicholas Allen in *South African Journal of Art History*. That article, "Is the Shroud of Turin the First Recorded Photograph?," was my primary source for shroud pondering. It has recently been expanded and reissued as the book cited below.

The Shroud Museum in Alamogordo, New Mexico, has since moved out of our shopping mall and into a prime location downtown, on New York Avenue. It sits, no joke, directly across the street from Joe Lewandowski's Atari-dig-funded project, the Tularosa Basin Historical Society museum, where the prize display is a bunch of Atari *E.T.* cartridges. So the Alamogordo shroud and the Alamogordo *E.T.*s are coupled, and overlooking the site of the Pit, less than a mile away. When you make your inevitable pilgrimage to that bizarre, tight triangle of technological ephemera, you will find at its center the Alamogordo Zoo, where the atomic cows were displayed in the wake of the Gadget's blast in 1945.

ADDITIONAL SOURCES

Allen, Nicholas. *Turin Shroud: Testament to a Lost Technology.* Lambert Academic Publishing, 2017.

Feder, Kenneth. *Encyclopedia of Dubious Archaeology: From Atlantis to Walam Olum.* Greenwood, 2010.

A MILLION TINY DAGGERS

337 *"Those ingenious labyrinthine inlets"*: The nineteenth-century English essayist Charles Lamb coins these descriptions for ears in his rant against fancy music, "A Chapter on Ears." He's upset the ears cannot be closed so easily as the eyes, that the sounds of music in particular are a kind of evil spirit his brain is not equipped to understand. It's satire, maybe. But then maybe he is right that we allow ourselves to be too easily lulled by pretty sounds, that to stay alert we need more than just melody, more than emotion:

Above all, those insufferable concertos, and pieces of music, as they are called, do plague and imbitter my apprehension. Words are something; but to be exposed to an endless battery of mere sounds; to be long a-dying, to lie stretched upon a rack of roses; to keep up languor by unintermitted effort; to pile honey upon sugar, and sugar upon honey, to an interminable tedious sweetness; to fill up sound with feeling, and strain ideas to keep pace with it; to gaze on empty frames, and be forced to make the pictures for yourself; to read a book, *all stops*, and be obliged to supply the verbal matter; to invent extempore tragedies to answer to the vague gestures of an inexplicable rambling mime—these are faint shadows of what I have undergone from a series of the ablest-executed pieces of this empty *instrumental music.*

343 *Nogier's acupuncture diagrams*:

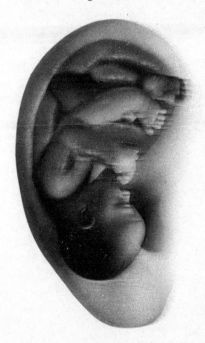

ACKNOWLEDGMENTS

Everybody gets a drink, on me. Sean McDonald for taking a chance on a bum from New Mexico, sticking with this book, and getting it into fighting shape. All the others at FSG, particularly Taylor Sperry for spotting it, and Maya Binyam for her insights as she ushered it across the finish line. Y'all get many more pounds of red chili pistachios too. Eleanor Jackson, for believing in the book before it existed, then getting others to believe in it too. John D'Agata for unleashing the magic of essays, and teaching me how to teach them. Geoff Dyer for yelling at me to quit aching for profundity, which I have not, but we remain friends anyhow. Many from Iowa, for reading and being pals throughout: Sandra Allen, Landon Bates, Gemma de Choisy, Keanan Faruk, Kristen Radtke, Helen Rubinstein, and all the rest. Carmen Giménez-Smith for first telling me I was unlikely to succeed as a poet, for which I am eternally grateful, and for her continued support. The Compound, RIP. All the Alamo boys. *Alamogordo Daily News* for my first job in journalism, the best job, chucking it at houses in the dark. And you, for making it this far. Finally, some dives where I wrote and moped, but mostly reveled in sloppy fellowship; I hope you will give me a break on the tab: El Patio (Mesilla, New Mexico), Red Garter (Tucson, Arizona), George's (Iowa City, Iowa), Radio (Baton Rouge, Louisiana).